C000145463

Reservoir Trout Fishing
with Tom Saville

Reservoir Trout Fishing with Tom Saville

Metropolitan Borough of Stockport
Libraries

C

0 00081033   799.1755
SAV

Metropolitan Borough
of Stockport

H. F. & G. WITHERBY LTD

First published in Great Britain 1991 by
H. F. & G. WITHERBY LTD
14 Henrietta Street, London WC2E 8QJ

© Tom Saville 1991

The right of Tom Saville to be identified as author
of this work has been asserted by him in accordance
with the Copyright, Designs and Patents Act 1988.

Photographs by Peter Gathercole
Text illustrations by Charles Jardine and
Andrew Mackintosh

A CIP catalogue record for this book is available
from the British Library.

ISBN 0 85493 210 0

Photoset by Rowland Phototypesetting Ltd
Bury St Edmunds, Suffolk
Printed in Great Britain by
St Edmundsbury Press Ltd, Bury St Edmunds, Suffolk
Illustrations printed by Krisson Printing Ltd,
Harlesden, London

Contents

List of Illustrations

Acknowledgements

No book can be written without the help of others, and mine is no exception. Firstly I must thank my wife Pat for her constant encouragement when I needed it most, and for her patient forbearance while I spent many long hours at the word processor. My thanks are also due to Ken Clower for reading the drafts and telling me how good they were! Michael Leney of Mercaston Trout Farm, Philip Tallents of Ryobi-Masterline Ltd, and Roger Thom of Rutland Trout, provided me with some of their specialist knowledge. Peter Gathercole gave unstintingly of his expertise in providing most of the photographs. The line drawings are the expert work of Charles Jardine and Andrew Mackintosh. John Goddard, Taff Price, and the Bristol Waterworks Company supplied photos from their collections. The makers of Partridge, Mustad, and Kamasan hooks allowed me to use their illustrations of the types of hook I prefer. My thanks are also offered to Sandy Leventon, Editor of *Trout & Salmon* and *Gamefisher & Fly-Tying Quarterly*, Chris Dawn, Editor of *Trout Fisherman*, and John Wilshaw, Editor of *Country Sport* and *Practical Gamefishing*, for allowing me to use some of my material which has previously been published in their excellent magazines.

'Thank you', too, to Ken Smith APGAI for introducing me to the pleasures of fly-dressing, and for tying some of the flies for the colour plates. 'Diolch yn fawr iawn' to that superb Welsh fly-dresser Mike Green for tying most of the other flies used in the photos. Both Ken and Mike are vastly better fly-dressers than I, and I wanted the best for my book.

I give my warmest thanks to Bill Goodale and all the other people in whose company I have fished, because we can never stop learning from each other.

Finally, David Burnett deserves my gratitude for his confidence in my ability as an author and for his enthusiastic help in the production of this book.

TOM SAVILLE
Bottesford
April 1991

Foreword

My first outing to Ravensthorpe reservoir, twenty years ago, was without doubt the turning-point in my own game-fishing career. Confident in my abilities on the tumbling streams and high country lakes of North Wales, I realised that I had been living sublimely in a state of arrested development. This was altogether a different game. Now the talk was of buzzers, sink-tip lines, running on the rudder, and catches of trout beyond my wildest dreams.

As founding Editor of *Trout Fisherman* magazine, I had the opportunity to fish with the pioneers of modern stillwater trout fishing. I drank in every word uttered by those original thinkers such as Arthur Cove, Dick Shrive and Tom Saville, passing on their latest radical thoughts to the now rapidly growing army of stillwater fly-fishers.

Many of today's best-known gamefishers owe their present status to their apprenticeship with Tom Saville, who, typically, passed on all he knew without any expectation of acknowledgement or credit. But that's Tom Saville. That anyone's sport should improve has always been reward enough.

And so you will still have to read between the lines of this long-overdue book to realise just what a powerful catalyst for development Tom Saville has been in our sport. No instant 'just-add-water' expert is Saville, but the genuine article. All I can say is 'Read on', for this is where we all begin to learn.

JOHN WILSHAW

Chapter 1

Early Days and Later Developments

Maybe I should have been born under the astrological sign Pisces (actually, I'm Libra, 1924, for those interested), because ever since I can remember, I have been interested in fish and fishing. 'Interested' really isn't the right word – I suppose I ought to admit to being the willing victim of an all-absorbing passion for fish and fishing! Water in its natural state, whether river, stream, brook, sea, lake, reservoir, pond, or even swamp, holds an irresistible attraction for me, and it has always been so. *Swamp?* Yes, the Florida Everglades offer some very interesting fish and fishing – freshwater garfish, largemouth bass, snook, and tarpon, to name a few. Music is almost as important in my life, and I have been lucky in being able to choose the three things I most enjoy as both hobbies and livelihood. I was a professional musician for some years before making fish and fishing tackle my business.

Until I was nineteen I lived in the village of Lymm, in the Cheshire countryside, and my father was a reasonably keen coarse-angler. So from the age of six it was natural that I should be taken along on some of his fishing trips to various Cheshire meres. I vividly remember the summer Sunday visits to a small lake at Arley, with its crystal-clear water, its border of pure white waterlilies and masses of feathery *Myriophyllum* weed among which dwelt all sorts of interesting underwater creatures for my investigative net and jam-jar. There were lots of water-snails and their rubbery masses of eggs which were laid on the undersides of the lily leaves. There were freshwater shrimps scurrying along, water-beetles and waterboatmen, dragonfly nymphs, leeches, even the odd newt. Equally vivid are the memories of muddy shoes and wet trouser-seat, and the smack from Mum ('Why do you always get yourself in such a mess, fiddling about in the water?') – quickly forgotten in the joy of cream tea with my favourite strawberry jam at the nearby farmhouse.

The various creatures and water-plants were taken home, identified as accurately as possible from a well-thumbed and well-loved book *Life in Ponds and Streams*, and kept in a big goldfish bowl on my bedroom window-sill. I quickly learned how they all lived, and which killed and ate which. And that although sunshine made the water-plants grow, too much sun heated the water to a state where many creatures died. All useful stuff for later life, as it happened.

My father and his brother ran a truly comprehensive country iron-mongery store in the village; there was even a shoeing forge off the big yard at the rear of the premises, where Jimmy Gould's shire horses were brought on Saturday mornings for old Joe the blacksmith to renew their huge horseshoes. If I was a good lad, I would be allowed to pump the bellows to make the coke white-hot, so that Joe could plunge the shoe into the furnace to heat up enough for another hammering session at the big anvil. Saville Brothers sold everything *including* the kitchen sink, and among their many agencies was one for fishing tackle by S. Allcock & Co. Ltd of Redditch. A very well-known name in those pre-World-War-II days, which in due course became the current Shakespeare Company. Allcocks made every kind of fishing tackle – game, coarse, and sea – but in Cheshire the only fishing available was coarse-fishing in the meres, ponds, and canals, so the stock at Saville Brothers was restricted to items suitable for local fishing only. Luckily for me, the village had the Bridgewater Canal running through it, plus a sizeable lake (Lymm Dam) only a few hundred yards from my home, and on my tenth birthday I was presented with a little fishing outfit. The rod was virtually a 7-foot garden cane fitted with a cork handle and rings of coiled wire, and the reel was a 2½-inch-diameter metal centrepin. The line was braided cotton, speckled black and white, and of unknown breaking-strain. There was a peacock quill float, a tub of split shot, and a little booklet of 'Hooks to Gut, size 14'. Dad used to go every week to a slaughterhouse in nearby Warrington to collect a big biscuit-tin full of maggots, which were sold by the pennyworth, and there were worms to be dug from the garden. No wonder I classed myself as a 'compleat angler'.

Although there were other inhabitants, the canal yielded only stickle-backs, the males in early summer resplendent in their brilliant green/blue and red, the females pot-bellied with spawn. A pair was carried carefully home in a jam-jar (what would little boys do without them?) and placed with equal care, complete with two *Argulus* fish lice attached to the male, in the goldfish-bowl aquarium. *Life in Ponds and Streams* identified the fish lice for me, once I had noticed them, and they were removed with Mum's tweezers and the care of a surgeon carrying out a heart operation. The book also said that the male stickleback made its nest in the green blanket-weed, and after the female had laid her eggs in it, guarded it until the eggs hatched. Sure enough, this is exactly what happened, but the fish ate most of my little nymphs and bit the water-snails, which was not part of the plan, so the sticklebacks were once again in the jam-jar – this time on a return journey to the canal.

The dam was a much better fishing proposition. Hardly anyone seemed to fish there, and it was easy to find a nice quiet spot where my clumsy efforts at casting would not be noticed. Perch and rudd were eager to devour the worm or maggots impaled on my size 14 hook and to pull the peacock float under; endless happy hours were spent 'really fishing' during the lovely warm summer holidays we always seemed to get, those many years ago. Already, the seeds were being sown which would blossom into my present-day passion for fishing.

It was at the age of twelve that another very strong influence came into my life. One of my pals told me about a bad-tempered man, Mark Rowlinson, who lived on his own nearby and had 'a greenhouse full of fish tanks'. The attraction of the fish was just enough to beat the fear of the bad temper, but it was with thumping heart that I knocked on Mr Rowlinson's back door the next Saturday morning and asked, 'Please may I see your fish?' To my surprise, his face broke into a smile, and in his gruff voice (which I gradually realised was shyness and not bad temper) he said, 'Of course you can, son', and led me round the corner of the garden to the famous greenhouse. It wasn't 'full of fish tanks'; in the humid warmth which met me as I followed him inside, there were, in fact, only two, but in those two aquaria were the most beautiful fish I had ever seen, and I shall never forget that moment as long as I live. 'What are they?' I gasped, and crikey, I wanted those fish more than anything in the world.

Only about two inches long, some (the males) had brilliant red and blue vertical stripes which glistened like jewels in the sunlight. He told me they were dwarf gouramis, and yes he had bred them himself, and no they didn't live in this country but were tropical fish which came from the Far East and yes the water had to be warm and no they didn't eat worms and maggots but daphnia (what on earth was that?) and yes they were pretty easy to keep and YES HE WOULD GIVE ME A PAIR!

After gabbling profuse thanks, I rushed home to organise 'a proper tropical fish tank, Dad' and between us we rustled up a glass accumulator jar (never mind that the glass wasn't perfectly clear) which was scrubbed clean and by good luck fitted exactly on a wooden margarine box. Heat was provided by a 60-watt light-bulb in a holder screwed to the inside of a hinged door cut out of one side of the box – thermostatically-controlled aquarium heaters had not then been invented.

The stream which fed the dam provided a layer of fine gravel for the bottom of the aquarium, and finally the contraption was reverently placed on a table near my bedroom window. I filled the aquarium with warm water from the hot tap in the bathroom ('better give it a good start') and a sheet of horticultural glass was placed on the top of the tank to 'keep the heat in'. I had no idea just how warm the water was supposed to be for the well-being of tropical fish, and never even thought of using a thermometer, but again luck was with me, for the 60-watt bulb kept the water temperature around what I later found out to be 80°F (27°C).

The following day, after what was for me a sleepless night, my father was persuaded to drive me round to Mr Rowlinson's ('We've got to get them home quickly in case they get cold, Dad') to collect my gouramis. My generous new friend also provided some *Vallisneria* and *Cabomba* plants, which grew luxuriantly in his aquaria, and enough daphnia for a couple of days' feeding. In my haste, I forgot to ask how and where he got the daphnia, but discovered that the fish would eat dried fish-food from the village pet shop.

Following Mr Rowlinson's careful instructions, the plants were quickly installed and the fish introduced after floating their jam-jar in the aquarium until the water temperatures were about equal. Sudden changes in water temperature are harmful to fish, I learned.

I can still remember the immense feelings of excitement, wonder, and joy which those two little fish gave me. I studied their every movement, marvelling at the lovely colours of the male and the more subdued hues of the female. Unbeknown to me, there was more than a little excitement on the part of the fish themselves, for they were in top breeding condition, and the following morning there was a tightly-packed mass of bubbles floating in one corner of the tank. The significance of this completely escaped me, although I had noticed that every minute or so the fish were in the habit of breathing at the surface. Mark Rowlinson had told me that they were members of a large family of fishes which were able to breathe air in addition to oxygen dissolved in the water, but he had omitted to tell me that they were bubble-nest builders for breeding purposes. A few days later, I was amazed to see a lot of minute black tadpole-like fry wriggling just below the bubbles. Not only was I a tropical-fish keeper; I was a tropical-fish *breeder*! I had no idea of the requirements of dwarf gourami fry, and of course they all died, but the whole series of events sparked off an interest in fish-keeping which was later to become my profession for a number of years and helped my angling to a surprising degree.

At school I was keenly interested in zoology and botany, of course, especially the aquatic side, and I was able to take a degree course at Manchester University which included those subjects. Just before Finals, I was taken ill (a condition which prevented me from becoming a member of the armed forces) and never actually sat the exam, but it didn't matter a great deal to me. It was sufficient that I had the factual knowledge the course had provided, knowledge which helped me directly and indirectly to enjoy my fishing more. I learned in great detail how fish evolved and how perfectly they are adapted to their habitat; I studied their brains and nervous systems, eyes, blood vessels, musculature, everything. I learned about algae and their biochemistry and about microscopic single-celled animals and plants, molluscs, insects, crustaceans, evolution, the lot! Some of it purely academic and boring, but much that was of absorbing interest. I'm not suggesting that every fly-fisher needs a university degree; I *am* suggesting that it is very useful to do some studying of the natural history of fish and aquatic life.

I mentioned just now that I learned about evolution and the nervous system of fish. Any thoughts I had about fishing being cruel to fish were quickly corrected as a result of this knowledge. It was obvious that fish did not have the ability to feel pain to the same degree as we humans do. Their nervous system is very primitive – one step higher than that of a worm, but not as advanced as that of a reptile. This was illustrated some years later when a python I kept as a pet hadn't the sense or feeling to unwrap itself from a heater, around which it had coiled, and cooked itself to death overnight! If a snake cannot feel the pain of intense burning, there is no way that a fish can feel any pain from being hooked. I fished, and still do, with a clear conscience.

Soon after leaving university, I decided that I could perhaps make a decent living as a musician. The money earned by players in the top-flight orchestras was high, and my parents had encouraged my natural talent for music with the result that I was a better-than-average pianist. Hearing Fats Waller at the age of twelve had awakened a feeling for jazz, and at the time it seemed a very enjoyable way of making money, playing the piano in dance bands. So for the next few years I threw myself a hundred per cent into the difficult task of becoming a successful professional musician, and fish and fishing had to take a back seat.

The late 1940s found me in Nottingham, working in the band at the local dance hall. I was buying my first house, a bungalow in the suburbs which had a garage. I couldn't afford a car to put in the garage, but it seemed a shame to waste the space so I insulated the walls and started to fill it with aquaria. A lot of what I had learned at university and the lessons of my childhood fish-keeping were put to good use, and pretty soon I was breeding tropical fish on such a scale that the money I got from selling the youngsters began to exceed what I earned as a musician – the post-war boom in tropical aquaria in the home having just begun. It seemed time for a change to what some might call a 'proper job'.

So I gave the band-leader notice, and became a full-time aquarist. The business grew to such an extent that I had to take in partners and form a limited company. I did, in fact, continue to take an active interest in playing the piano, but only at the local jazz clubs. It was there that I met

Ken Smith, a bass player who was also a very keen angler. Ken's expertise was to have quite an important influence on my future, as it turned out.

Lured by the close proximity of the River Trent, I had taken up fishing again, and on holiday in North Wales I caught my first trout, a 6-inch speckled beauty from the River Llugwy, on a worm. That little trout had almost the same effect on me as the dwarf gouramis had had all those years before! I was fascinated by its lovely colouring, its streamlined shape and, above all, the amazing strength with which this little fish fought. From that moment on, trout fishing became my main angling interest. Luckily, the Derbyshire trout streams weren't too far from Nottingham. Reservoir fishing was at that time very much in its infancy, and fishing for trout meant fishing moving water. Of course, there wasn't the fishing pressure which exists today.

I read every possible book on trout fishing, and quickly realised that fly-fishing was *the* method to use. The weekly *Fishing Gazette* carried an advertisement by Foster Brothers of Ashbourne, long-established and famous rod-makers and suppliers of game-fishing tackle in Derbyshire, so off I went to Ashbourne (thirty miles away, quite a journey) to buy my first fly-fishing outfit.

There, in the almost holy quietness of Foster's upstairs showroom, with the feeling that the ghost of Charles Cotton was looking down at me, I was taken by their sales manager, Arnold Moseley, through the ceremony of choosing a fly-rod. All the books had said that a 9-foot rod was the best all-round choice, so that's what I asked for. Split cane, of course – in those days there was no alternative. Six examples of Foster's 9-foot Champion model were brought out for me to examine, and even to my completely inexperienced arm they all felt different! Despite the undoubted expertise of Foster's rod craftsmen, the variation in the basic natural material was obviously a problem. Sensibly, I asked Mr Moseley (who I correctly assumed was an expert fly-fisher) to choose one for me; his choice of a medium-actioned rod proved very suitable. So, too, did a Young's Beaudex 3¼-inch fly-reel with braided backing and a Kingfisher double-tapered silk fly-line, size 2 to suit the rod ('Just a few minutes to splice the line and load the reel, sir'). What service! The line was loaded for right-hand winding, and to this day I always wind my fly-reel with the right hand.

Casts (as we called leaders then), Wheatley fly-box with a few flies (mostly dry), folding landing-net, fishing bag (two pounds it cost, and I've still got it!), and waders – oh and don't forget some line grease and fly flotant; all were slowly and carefully chosen. It seemed almost sinful to hurry things at Foster's, but finally the ceremony came to an end, and with a firm handshake and Mr Moseley's parting words 'Tight lines, sir' I was off back to Nottingham, a bit wiser and a lot lighter in the pocket.

Tight lines? First I had to learn how to cast the damn thing. The books gave only sketchy instructions, just enough to punch home the essential 'wait while the line extends behind you'. I didn't know of any local casting instructor, if in fact there was one, so I struggled on alone, mostly on some floodwater lying well away from the public gaze, until I could cast what I felt was a reasonably good line, all of 15 yards! It took me from October until the following February to find out how to cast, and even then I hadn't actually cast a fly to a trout or to any other fish for that matter. Then I remembered the bass player I had met at the jazz club. Hadn't he talked about fishing the River Derwent?

I went round to Ken Smith's house that evening, and we had a good chat which turned out to be very beneficial for both of us. Ken was even then an experienced caster and fly-dresser (he became an Association of Professional Game Angling Instructor in both) but couldn't read jazz bass parts very well. We did a swap – I taught him the jazz and he polished up my casting and showed me how to tie flies.

We had some hilarious evenings. Ken was on a wine-making kick, and this resulted in some fairly potent brews. During the bottling process there is always a little drop left, and Ken used to pour all the leftovers into a special bottle labelled 'Jungle Juice'. Naturally, it was bad manners not to try a taste. You should have seen my attempt at an Alexandra after a couple of glasses, and Ken's valiant efforts to read a syncopated bass part ('one-*and*-two-*and*-rest-*and*-*four*') would hardly have pleased Duke Ellington. Fortunately, there were plenty of 'serious' evenings too, and we both learned a lot.

I joined the Ashbourne Fly-Fishers' Club, after much soul-searching as to whether I could afford the twelve-pound subscription. In the early 1950s it seemed an awful lot of money. By now I was 'mobile' – the business had merited a van – so the thirty-mile trip to Ashbourne was not too much of an obstacle. The club had the fishing rights on a small pond owned by Nestlé's, who had a factory in the town, and on stretches of the Henmore Brook and the Bentley Brook, both tributaries of the famous River Dove. The stock of native brown trout was augmented by a few hundred from a local trout farm each spring. Both brooks were only four or five yards wide, and much of the banks was quite heavily bushed. Really, not the best sort of water for a beginner, but how was I to know?

So it was with great hope and excitement that I made the journey to Ashbourne one morning in late April, arriving around 10.30 a.m. at the little bridge where the road to Ilam crosses the Bentley Brook. It was a lovely spring morning; just enough sun to take the chill out of the air. Buds bursting, birds singing, and the murmur of the water tumbling over the little weir downstream. I felt very much at peace for a moment. Then the excitement took over. With trembling hands I put the rod together, fitted the reel, threaded the line through the rod-rings. (Yes, missed a ring in my haste and had to do it again.) I knotted a 9-foot tapered cast to the tip of the fly-line. Now, which fly to use?

I couldn't see any natural flies in the air, and the books had said one should always try to match the artificial fly with the natural fly the trout were feeding on. Very occasionally, there was a ring on the surface of the brook, so the trout were feeding on *something* floating on the water. Right, dry fly was the choice. But which one? One of the books had said that the Cochybonddu was a good general pattern to use, and because it was an easy fly to tie, I had made a few on size 14 up-eyed hooks. Let's try the old Cochybonddu, then.

I had been practising the half-Blood knot, so that part was easy. The difficult bit was getting the end of the cast through the eye of the fly – my fingers were shaking so much by now. Finally I did it, and even remembered to get out the little bottle of Mucilin Dry Fly Oil and to brush some on the fly. Damn!! I'd forgotten to grease the line! Out with the tin of Mucilin . . . why, oh why, do they make the lid so hard to get off? One broken fingernail later, felt pad thick with grease, some ten yards of the silk fly-line were pulled through the rod-rings and made to float.

Several yards upstream of the bridge, there was a stretch of the left-hand bank which was clear of bushes, with no shrubs or trees nearby to ensnare the back-cast, and a fish was rising every few minutes in midstream. Mustn't frighten it! Hoping there would be no passers-by to see me acting so strangely, I crept on my knees across the grass until I was opposite a clump of celandines which grew on the top of the bank close to where the fish rose. Cautiously, I raised my head for a peep – yes, there it was again!

Somehow, I can't remember exactly how, the cast was made, and the fly miraculously landed a yard upstream of where I thought the fish was. Would it rise and take? The fly floated along, past the celandines. Had it passed the fish? Suddenly there was an explosive splash and the fly disappeared. I was so startled that it was a couple of seconds before I realised what had happened and raised the rod (actually, just the right amount of time you should allow to hook a trout which has taken a dry fly) and felt the power of the fish as it bored away downstream. The trout leapt a couple of times ('Oh God, please don't let the hook come out') and turned upstream. I wound the reel-handle furiously to regain control – 'keep the rod up; keep a tight line', the books had said. A couple more attempts to bore away were easily foiled by the inherent power of the rod, and the fish seemed almost ready for the net.

The net! Where was it? Clipped to my brand-new fishing bag lying where I'd dropped it several yards away. Luckily, the trout was tired and I was able to back away to pick up the net, easing line off the reel as I went. I flicked the net open – miraculously it didn't tangle – and tucked it under one arm. Reeling in steadily to keep that all-important tight line, I got back to the edge of the brook, knelt down, and drew my prize into the net. What a beauty! My first trout on the fly, and about a foot long. I'd forgotten to check the rules for the size-limit, so I wasn't sure whether I could take the fish or not. Better safe than sorry. I quickly removed the fly (nicely in the 'scissors' of the jaw, I noticed) and slipped the trout into the water.

Later that morning, chatting to another club member, I learned that the size-limit was in fact 10 inches, and my 12-incher was quite a good trout for the water! I also learned that it was a good idea to mark a 10-inch length on the landing-net handle so that the size of any trout caught could be quickly checked against the limit. While wandering along the brook and trying to cast to various rising trout, I learned too that a 9-foot rod was really not the ideal length for a small brook like the Bentley; there were far too many places where overhanging bushes prevented a proper cast. I resolved there and then to buy a 7-foot rod at the earliest opportunity, like that very afternoon!

Fosters' Airsprite rod turned out to be an absolute gem, and served me well for many years. It was ideal for the Ashbourne club's streams, and I ended the day with a second trout (exactly 10 inches, this one) and a grayling, both on the dry Cochybonddu. A most satisfactory day's sport for a rank beginner, and the start of what were to be many happy years fishing those small Derbyshire streams.

The 9-foot rod, though of little use for the brooks, was fine for the Ashbourne lake, which I started to fish late in May. The first day at the lake was sunny with a strong cool wind. I had absolutely no idea of how to fish a small stillwater (not that I had much idea of how to fish anywhere!) and stuck to the only method I knew caught fish – dry fly. I hadn't yet read Tom Ivens' pioneer book, *Stillwater Fly Fishing*; in fact, at that time the literature on fishing lakes and reservoirs was pitifully small. I had no real source of information to help me, so I plugged away with various small dry flies from eleven in the morning until four in the afternoon.

Bright sun with a strong wind – certainly not the ideal conditions for floating line and dry fly, but how was I to know? Not a single fish rose, either to my flies or to anything else, so I moved over to the nearby Henmore Brook, where a few mayflies were in evidence, easily recognisable even to this novice. I had nothing in my box to represent a mayfly, but managed to get a couple of trout to rise to a dreadful overdressed striped 'Bee' dry fly which someone had given me (probably glad to get rid of it!). The first kicked off and the second was just pricked. The wind gradually lessened, and when I returned to the lake at 9.00 p.m. it was flat calm, and trout were rising all over the place. A wonderful sight. Several anglers were flogging away, with little result to either dry or wet fly.

In those days, the significance of chironomid midges was virtually unknown, and no one could tell me what was causing the hectic activity of the trout. In fact, it was not until three years later that I realised these enthusiastic evening rises were due to what we now call 'buzzers', and that was only when I belatedly discovered the amount of information that examining the stomach contents of a trout could provide. After that, the Ashbourne lake evening rise was easy – a black buzzer nymph fished very slowly.

That first evening, though, was a different matter. I caught one 11-inch brown on a size 15 (yes, we could buy odd-number sizes of hook then) dry Gold-ribbed Hare's Ear. A random choice of pattern, the winged wet version of which I found later was quite effective when ginger buzzers were hatching. There was so much to learn about what to do and what not to do in my new hobby, that I started a fishing diary in a little notebook. Taking notes at university lectures had taught me that in my case the written word, and particularly the act of writing, had a greater impact on what was obviously a 'photographic memory'. Each time I went fishing I jotted down details of the venue, time of day, weather, flies, etc., and found it so useful that I've kept up the practice ever since. Hence my ability to recall in such detail the early experiences I have just recounted. I advise every reader to do the same.

I mentioned earlier that I had already begun to tie flies, a hobby which has added so much to my fishing enjoyment. Fly-fishers who aren't fly-dressers miss a great deal of pleasure and interest. As you learn more and more about the habits of the trout and the tactics required to catch them – and, believe me, you never stop learning – you can sit down at the vice and create new and improved patterns. How satisfying it is when you next go fishing and the new fly catches fish! There's really no substitute for the feeling it gives.

When, like me in those early days, you know so little about which flies to use, there is a tendency to amass a vast number of flies in the hope that you will stumble on *the* fly which will work every time. To tie that vast number of flies, you need a huge range of materials. So I started to collect fly-tying materials with unbridled enthusiasm. This began to drain my finances to a dangerous degree, when it suddenly hit me that because I had a retail shop why not buy materials wholesale? The natural progression was that we started to sell fly-tying materials and soon extended the stocks to include fishing tackle. We formed another company to run the aquarium trade outlet. And so a business was started which grew into a nationally-known specialist game-fishing concern of some repute.

Meanwhile, as the weeks of my first fly-fishing season sped by, I fished the Ashbourne club waters as often as I could, mostly with dry fly, which I found easier to fish compared with wet fly. Because the brooks were so narrow, and the pools so small, there was no real opportunity to practise across-and-down wet-fly tactics. My casting was getting more accurate, and a properly aimed dry fly usually brought a rise, though I didn't always manage to hook the fish. Fishing these small streams taught me a lot about how not to scare trout; there was much creeping and crawling on hands and knees, Red Indian-style, in order to get into a suitable position from which to cast to a fish. The author of one of the books I had read stressed that the angler's approach to the water should be 'unseen, unheard, and unheralded', and where those Derbyshire streams were concerned he was absolutely right. I used to say later that if you could catch trout on the Bentley Brook you could catch trout on any river in the United Kingdom. Certainly when I joined the Cromford Fly-Fishers in 1957 and fished their stretch of the River Derwent, I found the fishing much easier due to the increased size of the river. It was there that I learned to fish downstream wet-fly and upstream nymph, but that's another story.

My stillwater fly-fishing didn't develop much that first season, mainly because I persisted in fishing mostly dry flies more suited to river fishing. I wonder what would have happened if I had used the modern reservoir 'dries' devised by Dave Shipman many years later? Progress wasn't helped by well-meant advice I was given by two expert anglers who specialised in fishing dry fly. The first was Tommy Tulett, who ran a small firm making dog biscuits and was a season-ticket holder at Ladybower reservoir up in the Derbyshire hills. Ladybower had steeply sloping banks, the slope of which continued underwater – ten feet out it was ten feet deep – and the water was of rather acidic moorland origin; this meant there was little underwater food available, and the fish were often on the lookout for surface flies. Tommy was frequently top-scorer at Ladybower, with small Black Gnat dry flies cast along the bank to the edge of the ripple, so naturally he advocated this method when he invited me to share a day there with him. It was Tommy who invented the saying 'Wait till the rings are the size of a dustbin lid' regarding the timing of the strike to dry fly. I was treated to a perfect demonstration, as Tommy got the four-fish limit and I missed the two fish which rose to my fly.

The second source of advice was old Alan Hardy, who had fished the Ashbourne lake for very many years. He was the first man I knew who used fluorescent flies; his most successful pattern on the Ashbourne lake was a simple hackled fly with a fluorescent scarlet body and black hackle, especially for the evening. Chatting to me as we left the lake after he had had five trout and everyone else had caught nothing, he told me to leave the fly static most of the time, with an occasional twitch to simulate life. What could I do but follow his advice?

The season was almost over when I found out that the Ashbourne club had access to a small pool at nearby Bradley. Very few fished it because only a few yards of one bank was fishable; all the remaining banks were overgrown with bushes and quite marshy. The pool held only a few fish, again all browns, and these were of better average size than those in the town lake. I ended the season there with two trout, of 1lb 5oz and 1lb 10oz, and to me they were absolute whoppers. Both were caught on a dry sedge pattern which Tommy Tulett had given me; it had a wing made from a body feather of a melanistic pheasant, varnished to stiffen it and enable it to trap air so that it floated well. Tommy was probably the first person to show me that it was possible to create artificial flies which looked quite like the real thing.

By the end of the season I had fished on 36 occasions and caught 38 trout, 19 of which were of takeable size: a season good enough to ensure that I was well and truly 'hooked' on fly-fishing.

For a couple of years I was mainly a river fisher. Occasionally I went along with friends to Eyebrook, Ladybower, even Blagdon, but caught very little, despite the reputed ability of the rainbow trout to give easier sport than browns. Usually, the weather on those random days was terrible for fishing – either freezing cold and blowing a gale, or flat calm and brilliant sun. No wonder I wasn't a very enthusiastic reservoir man!

The cost of a day-ticket at Eyebrook was one pound at that time, and it was on my fifth spasmodic visit there that I caught my first Eyebrook trout. I remember looking at it in the net and saying to it, 'Yes, you bugger, you've cost me a fiver!' and I vowed right there and then that I would master Eyebrook. To that end, I fished Eyebrook virtually twice a week for several years (in fact, until Grafham opened in 1966) and although one can never 'master' any water, I learned how to catch Eyebrook trout from both bank and boat. I learned which drifts and which stretches of bank fished best in certain winds; I learned which flies appeared as the season progressed, and what fly patterns to use to best imitate them; I learned how important depth is; I learned about different speeds of retrieve, and a lot more. I learned how to row a boat and how to position it for an accurate drift. I learned that a slight break in the wave-pattern, with ripples going the other way, meant that a trout had risen, and that you didn't need to hear a splash. Oh yes, how I learned. And it all went down in my little notebooks.

As the 1950s gave way to the 1960s, craftsmanship began to give way to technology in the fishing-tackle industry. The Gladding Bubb-L-Ette floating fly-line appeared from America, followed by the same company's Aerofloat line, plus floating lines by AirCel, Shakespeare, and several others. Although more bulky than the silk fly-lines, particularly at the tip, so they didn't present a fly quite as delicately, these early plastic lines freed the fly-fisher from the chore of greasing the fly-line to make it float. The demise of the silk fly-line was inevitable, and made even more certain by the gradual introduction of sinking lines with controlled rates of sinking. My own silk line was discarded – I liked the new lines. Next, fibreglass fly-rods were invented. The first examples were solid and therefore heavy, with terrible actions; built-cane craftsmen felt no threat. Then it was discovered that beautifully light, hollow rods could be made by wrapping resin-impregnated fibreglass cloth round tapered mandrels, and fly-fishing with a 10-foot rod no longer required the arm muscles of a blacksmith. The action of some of the early fibreglass fly-rods left much to be desired, but it was soon learned that wall thicknesses were equally as important as tapers, and some excellent rods became available.

By 1964 I had got rid of all my built-cane trout fly-rods except for the 7-foot Foster Airsprite, and was the proud possessor of two American hollow fibreglass rods assembled from blanks made by the Lamiglas Corporation: the 9-foot Hurricane for the river, and the 9½-foot Galaxy for the reservoirs. At that time, the importance of the weight of a fly-line, rather than its diameter, was being realised, and the American Fishing Tackle Manufacturers' (AFTM) system of numbering line-sizes according to their weight became the accepted formula by which both fly-rods and fly-lines are rated. My Hurricane was rated 6, the Galaxy 8, and they were a joy to use until the advent of carbon-fibre produced even better rods.

I suppose it was the opening of Grafham Water in 1966 that really turned me into a dedicated reservoir fisher. Some super-human once coined a description of the evolution of a fly-fisher: 'First he wants to catch the most, then the biggest, then only the most difficult.' Maybe he had reached stage three, but I must confess that I was then, and still am, still at stages one and two – why make life too hard? Although Chew Valley Lake held big trout, it was too far from my home for me to fish there regularly. Grafham, however, was only one-and-a-quarter hours away, and its big rainbows were like a magnet. I even used to belt down the A1 for a couple of hours' fishing in the evening. I had become a 'Grafham regular'. I did, of course, fish other reservoirs from time to time; I even tried one or two of the small stillwater fisheries which had begun to spring up, but these seemed too artificial for my liking.

Some years later, I moved to Bottesford, a village near Grantham, so was ideally situated to become a 'Rutland regular' when that huge water opened in 1977. Rutland has been my main fishing venue ever since although I've fished most of the major waters including Draycote, Derwent, Pitsford, Brenig, Toft Newton, Bewl, and, of course, Chew, Blagdon, and Grafham. Even wider experience was gained on the big natural lakes – Loch Awe, Lough Sheelin, Lough Conn, and the like.

Nowadays, I fish rivers only occasionally – mostly in the winter months, for grayling. I find reservoir fishing far more interesting, so much more of a challenge. I maintain that you earn every fish you catch from a big reservoir, using every bit of experience gained over the years. My experience – I hesitate to call it expertise – is detailed in the following pages. I sincerely hope that it will help you to enjoy your own reservoir fishing as much as I do mine.

We all like to catch fish, and it's nice to go home with a limit bag, but if you expect a limit every time you fish, you will be disappointed. Too many people nowadays want 'instant fishing', thinking that payment for the day-ticket entitles the holder to a guarantee of the maximum number of trout allowed to be taken. These people feel cheated if they don't catch the limit; 'bag up' is the usual expression. I always suspect that those anglers who grumble about 'limititis disease' secretly wish that they had the skill to catch a limit. Until 1990, Eyebrook had no limit; you could catch as many as your ability, luck, and conscience allowed. On some difficult days, all the effort you could muster only brought a couple of fish to the net; the satisfaction of catching those two fish was worth more than any easy-day limit elsewhere. Approach your fishing in that frame of mind, and you will enjoy every day.

Okay, lecture and moralising over! Now, come reservoir trout fishing with me . . .

Chapter 2

The Reservoir Trout

Before we actually start fishing, I suggest it would be a wise move to learn something of the way trout live and behave. Such knowledge has helped me to understand my quarry better and ultimately to get more enjoyment from my sport. Successful trout fishing is partly a study of trout behaviour, which is influenced not only by what creatures the trout is feeding on but by its physical make-up, and its surroundings (including the weather). We will take a look at each of these factors in detail, so that you will be better able to predict the location and feeding activity of the trout before starting to fish. Let's face it – finding the fish and discovering what they are likely to be feeding on is more than half the battle in reservoir fishing.

If you haven't had an offer of some sort from the trout during the first hour of fishing your chosen spot, it is fairly safe to assume that no fish are there at the time, especially if you feel that you have fished it properly. Yet so many people continue to 'stick it out' in the hope that the trout will show up. I always think it's better to move elsewhere and try to find some fish; you can always return to the original area later – very often the trout will move into a particular location in the evening, perhaps attracted by a hatch of insects there, even though it has been unproductive during the day. 'Finding the fish' doesn't only mean ascertaining which parts of the reservoir hold reasonable numbers of trout; it also includes finding out the all-important depth at which they are living. Once those two problems are satisfactorily solved, I suggest that success in much of the remainder of the battle involves good casting technique and the correct manipulation of the right flies. There are some areas of every reservoir which rarely hold fish, and others which are rarely unpopulated – the latter referred to as 'hot-spots' – because the depth of water, the topography of the bottom, and the abundance of food, are all ideal for the trout. Knowing what makes for these ideal conditions gives you the edge over those who do not. Of course, it's easy to follow the crowd and tag on to the end of a shoulder-to-shoulder line of anglers on the bank, or to join an armada of anchored boats. Neither, however, ensures that you will catch fish. The line of bank-anglers could possibly be there because the wind direction is conducive to easier casting (not always the best place for catching fish) and the huddle of boats is often the result of the peculiarly magnetic attraction which a static boat has for others ('He's been over there for ages – must be catching fish') and one boat becomes two becomes ten.

How much nicer it is to assess the situation properly and to find a productive spot on your own, a direct result of your own thinking. I found one such location some years ago, along the north bank of Hambleton Peninsula at Rutland Water. Looking at it from the track, it seemed to be a featureless length of bank, but there was a nice slope to the reservoir bed there, with a shelf drop-off within casting range, plus correctly-sited weed-growth. Everyone used to drive past it, the regulars smiling and no doubt saying, 'There's Saville on his travels again' when they saw the lone angler, having recognised the car parked nearby. For a long time I had the place to myself and caught a lot of fish there. Of course it was too much to hope that it would be my exclusive territory for ever. Others finally discovered its potential for themselves, but it is still identified on the map of Rutland Water as 'Saville's Travels'. Immortality at last!

Another easy ploy is to ask the bailiffs or the fishing-lodge staff where fish were being caught earlier. Again, this is no guarantee that you will catch fish. A subtle change of wind can move fish overnight. I've long ago stopped asking reservoir staff for such information; the information given, though well-meant, was rarely helpful enough.

To enable you to make your own independent decisions on where and how to fish, we must first examine the trout themselves. There are two major species of trout normally stocked in reservoirs – brown trout and rainbow trout. There have been trial stockings of other species from time to time, such as brook trout (actually a char) and odd hybrids like 'tiger trout', but these have not been successful enough to merit repeating. The waters are usually stocked with either or both major species at the minimum takeable size, which more often than not is 12 inches; some less fertile reservoirs have a lower size-limit. Most reservoirs have a rule which insists that all trout landed must be killed, hence the stocking of fish which are takeable.

Returning played-out trout to the water demands very careful handling indeed, even if barbless hooks have been used. Rainbows especially fight very hard and are completely exhausted when netted; they do not always recover if released. Brown trout fight less energetically as a rule, so may be returned with less risk, provided the fish are not damaged. While on the subject of returning trout, I must say that I am totally against introducing 'catch-and-release' methods where reservoirs are concerned. Apart from the unfortunate fact that many anglers carelessly mishandle fish and damage them, which is detrimental to the well-being of the fish, my main concern is that using the catching of fish solely for sport gives important ammunition to the anti-bloodsports brigade. At least when we catch and

Above: Fishing in front of the Lodge on Blagdon Lake

Right: Bentley Brook, Ashbourne. The exact spot where I caught my first trout on the fly

Right: River Derwent, Derbyshire, July 1957

Below: Grafham Water, where the first Muddler was fished

Above: Brown trout   *Below:* Rainbow trout

kill our trout we can claim that they are used as food. There are so many dangers lurking which can seriously affect game-fishing in the future, and we must all be careful to guard against attacks from often ill-informed 'do-gooders'. Furthermore, we must be prepared vociferously to defend our fishing when defamatory remarks are made in the media; letters published in the newspapers are a typical example – so rarely do we see individual anglers, or, more importantly, top representatives of angling organisations, replying to criticisms of fishing. We would all prefer to get on quietly with our fishing but nowadays this isn't enough. No longer can fishing of any sort be simply 'the contemplative man's recreation'. We have to fight for our recreative sport, whether we like it or not. Sorry to have digressed, but this needed to be said!

Now let's get back to our fish . . .

In addition to normal stocking, one or two reservoirs, notably Chew and Rutland, have stocked some brown trout at yearling size – between 5 and 7 inches – with the idea that those which survive predators such as cormorants and pike (not to mention some 'fish-mongering' humans!) will grow into decent-sized fish. Because yearling browns are much cheaper than 12-inch browns, this is economically quite feasible. Experts predict a 20 per cent survival rate over five years, at the end of which the browns should be at least 4lb in weight. A brown trout of this size, grown on virtually as a wild fish, is a trophy to be greatly prized. While they are below the takeable size-limit, however, these small browns must be returned to the water if caught. If bank-fishing, the best way to do this is to rush the fish into the landing-net (do not under any circumstances haul the fish flapping up the bank, as this damages skin and scales) and, holding the fly in your forceps or scissor-pliers, shake the fish off the hook without handling it in any way. If boat-fishing, this can be done without resorting to the landing-net; just suspend the fish half out of the water at the side of the boat.

One other point while we are on the subject of these under-sized fish: they tend to shoal, especially for a couple of months after stocking, so if you start to catch them, move to another place. There's absolutely no sense in staying there and having to shake off fish after fish. Apart from providing no sport worthy of the name, these babies are possibly the whoppers of the future, so why put them at risk?

Reservoir fishery managers have found that it is usually not worth stocking under-sized rainbow trout in the hope that they will grow on into sizeable fish. Although rainbows tend to grow faster than browns, they do not live as long (the average lifespan is four years), and for some unknown reason a large percentage do not seem to over-winter too well. The usual 'stockie' rainbow, at 12–14 inches, is two years old and weighs from

1–1¼lb. In a fertile Midland reservoir like Rutland Water, those stocked in March which remain uncaught are often more than double that weight by the following September, and the lucky ones which survive a mild winter can be 3½–4lb by the next May. And what fantastic fish they are! Fully-finned and full of fight, they can strip a full fly-line and yards of backing off the reel in seconds. What a difference from those dreadful big tail-rotted stockies you find in some small stillwater fisheries. The weekly angling press love to publish pictures of an angler holding one of these stewpond monstrosities, with a typical caption reading: 'Joe Bloggs with a superb 14lb 3½oz rainbow'. They fail to tell you that it was probably stocked the day before it was caught, and fought like a wet sack. How they dare to describe such a fish as 'superb' beats me. One more reason why I prefer reservoir trout fishing!

Whilst on the subject of undesirable stocking, one or two reservoirs are now putting in some of these big 'tail-less wonders' in an effort to boost attendances. I do wish they wouldn't. I would hate to see the day when to catch such fish becomes the accepted norm. The fish I am holding in the jacket photograph is one caught at Draycote Water.

Similarly, I don't like the increasing practice of introducing farmed salmon into the smaller reservoirs. Okay, it gives Mr Average a chance to catch a salmon, but in my opinion a salmon should be a wild fish in a river if it is to give proper sport. Or at least a wild fish in a big natural lake connected to the sea.

Now, having got that off my chest, here's some background on our two major reservoir trout species. First, the brown trout (*Salmo trutta*), which in fact is rarely brown in colour, but often a mixture of olive, bronze, yellow, gold, silver, or grey. The colour is extremely variable, according to location. The peaty waters of some upland reservoirs hold dark fish, whereas the 'Loch Leven' strain is silver. At one time, these colour variations were thought to be different species, but modern zoologists agree that they are all *Salmo trutta*. Often referred to by those of a poetic nature as 'the speckled beauty', the brown trout carries black spots which are sometimes mixed with red or ringed with blue. These spots are not continued on to the tail fin.

Browns don't like water which is too warm. They usually retire to the cool depths during summer, although they can be tempted to venture temporarily into unsuitable temperatures by an evening hatch of big sedge-flies or a shoal of coarse-fish fry. This preference for cold water isn't surprising, because expert zoologists tell us that the brown trout originated in the Arctic seventy million years ago. As the ice of the Glacial Era spread southwards, the brown trout moved in front of it, to become very widespread in distribution. As well as being native to Britain, browns are found naturally in Scandinavia, France, Austria, Spain, Yugoslavia, Germany, Russia, Algeria, parts of Asia, and even Morocco. It has also been introduced to many other countries, including India, South Africa, Australia, New Zealand, Kenya, USA, Canada, the Falklands, and parts of South America. In the hot countries, it is of course restricted to the cold mountain streams.

The brown trout is looked on with affection, almost respect, by many reservoir fly-fishers, to whom the capture of a 'brownie' seems to have greater value than any other fish. This is perhaps based on its reputation to be more wary and more wily than the rainbow, characteristics possibly more imagined than true. When first put into a reservoir, stockie browns tend to shoal, and are often too easy to catch, especially by the bank-angler. The onset of warm weather sends them out of the margins into the depths, where they can only be caught by sunk-line methods. As they grow and acclimatise, the bigger browns become 'loners' and less conspicuous. This comparative unavailability is perhaps what gives them their special status.

Brown trout do not breed in reservoirs to any great extent. They will enter feeder streams if allowed to, and spawn on suitable gravelly stretches. They will also spawn in the reservoir itself in shallow areas with a stony bottom, but the eggs need a proper flow of cold aerated water for hatching, so rarely come to anything. The spawning season is November/December.

The rainbow trout (*Salmo gairdneri*) is originally an American species, native to the western United States from the southern part of Alaska down to California. There are several different strains or sub-species of rainbow, notably the attractive November-spawning Shasta type, which inhabit the McCloud River near Mount Shasta in the Sierra Nevada (first introduced into the UK in 1928 by D. F. Leney of the Trent Fish Culture Company at Mercaston in Derbyshire), and the Irideus type, which is the one mostly used nowadays. Unfortunately, Irideus rainbows spawn in spring, and many are out of condition at the start of the normal trout-fishing season. The males particularly are noticeably dark-coloured (the infamous 'black' rainbows), easy to catch due to their pugnacity, squirting white milt when handled. The Shasta type spawn in November, so it is a great pity that British fish-farmers don't use them. The original idea of Leney's was to get all the hatchery work over at the same time, browns and rainbows, but this didn't meet with universal agreement. It has been whispered that fish-farmers choose to breed the Irideus rainbows because they can be stripped after the browns, thus spreading the workload. The modern tendency is to carry that approach even further by importing fish from such faraway countries as Australia, in order to get eggs at different times of the year and provide more regular sizes of trout for the stocking of reservoirs throughout the season. There are some trout farms working on 'photo-period' spawning, i.e., changing the length of daylight hours by artificial lighting, in order to control the times of spawning.

When fishing in April, if you happen on 'black' fish, leave them alone; the flesh is in poor condition and they are simply not worth taking. In an effort to overcome the problems created by out-of-condition fish, many reservoirs began to stock with females only, which although not as silvery during the breeding season as they would be later, are more attractive than the males. In recent years, an ideal solution seemed to have been found – genetically-engineered 'sexless female' rainbows termed 'triploids', which could never be out of condition. Triploids are rainbows resulting from an alteration of the chromosomes in the egg from two (diploid) to three by heat treatment immediately after fertilisation; there is also an alternative pressure treatment which is said to be more reliable. Creating triploids can be rather a hit-and-miss affair and also entails extra work on the part of the trout farmer, so, to my knowledge, few breeders currently produce triploids in quantity. After all, the major percentage of output from most trout farms goes to the food market, and the housewife isn't concerned with the sex of her fish course. The main difficulty has been the use of normal eggs (fertilised by normal males) for triploid treatment; triploiding these can result in some of the trout still showing male characteristics. Ideally, to produce a type of egg which is more likely to hatch into a 'sexless female', it is necessary to add an extra stage to the process.

This extra stage involves the fry from normal eggs being fed with carefully-calculated amounts of hormones so that the males become 'reverse males' with testes producing sperm but no ducts through which the sperm can be released. Mature 'reverse males' are killed, opened up, and the milt removed and used to fertilise eggs from normal females. These special fertilised eggs are then treated for triploiding, and should hatch into completely sexless fish which will look attractive and remain in the best possible condition. Unfortunately, there have been reports of high mortality among the alevins. All this means more costly fish, so if we anglers want the benefits of triploid trout we must be prepared to pay more for our fishing in the long run. When in its non-breeding livery, the rainbow is a lovely fish, bright and silvery with a pale magenta stripe along each side. (This stripe is much deeper in colour in rainbows which have bred in the very few rivers in the UK where they have become naturalised, such as the little River Wye in Derbyshire.) The upper parts of the body are decorated with black spots, and these extend on to the tail fin (unlike the spots on a brown trout).

Rainbows tolerate higher water temperatures than browns, so they are able to venture more often into the margins and the upper layer of the reservoir. They seem to have a curiosity, pugnacity, call it what you will, which makes them willing to take our artificial flies or lures fairly readily. When hooked, rainbows fight really hard, with spectacular runs and strong rod-bending dashes. These characteristics combine to make the rainbow the ideal game-fish for the reservoir fly-fisher. Both rainbows and browns are reared in the trout farm stewponds on pelleted food which contains carotene to pigment the flesh pink. This pink coloration is maintained in the reservoir if the trout feed on freshwater shrimps, snails, and daphnia. Pink-fleshed trout always look so much nicer on the plate!

Rainbows seem to be more inquisitive than browns, and sometimes more disposed to feed on a wide variety of food items. Perhaps it is this natural curiosity which causes the rainbow to roam from place to place in the reservoir? It will find an abundance of food in a certain area, and stay there while the food is present. If a change of wind, for example, moves the food supply, the rainbow is prepared to move with it.

Since most of the 'stockies' in a reservoir are rainbows, it is worth studying their behaviour. They have been used to living in a crowd in the stewponds and cages, which explains why, for some time after being released into the reservoir, they tend to shoal. Not being used to fighting any water current, they often drop downwind in rough weather. Because they are unaccustomed to deep water, stock fish will patrol the shallows, often at the edge of a sudden drop-off. It takes quite a time for them to acclimatise to the vast expanse of the reservoir. Having no experience of feeding on natural foods, curiosity makes them nip and tweak at anything which moves, including your fly!

Whether brown or rainbow, the trout is anatomically a primitive form of life, yet with a body perfectly constructed for rapid swimming. The trout's brain is quite rudimentary when compared with the human brain, yet anglers constantly credit trout with having feelings, thoughts, memory, and intelligence as if they were human. Believe me, the brain of a trout simply does not have the ability to think. A trout behaves by reacting instinctively to various stimuli such as light, movement, temperature, and so on.

A trout has no intelligence as such, otherwise it would never be caught. It can learn, for example, that trout food pellets are good to eat and that these pellets make splashes when they enter the water. Get a handful of gravel of similar size to trout pellets, and throw it into a stewpond; the trout will immediately react as if the gravel was food, boiling at the surface and trying to swallow the falling particles. Even after having discovered that they have been fooled, they react in the same way every time you throw the gravel in. Educated but still stupid!

There are lots of other examples of this lack of intelligence. Having been fooled into taking an artificial lure, and having broken the line, a trout will still take another artificial – we have all caught a trout with someone else's fly still in its jaw. The more you think about it, the more you realise how much the behaviour of the trout is due to instinctive reactions.

Now let's take a look at the trout itself. The scales which cover the body grow in the same way as human fingernails, the scale material being thrown off by root cells. Each growth period shows as a 'ring' on the scale, so by microscopic examination of a scale the age of the fish can be determined. Along each side of the body is a row of sensitive cells, the 'lateral line', which pick up waterborne vibrations and carry them to a mucus-filled tube under the skin, with sensory cells connected to the nervous system. Like sonar, this warns the trout of possible danger. Anglers must therefore avoid any actions giving rise to sudden sharp vibrations which can be transmitted through water – jumping down a bank to the water's edge, banging anything whatsoever in a boat, throwing an anchor into the water, etc. Although trout do have ears internally, these are not concerned with hearing, but with maintaining balance. You can talk as loudly as you like and it won't disturb the trout (although it may well disturb nearby anglers!). Low-flying jet aircraft also don't seem to have any effect on them.

Trout can detect odours in the water, using twin nostrils situated on either side of the snout. They can also taste food; the mouth is generously supplied with taste-buds. Perhaps this explains why certain insects are ignored by feeding trout.

A very thin coating of mucus covers the body, helping to protect it from infection, and reducing friction for speedy movement through the water; this mucus also slows down the process of osmosis and helps to keep the trout's body-fluids stable. It is therefore most important not to handle fish with hot dry hands if you intend to return them to the water. There are eight fins, including the tail fin which acts as propellor and rudder. The main locomotive thrust comes from the body muscles, so the eroded tails of some stockies are not really a physical handicap. The dorsal and anal fins keep the fish on an even keel. The paired pectoral and ventral muscles act as brakes, stabilisers, and auxiliary rudders. The little adipose fin, situated at the back just in front of the tail, does not appear to have any function. It is a commonly accepted fallacy that only game-fish like salmon, trout, and grayling have the adipose fin. In fact, several other families of fish sport an adipose fin, such as the characins, the popular tetras of the tropical aquarium.

An active fish like the trout needs highly-oxygenated water in which to live, hence its need for comparatively cool water temperatures. Warm water holds less dissolved oxygen. To extract oxygen from the water, the trout has efficient gills, which are attached to bony arches on each side of the mouth cavity. So that blood can be easily pumped to the gills, the heart is situated right at the front of the body cavity; the rate of heartbeat is directly affected by water temperature, slowing in cold, quickening in warmer water. This is typical of the 'cold-blooded' animal whose activity is related to its body temperature.

The actual gill filaments are delicate and easily damaged; they are protected from external damage by the gill covers. In addition to this protection, there are strainers called gill-rakers, which sieve bits of debris from the water. The trout can therefore swim and 'breathe' in water containing particles of suspended algae, or dirt stirred up from the bottom by wave action, without the gill filaments becoming clogged. This breathing action is worth explaining. As a fish opens and closes its mouth, many people think it is drinking water, whereas in fact it is pumping water over its gill filaments. When the mouth opens, the gill covers close, and water is sucked into the mouth cavity. As the mouth closes, the floor of the mouth cavity rises and pushes water over the gills and out through the now-open gill covers. Why doesn't the water go down the throat? Because the constricted pharynx at the top of the throat is constantly closed unless food is to be passed down into the stomach.

When feeding, water is inevitably taken into the mouth and then pushed out again when the mouth closes, leaving the food to be swallowed 'damp'. Food passes down a short gullet into the U-shaped stomach, which at its hind end bears several creamy-coloured 'fingers', the pyloric caeca; these are sometimes mistaken for tapeworms when gutting the fish. Their function is not fully known, but it is thought that they aid digestion. Even if I haven't previously bothered to discover exactly what the trout has been feeding on, I always make a point of examining the stomach contents when gutting the trout. Having cut the upper end of the stomach away from the gullet, it is easy to run finger and thumb along the stomach from the lower end, squeezing the 'sausage' of food into water in a plastic dish or cup. A quick stir with the finger separates the mass into individual items, and these can then be identified. Separation of the contents in water is essential for proper identification; rarely can much information be gained from a cursory glance beforehand. It's interesting to correlate what is in the stomach with the pattern of fly which has taken the fish, making future fly selection much easier.

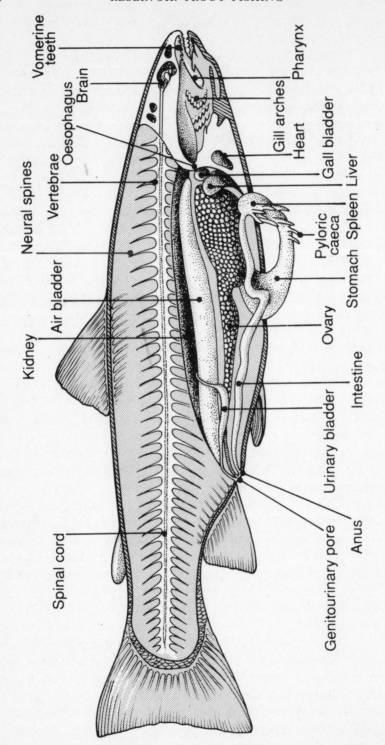

The anatomy of a trout

The stomach leads to a short intestine (typical of a carnivorous creature), then to the anal opening just in front of the anal fin. The trout's digestive system is quite complete, having also liver, gall-bladder, and spleen.

The kidney of a trout is not the usual bean-shaped organ found in higher animals. It is the dark layer of tissue lying along the top of the body cavity next to the backbone. Near the kidney layer you will see a glistening membrane, often partly inflated. This is the swim-bladder, which has several functions, some of which are not fully understood by our scientific friends. From the angler's point of view it is sufficient to say that automatic regulation of the amount of gas in the swim-bladder enables the trout to maintain its equilibrium according to the depth at which it needs to swim.

Now we know where everything is and what it does, this is perhaps an opportune moment for some instruction on how best to gut a trout. My own method stems from my university training in dissection, and it's quick and easy. The only tools needed are a large pair of kitchen scissors and a table knife. Do the job over the kitchen sink, and have a newspaper handy to receive the innards.

My method is, I feel, the more acceptable if you prefer to leave the head of the trout on – some people like to see the fish as a fish and not as a lump of meat. Holding the trout upside-down, insert the point of the scissors into the anal opening and cut open the abdomen in a straight line, ending at the gills. Try not to puncture the intestine. Open the slit and you will see the liver and little heart near the head. Pull them out with your fingers. If the fish is a mature female you will see two orangey egg-masses; fingers remove these too. With your scissors, snip the gullet at the front end of the stomach, as close as possible to where it disappears into the head. The stomach and intestine are now easily pulled out in one piece. (Don't forget to examine the contents of the stomach.)

In a male fish you will see the two creamy-white testes (soft roes) which are easily removed. Pull out the swim-bladder next, exposing the dark kidney tissue. Scrape this away from the backbone with the knife, working from head to tail; make sure you remove every scrap. I find it better to do this under a running tap, although the 'bits' must then be removed from the plug-hole. If you don't want to keep the head and tail on, now is the time to cut them off, using a sharp knife; much less messy than chopping the head off first. This is best done on a chopping-board, of course. Then swill the body cavity under the tap, at which time you can get rid of any lingering bits, and wash out any blood from the gills by letting the water run through the opened mouth of the fish. A quick shake to remove surplus water, and into the plastic bag, ready for the freezer.

There's one more important item to discuss before we leave the subject of trout anatomy – the eye. Sight is essential for a trout to survive. A blind trout cannot feed, and quickly becomes emaciated and dies. What a trout sees is important to the fly-fisher too, because this has a very great bearing on the colours and designs of the flies we use.

The eye of a trout is well-developed and very similar to the human eye. Both can be likened to a camera – the iris aperture allows light to pass through the lens, which focuses the image on the retina. A trout, however, has no eyelids, and there are other differences. The lens in the trout eye is spherical instead of elliptical, for better vision in water; it can be moved forward or away from the retina to give long-range or short-range focusing. The iris cannot be opened or closed, so there is no protection from bright sunlight.

The retina can be thought of in the same way as the screen of a colour television. It has two important types of light-receptive cells – rod-shaped for black-and-white, cone-shaped for colour. The retina of the trout eye is adapted for seeing in dim light, having a majority of rod cells. It also has cone cells, so don't let anyone tell you that a trout cannot see colour! Trout can distinguish colours and shades of colours, so our artificial flies sometimes need to be accurately-coloured representations of living creatures, or at least lures of a certain colour.

In trout, each eye has its own field of vision to the side, but there is also a straight-ahead binocular vision, enabling distance to be judged when taking a fly or any other food item. It is wise to remember that trout can see outside their watery element, through the surface. The frightening effect of sudden movement or flashing reflections from rods or fly-lines, whether on bank or boat, needs to be eliminated as much as possible. Imagine that the trout can see you at all times, and you'll behave in a way which will increase your chances of catching them. Never wade straight into the water, for example. You could scare off a trout from the shallows, whereas by a stealthy approach you might have caught it. I remember one dawn session at Chew, when I caught a beautiful 3-lb rainbow which was cruising in water no more than a foot deep, six feet from the edge, by kneeling in the grass and casting across fifteen yards of dry ground to the little swirl it made on the surface. I would never have caught that fish if I had stomped straight in.

I hope that you will now agree that simple biological study such as we have just done helps you to understand how and why a trout behaves as it does, and gives you a better chance of a good catch. Let us next find out which parts of the reservoir offer us the *best* chances of a good catch, and how the weather affects the location and method we choose.

Chapter 3

Reservoirs and the Weather

The answers to the all-important questions of where and how to fish are determined by the type and topography of the reservoir you are fishing, and by weather conditions. So let us now take a look at those factors.

I must remind you that this book is about fishing in water-supply reservoirs containing stocked trout and usually offering bank-fishing and boat hire; it does not deal with fishing in natural waters like the lochs of Scotland, the llyns of Wales, the Irish loughs, or the English lakes like Ullswater.

The geographical location of a reservoir gives an indication of what to expect regarding water fertility and the contours of the reservoir bed. Reservoirs situated in moorland or mountainous districts are likely to contain acid water of low pH content, and are usually deep, with steeply-sloping margins often lined with coniferous forests. The water comes off peaty land, in which case it is stained amber or brown, or insoluble rock such as granite, when it is gin-clear; it contains little nutrients and few situations where trout food can thrive. Due to frequent drying-out of the steep margins when water is drawn off, there is no chance for nymphs or even acid-loving water plants to survive. Trout therein are usually small browns relying on insects blown off the surrounding land for much of their food, plus a few larger 'Ferox' specimens which feed on the small ones. Rainbows rarely do well in such waters. There are exceptions such as Ladybower, where some alkaline water comes into the reservoir from limestone sources, making the conditions a little more suitable for stocked trout to thrive. Llyn Brenig in the hills of Clwyd in North Wales is another upland reservoir worth fishing; it is stocked with rainbows and browns, both of which do well and put on some weight, though they darken in colour due to the peaty water. Two kinds of flies give success in this class of reservoir – black or dark brown patterns suggesting the limited insect life (Bibio, Black Pennell, Mallard & Claret, for example), or bright fluorescent patterns which are more visible in the stained water.

When bank-fishing this type of reservoir, short casts out or long casts along the bank will cover the most productive water; boat-anglers should either hug the shoreline with floating lines or fish fast-sinkers further out unless there is an obvious rise to an abundance of surface insects.

Normally, however, the acid upland reservoirs offer little of interest except to locals. Their effective season is short, due to the altitude; the water doesn't warm up sufficiently until late May and cools off sharply in September. Fishing methods are usually best restricted to dry-fly imitations of land-bred insects such as heather fly, various beetles, and perhaps crane-flies and grasshoppers if there is some grassland nearby. However, small dark wet-fly patterns also work. I had an enjoyable day a few years ago, bank-fishing Loch Nant, a small reservoir in the hills above Taynuilt, Argyllshire. It was a hot sunny day in June, with an easterly breeze rippling the surface. Flies were being blown on to the water from the surrounding heather, and the trout were rising spasmodically. Travelling light, I had no dry flies with me, but a size 16 winged wet Alder on a floating line brought me seventeen little brownies, the best weighing about 12 oz. I fished with my back to the breeze, casting into the ripple. It was great fun, once I had learned to strike at the slightest touch, but no substitute for a day at Rutland!

Yes, it is the lowland reservoirs that give the greatest potential for good sport with trout of a very satisfactory size, and incidentally offer the greatest challenge. Reservoirs located in lowland countryside are usually shallow by comparison, often with gently-sloping margins, and have basically clear water of neutral or even alkaline pH value. They are fertile, full of water-plants and trout food. Both rainbows and browns thrive in such waters, and can reach a large average size. Surrounded by farmland and adjacent to urban areas, lowland reservoirs are threatened by high concentrations of dissolved nitrates and phosphates from fertilisers and detergents. Under certain conditions of prolonged summer sunshine, these can give rise to heavy blooms of microscopic unicellular algae which feed on such nutrients. Certain of these algae – the blue-green types (identified by their bright bluish-green colour and a distinctive nasty smell) – include species which in very high concentrations can be toxic if ingested by small animals, especially when left as a thick scum by receding water-levels.

From an angler's point of view, these blue-green algae offer no physical threat, except perhaps the possibility of a rash on extra-sensitive skin. The danger lies in the water being closed to angling by the company controlling the reservoir, such as occurred in 1989 at Rutland and other major trout waters. My opinion is that these closures were panic moves in a 'better safe than sorry' vein, exaggerated by media coverage at the time when privatisation of the water industry necessitated good public relations. We must fervently hope that a more sensible attitude prevails if severe infestations of blue-green algae occur in future. At Rutland, for example, none of the almost two hundred members of the Rutland Water

Fly-Fishers' Club (many of whom are locals and season-ticket holders, fishing the water several times a week) reported any adverse effects before or after the 1989 closure. It must be remembered that blue-green algae is not a new phenomenon; it has always been present in lowland reservoirs, but rarely at dangerous heavy-infestation levels.

Much more common, in fertile lowland reservoirs, is the presence of harmless microscopic green (or perhaps brown, such as occurs at Chew from time to time) algae suspended in the water, giving it colour which can range from a slight tinge to something resembling green soup. At one time, I was very unhappy to see water coloured in this way, especially when boat-fishing. I felt that clearer water enabled the trout to see my flies properly, and that in 'thick' colour they couldn't see the flies at all. However, I discovered over the years that the trout *could* see my flies in soupy water – in fact, it's amazing how many takes you get.

Some experienced bank-fishers have told me that they find the fishing much easier when the water isn't clear. Even so, although I'm not quite so worried as I used to be about fishing water coloured with algae, I do prefer water showing a 'visibility factor' of around 5 feet. I have a simple little trick to find how far I can see into the water. I push my rod down below the surface and check when I can't see the tip. If I can see half of my 10½-foot rod, I'm happy. Normal green unicellular algae blooms are potentially harmful (to the trout) only if they reach 'green paint' saturation level and then begin to die off, exhausting the water of oxygen. Luckily, this rarely happens, because daphnia and other plankton feed on this type of algae and clear the water naturally, to the ultimate benefit of the trout.

A typical lowland reservoir offers varied bottom geography, from gently-sloping shallows to sudden deep drop-offs. If bank-fishing, the shallows require 'long-distance' wading before you reach water of a suitable depth, and are subject to high water temperatures and infestation by filamentous algae (blanket weed) in summer. Shallows like these are difficult to fish, but can at times hold some very large trout attracted by the shelter of the weed and the abundant food to be found there. The western end of Rutland's North Arm is a typical example.

The deep drop-offs are interesting in that they frequently hold trout in conditions of summer heat; trout lurking in the cooler water deep down can be reached with fast-sinking lines. There are hopefully lots of banks where the bed slopes gradually, to give a water-depth of between 6 and 10 feet at a distance of 20 yards from the edge – excellent places to fish. There are points, bays, sunken roads, tree-stumps, and we mustn't forget the dam wall (although some reservoirs don't allow access to the dam area) – all potential hot-spots because they either concentrate food supplies or offer acceptable depths of water.

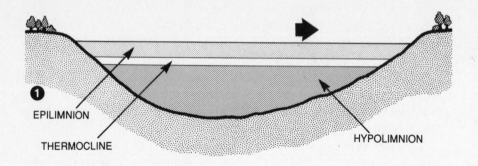

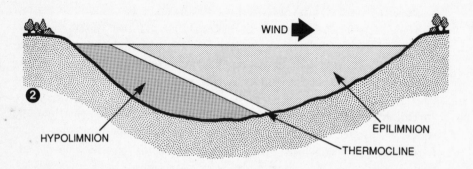

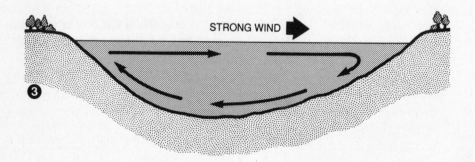

The stratification of water in a reservoir

Fig. 1 The situation in calm conditions
Fig. 2 Continuous wind tilts the layers
Fig. 3 A lengthy period of strong wind mixes the layers

A point or promontory usually has fishable water on all three sides, and enables the bank-angler to reach well out into the surrounding bays; it creates currents which attract the trout to such a degree that sometimes there is an almost constant procession of fish passing upwind past the tip. Sunken roads, usually lined with hedges or stone walls before the land was flooded to create the reservoir, offer sanctuary to small fry and homes for caddis and other larvae, so the trout hang around such places. Dam walls made from rough rocks, as at Draycote and Rutland, offer homes to water-snails and other trout food; even the comparatively smooth concrete dams such as we find at Grafham and Eyebrook bear a growth of algae and therefore contain snails and other food for the trout.

The larger reservoirs are affected by stratification of the water into 'layers' of different temperatures. The basic cause of this stratification is the fact that at 39°F (4°C) water is heavier than at higher temperatures, so water cooled in late autumn or winter to this degree sinks to the bottom. Surface water, warmed by sun or wind, remains lighter and stays at the top; it is affected by wind action which circulates and aerates it. In calm weather, in reservoirs of suitable depth, these two major layers remain undisturbed; there is a narrow layer of cool oxygenated water between the two, which is termed the thermocline. Trout tend to inhabit the thermocline, hence the need to discover its depth when fishing sunk lines.

At some reservoirs, the water engineers have reduced the effect of stratification by installing aerator pumps on the bottom in the deep parts. When in operation, these act like giant aquarium diffuser stones, causing water from the lower depths to be brought to the surface in a huge fizzy turmoil, with resultant circulation and breaking-up of the strata. Particularly in summer, boat-anglers know the attraction these aerator 'boils' have for the trout, providing well-aerated water and a supply of food items.

Reservoir hot-spots, whether geographical or thermal, are far from constant, and the reason for this inconsistency is the British weather. Weather conditions have a very great effect on reservoir trout fishing. Not just the weather on the day we are fishing, but that which has occurred during the previous week. If you are able to have a free choice of days when you can fish (like we lucky retired folk!) be sure to watch or listen to the week's weather forecast given in the TV or radio farming programme. Although it is impossible for this to be always a hundred per cent accurate, it gives a good idea of the weather we are most likely to encounter during the coming week, making the choice of fishing day a little easier. Even more important is the late-night radio or television weather forecast before your chosen day; this is as accurate as it is possible to get.

Basically, there are five weather features which affect our fishing –

wind, temperature, sun, cloud, and barometric pressure.

Let's start by looking at the first two:

Most reservoirs are large enough for the wind and temperature to have important effects on the fish which inhabit them. Wind affects water temperature, and water temperature dictates the activity and location of the trout, as explained in the previous chapter. So the weather tells us where and how to fish. One of the most useful items of equipment for the reservoir fly-fisher is a thermometer, for checking the temperature of the water.

Wind blowing on water creates a surface current flowing in the direction in which the waves are travelling; it also causes the surface water to change temperature, either up or down, according to whether the wind is warmer or colder than the water. If the wind direction is constant over a period of several days, its effect is more pronounced and the behaviour of the fish more predictable. And there is no doubt that a sudden change of wind direction affects the fishing very badly – the fish certainly do not like it.

A warm wind blowing on cold water makes the water warmest towards the downwind shore of the reservoir. As this warmer water reaches the shore it will be pushed downwards and will start to create a circulation which will result in cold water from the deeps rising to the surface on the upwind shore. This means that if you fish the upwind shore (with your back to the wind) or near the upwind shore (with the more preferable side-wind) you will be fishing in the coldest water. Remember, this is where the fish, and incidentally their food organisms, will be at their most lethargic if the water is really cold. In summer, however, this area could be where the water temperature is just cool enough for optimum activity.

If the wind is colder than the water, the surface water is cooled and the coldest water will be found on the downwind shore. Warmer water will be pushed up on the upwind shore and in cold weather this is where you should be fishing. In summer heatwave conditions, however, always check for water too warm for fish to be comfortable, where insect life will also be below par. Ideally, look for water between 45°F (7°C) and 60°F (16°C), according to the season. I remember one day at Blagdon, when a dawn session at Rugmore Point gave me four lovely fish; returning there in the evening, I found that the wind had changed and was blowing into that bank. No matter, I thought, it's not too strong for casting, and set up for the expected buzzer rise. When this failed to materialise, I couldn't understand why, until I happened to put my hand in the water; it felt warm. A thermometer check gave a reading of over 70°F (21°C), too warm for any action. Rushing round to the other side of the reservoir, I found the water at 55°F (13°C) and trout rising well to a superb hatch of buzzers!

Llyn Brenig, a typical upland reservoir

Rutland Water, a huge but typical lowland reservoir

Above: Nymphing from the bank. Note the correct position of the rod for this technique.

Left: Choosing a fly. I find the big fly box a great help, as every fly is visible at a glance.

I would say that this was a perfect example of how temperature and wind affect the fishing.

The direction of the wind is important, too. The prevailing westerly or south-westerly winds are, thankfully, usually accompanied by reasonably comfortable temperatures and a certain amount of cloud. These winds give excellent evening fishing conditions, because a westerly wind usually drops to a nice breeze before dusk, ideal for fishing a hatch of buzzers or sedges. Southerly winds are also liable to provide good fishing. North and east winds are not so good, especially if they follow a long period of wind from the opposite direction. The old rhyme was based on quite sound principles:

> When the wind is in the North,
> the skilful angler goes not forth.
> When the wind is in the South
> it blows the bait into the fish's mouth.
> When the wind is in the East
> 'tis fit for neither man nor beast,
> But when the wind is in the West,
> 'tis then the fishing is the best.

Any sudden change of air temperature can be bad. Night frosts, especially in September or later, can immediately send fish down and kill any hope of surface fishing with floating line. Sunk line is then the only method to use.

Wind strength, or lack of it, is important too. A howling gale makes fishing extremely difficult, if not impossible. If boat-fishing, you cannot control line or flies properly, and even if fishing behind the boat, it may be drifting too fast. A drogue slows the speed down but prevents tacking to give the lure proper movement. In any case, winds above 20 mph make casting hazardous, whether boat- or bank-fishing. A strong wind blowing from the side of your casting arm can mean a fly in your face if you try to aerialise too much line. If blowing from behind, you have to duck on every forward-cast, even if you manage to make a decent back-cast! Casting into a gale-force wind is damned hard work and not always worth the effort; many writers tell us that the trout will always be stacked up along the bank into which the wind is blowing – unfortunately the trout haven't read the books! (If you do feel that you need to cast into the wind, be sure to shorten your leader and to fish no more than two flies.) Even when a strong wind is blowing from a 'safe' side, it puts too great a bow-curve in the line even before it lands on the water. You will have gathered that I don't like fishing in a gale!

Lack of wind, the dreaded 'flat calm', doesn't bother me quite so much when bank-fishing. Casting technique has to be spot-on, of course – it's no use if the flies land in a splashy heap. Don't try to cast too far, for one thing. A quick jerk on the line just before it lands helps to turn over the leader nicely if your casting isn't perfect. At least you can see every movement the trout make; gentle rise-forms which you would not notice in a wave become quite obvious now.

It's when boat-fishing that the flat calm becomes a real problem. The only possibly productive methods left open to you are: (a) cast out a dry fly in the hope that something will come along and take it; or (b) rake the bottom with a deep-sunk nymph. In my experience, it's not worth chasing over to a batch of rising fish – the arrival of the boat usually puts them down! Sit tight and let the fish come to you. Keep a lookout for the advent of a decent ripple, and then get over to it as fast as possible without making too much disturbance with the motor; careful rowing is usually better.

Now let's take a look at sun and cloud.

You will remember that trout have no eyelids, so cannot shut out the sun. Also that their eyes are adapted to seeing best in dull conditions, so they don't like bright sun. Neither do daphnia, those tiny crustacean 'water-fleas' which form an important part of reservoir trout diet, particularly rainbows. Trout feeding on daphnia follow it down to the deeper water in bright weather. So it's pretty obvious that when the sun is shining brightly, you fish deep, unless a hatch of buzzers brings the trout to the surface. If a good hatch occurs, trout don't seem to be able to resist following the ascending buzzer pupae up from the bottom. But as soon as the hatch is over, down they go again. The effect of sunny conditions is not so drastic if the water isn't clear. Water coloured by suspended algae, or whatever, acts as a filter and reduces the brightness, allowing the trout to come higher in the water. We also mustn't forget the shade afforded by waterside woodland, which can create good conditions when the sun dips behind the trees.

There are two words which should not be used when discussing fishing – 'always' and 'never'. 'Usually' and 'not very often' are better substitutes. The combination of clear water, bright sun, and an east wind, which occurred at Rutland for the first three days of May 1990, should have offered very difficult conditions. Instead, I caught three successive limits from the 'Stones' bank, using a floating line and 22-foot leader; every fish took the leaded point fly, a special orange-tailed version of the Gold-ribbed Hare's Ear Nymph. Fishing over deepish water, the secret was to count to forty slowly before starting a very slow retrieve. The air temperature was a comfortable 59°F (15°C) and the wind came from behind.

One more point, before we leave the subject of sunshine, that is of particular interest to the loch-style boat-angler. Trout tend to face into any current of water, so they usually travel up against the waves when they are in the top layers of a reservoir. A wind blowing 'out of the sun' creates blinding conditions for trout which perhaps have been drawn up to the surface by a movement of buzzer pupae. Provided the wind direction doesn't change, the movement of the sun around from east to west has a noticeable effect on the fishing at first one end of the boat and then the other, not to mention the boat as a whole. This alteration of angle of sun can explain why success sometimes comes to one end of the boat and not the other.

Without doubt, cloudy weather is the optimum for reservoir fishing, especially when the cloud cover is in the form of a totally grey blanket high in the sky. There is no sunlight to trouble the trout, and the daphnia is high in the water. Total cloud cover is an insulator, keeping the air temperature comfortable and stable. Think of those summer evenings when suddenly the clouds evaporate to leave a clear blue sky; the air temperature takes a quick dive and you reach for your coat. The hoped-for 'evening rise', if it happens at all, is nothing like it should be – the air is now colder than the water, and conditions are simply not right for a catch.

Rain, although unpleasant to fish in, rarely puts the fish off. One of my best days ever was on Chew in a gale combined with an unrelenting downpour. Boat-fishing with my wife Pat, we caught sixteen trout totalling 50lb.

Immediately after rain can also be a good time for catching fish, possibly allied to a change in air pressure which can then occur. This last weather factor, barometric pressure, is rarely mentioned by angling writers, but I am sure that it has quite an effect on our fishing. A rising barometer usually brings good settled weather, albeit perhaps too sunny and calm sometimes, whereas a falling barometer means rain and wind. Sudden major changes, either up or down, can cause problems which do not arise when the pressure remains steady. For example, if the air pressure falls after a prolonged period of steady pressure, the fishing suffers, but it will recover if the pressure stays low, despite the rain.

The heavy 'close' air which precedes a thunderstorm usually puts fish down, but they often come on the take immediately after the storm when the air clears. Perhaps air pressure affects the swim-bladder of the trout? Or maybe this sudden minor change triggers off a rise of buzzer pupae to the surface?

British weather is notoriously fickle. I make my American friends laugh when I tell them that we can have all four seasons in one day! One thing is certain – on most days, you can't afford not to have your waterproof clothing with you when you go fishing. Which leads us neatly to the next chapter . . .

Chapter 4

Equipment and Tackle

Actual fishing will have to be delayed a little longer while we discuss tackle, although I'll be outlining various techniques when recommending suitable items. Too many people try to fish reservoirs with equipment which is quite wrong for the job. Often this has been advised by a well-meaning friend with very limited knowledge, or sold by a tackle dealer who has no practical experience of reservoir fly-fishing. To get the most enjoyment out of your fishing you need the right tools for the various methods, and my long experience in the game-fishing tackle trade will, I hope, help you to choose these from the vast and bewildering array currently on offer.

My first piece of advice is that you buy your reservoir tackle from a specialist source carrying a comprehensive range of gear, with a proprietor (or staff member) who fishes reservoirs regularly. Such shops should be able to keep up-to-date with what is happening on local waters in addition to stocking everything you may need. If there isn't a specialist supplier in your area, the large long-established mail-order firms who advertise their catalogues in the game-fishing magazines are a safe bet.

CLOTHING

You won't be able to give your full attention to fishing if you are not comfortable, and this means proper weatherproof clothing and footwear. A good fishing jacket is essential for personal comfort in bad weather, and that means not only rain but cold and wind. It must be designed correctly – so many lack what I feel are necessary features.

The jacket must be light in weight. Casting is an energetic exercise, and a heavy jacket hastens the onset of fatigue and perspiration as well as hampering free movement. It should have shoulders designed to prevent the sleeves riding up when casting, thus exposing to rain the sleeves of any garment worn underneath; knitted storm-cuffs inside the sleeves are a useful feature. The jacket must be long enough to cover the tops of thigh waders so that rain doesn't run off into the waders. It must have a deep 'wading flange' along the bottom edge, because everyone at times feels the need to wade deep, and the jacket must not soak up water while doing so. It should have a hood permanently attached, large enough to be immediately and easily pulled over a fishing hat, and with a drawstring for complete protection in very heavy rain and wind. The main pockets must have double flaps which are extensions of the pockets themselves, so that when folded over they prevent rain entering; these pockets should be large enough to hold a sizeable fly-box in one and a towel and priest in the other – items which need to be readily accessible. There should be a D-ring above the breast pocket, to which you can tie a pair of scissor-pliers; another D-ring at the side is useful if you wish to clip a telescopic folding landing-net on to your jacket. A stormproof front, with studded flap and strong two-way zip, is normally a feature, but the collar is often not high enough to keep your neck dry and warm. The traditional waxed-cotton jacket has never been my choice, because I feel that the water-proofing method isn't completely suited to fly-fishing activity; wear or actual cracks can appear in the sleeves and this is quite unacceptable (although the makers will replace the jacket if this happens). I don't like the alternative woven-cloth 'breathing' materials either; although very comfortable to wear, these have rarely proved to be completely waterproof in a prolonged downpour.

I prefer PVC material, which keeps out wind and rain a hundred per cent and, incidentally, is comparatively cheap. It is said that a PVC jacket causes excess sweating, but I haven't found this. The Peter Storm 205 jacket is pretty good, but I would prefer it to have some of the above-mentioned design features.

Boat-fishing necessitates wearing fully-waterproof over-trousers, not only in wet weather but to protect against splashes from heavy waves in dry weather when moving from one part of the reservoir to another, and boat seats are often wet first thing in the morning, from dew or overnight rain. The only fully reliable waterproof over-trousers are again those in PVC. None of the others will withstand being sat in on a wet boat seat – the pressure forces water through the pores of any woven material. Over-trousers should have an elasticated waist and no side-slits or fly-front to let rain in. The legs should be wide enough for the garment to be easily put on and taken off over calf-length footwear such as Derriboots or wellingtons.

I'm keen to keep my hands warm and dry when I'm fishing. It's impossible to fish properly if your hands are numb with cold, and wet hands soon get cold when the wind blows on them. So I always carry a towel and dry my hands frequently in cold weather. The towel is also needed after handling a trout; washing off the slime, then drying the hands, enables you to carry on fishing comfortably. In cold, windy weather

I also like to wear shooting mittens which keep the backs of my hands and my wrists protected from the cold whilst allowing free movement of the fingers.

Some form of headgear, with a wide brim to shade the eyes, is advisable. There are plenty of cheap peaked caps available if you are prepared to advertise a brand of tackle on the front. My choice alternates between one of these and a camouflage hat I bought in America; similar hats are available in the UK. Whatever type you choose, try to fight the urge to stick flies in it. I have been guilty of this in the past, and I can tell you that all it does is ruin both the flies and the hat! If you don't wear a hat or cap, eyestrain can become a problem, and you should also remember that the body loses a lot of heat from an unprotected head. A towelling scarf or cravat prevents heat loss at the neck in cold weather, and helps to keep the neck dry in rainy conditions. I wouldn't be without mine.

Whilst on the subject of clothing, perhaps it would be a wise move to follow the advice of Peter McKenzie-Philps and take along a spare pair of trousers, socks, and underpants – in case you fall in (it has been known!). Lady anglers will know which necessary garments to include in their 'falling-in kit'.

POLARISED SPECTACLES

I mentioned eyestrain just now. Even with the help of a hat-brim, this can become a real problem when you're concentrating hard all day on a glaring rippled water surface, so a really good pair of polarised sunglasses is very necessary. In addition to reducing eyestrain they protect the eyes from damage by hooks flying around in strong blustery winds. You only have one pair of eyes, and it is stupid to risk your sight. Ordinary sunglasses are better than nothing. Polarised lenses give much better visibility and in my opinion the Optix Cormorant Crylon HLT (High Light Transmission) models are the best. The lenses are made in either grey or amber; the latter colour seems to be preferable. Clip-on models are available for spectacle-wearers like myself; make sure they are light in weight – slightly too heavy, and they gradually push your spectacles down your nose, which is most uncomfortable. A handy feature of any pair of polarised glasses is the flip-up lens – you don't always need to look through the glasses.

TACKLE CARRIERS – WAISTCOATS, BAGS AND BOXES

My fishing waistcoat is an indispensable item, holding almost every item of equipment I need, readily to hand. Much better than a shoulderbag or haversack, because the gear is distributed among many pockets, so it's easier to find an individual item quickly (provided that – like me – you are orderly and always keep the things in the same pockets!), and the total weight isn't concentrated on one shoulder. If you are wading, you don't have to keep plodding back to the bank every time you need to change a fly, for example.

There are lots of waistcoats on the market, including some which incorporate buoyant flotation material, such as the Heron range. These are a wise buy for the boat-angler who can't swim. I bought my own Stream Designs waistcoat in America; it was costly, but superbly designed, with a great number of pockets, some of which are specially shaped to hold specific items such as sunglasses. There are even six internal pockets along the lower edge for different spools of nylon. Whichever waistcoat you choose, make sure it has plenty of pockets and that these are the 'bellows' type which are more roomy, so that you can carry a spare reel or spool in one of them.

When choosing a waistcoat, think of the items you will want to carry on your person, and make sure that it has enough suitably-sized pockets to accommodate all these; there are several brands on offer which don't meet this requirement. The only item of tackle I don't carry in my waistcoat is my big 'stock' fly-box. When bank-fishing, this goes in a big strong plastic sack which also holds my food and flask; I leave this on the bank, top folded well over, so all is safe if it pours with rain. I never find that I need the old-fashioned 'fishing bag' nowadays.

When boat-fishing, these items are transferred (together with a drogue and various extra fly-lines on reels or spools) to a good-sized plastic tackle seat-box, the sort which coarse-fishing anglers use nowadays instead of a basket. The Shakespeare model 9267 is a popular choice. This keeps everything dry and in one place – there's nothing worse than clutter in a boat! Steve Parton was the angler I first saw using such a box, and there is no better-organised boat-angler than Steve.

WADERS AND FOOTWEAR

Most reservoir managements ban the use of chest waders for safety reasons, on the grounds that if you wade too deeply you could drop into an unseen hole in the reservoir bed, and drown. I often wish they would allow trouser waders (those which only come up to the waist and, incidentally, are very difficult to find). These would let us wade just that little bit further should the need arise, without the danger of the water running in over the top, as happens all too often with thigh waders. However, it's thigh waders we bank-anglers are stuck with, and what a hazard these can be. The problem is durability, or rather, lack of it.

Rubber thigh waders perish and leak all too soon, even if looked after as carefully as possible. The olive-green ones beloved of fly-fishers are the worst in that respect; something to do with the additives the makers use. Black ones are said to be longer-lasting, but are often clumsy 'industrial' models. I've tried them all in my time, from the dearest to the cheapest, and have come to the conclusion that the PVC models last the longest. Some PVC waders have uppers which are too flimsy (all in the name of lightness) and these can quickly delaminate and leak. Mukluks brand (what a horrible name!) are good, as are Ocean.

For reservoir fishing there is no need to buy waders with studded soles; a deeply-moulded 'tyre-tread' pattern is fine. If your legs aren't of adequate proportions to hold the waders up without support, use the belt straps to hitch them to your trousers – it is essential that folds and creases are eliminated if the waders are to last as long as possible. Whether you choose PVC or rubber waders, invest in a pair of wader hangers so that you can hang your waders upside-down in a dark cupboard, or at least hang them up by the straps. Keep them out of sunlight and heat – the back seat of a car isn't a suitable place. Buy waders of the correct size. Some makers' definition of a size differs from others, and the oft-quoted European sizes don't exactly match the traditional English sizes. Too small, and you'll be uncomfortable, too large and you'll get blisters, so always try them on before you buy. For comfort, wear thick woollen stockings or padded foot-sox such as the Bama type. Boat-anglers, and those who fish the banks of 'concrete bowl' reservoirs like Toft Newton where wading is prohibited, can get by with calf-length boots – I like Derriboots for comfort and durability. Again, avoid studded soles, which are too noisy in boats (remember that sensitive 'lateral line' I told you about in Chapter 2) and too liable to slip on sloping concrete.

Having dealt with items relating to your personal comfort, it is now time to deal with fishing tackle. Open any game-fishing supplier's catalogue, or look at the advertisements in the well-known monthly magazines, and it is at once obvious that there is a mind-boggling array of tackle on offer. Reservoir fishing, however, demands only certain specifications of tackle, so we can eliminate a lot of unnecessary stuff right away. Even so, you must be resigned to becoming the proud owner of several rods, reels, fly-lines and so on, if you are to be a 'compleat' reservoir fly-fisher. Of course, you may decide to restrict your activities to one method only, such as nymphing from the bank or loch-style boat-fishing, in which case you will need less tackle, but you will miss out on a lot of opportunities for good sport by such a restriction. There will be times when your chosen method is just not the most suitable for the prevailing conditions. There are certain styles of fishing which I prefer, and these are naturally my main methods, but I've tried them all, and I think I'm a better angler for it. I have certainly gained in interest and enjoyment, and that's what it's all about. Some people look down on fishing 'Northampton-style' behind the boat, for example – 'Nothing short of trawling' – but having done it under the guidance of experts like Steve Parton and Jim Clements, I can tell you that, done properly, it is extremely skilful and demands a great deal of knowledge.

No matter whether you decide to concentrate on one method of fishing or try the lot, you must first decide on how much you want to spend. That will narrow the choice down for a start. There are some quite satisfactory items of tackle in the lower price-brackets but you must accept that you 'get what you pay for', and higher price usually means higher quality. Stick to the established name-brands and you won't go far wrong. The correct choice of tackle is so important that I am devoting a lot of space to describing the various items you will need.

LANDING-NET

There is a nasty tendency nowadays for bank-anglers to 'beach' trout instead of using a net. I hate to see a beautiful fish brought flapping up the bank, and there's always the danger that it will come off and flip back into the water. In any case, it's so much easier to grip a trout while in the net, for hook removal and despatch of the fish. So I do implore you to use a net if you intend keeping the trout, no matter if the fish is a small one (no one but an idiot would attempt to beach a big one). For boat-fishing, a landing-net is, of course, an essential item.

Where landing-nets are concerned, my motto is: 'You can get a small fish into a big net but you can't get a big fish into a small net'. In other words, have a decent-sized net, with a strong, light frame at least 20 inches wide, preferably 24 inches, and a depth of at least 30 inches. Some bank-fishers like a folding telescopic-handled net which they can hang from a suitable point on the body, but I prefer one with a rigid 4-foot handle which has a spike at the end for sticking into the reservoir bed.

This, I hasten to add, is not to stake out a place, but merely in order that when I am wading the net is immediately to hand for landing a trout. Stuck in the reservoir bottom at an angle, the net can serve as a receptacle for retrieved fly-line instead of a line-tray.

The problem is finding a choice of nets with spiked handles. For some reason, manufacturers currently don't include this feature. The only one I know of is actually an excellent choice; it's marketed by Bob Church, with a strong lightweight handle and good-sized folding net-frame in poly-carbonate. It's handy if the handle floats – a net can fall over if not pushed into the bottom quite firmly (a difficult undertaking if the bottom is a bit stony). A landing-net is awfully difficult to retrieve from under two feet of water!

A long telescopic handle is an advantage when boat-fishing, so that the trout can be netted without bringing it right to the side of the boat. The sooner a fish is in the net, the better. In competition fishing, this time-saving is very important.

Check your local water company's ruling on the type of mesh your net must have. Yorkshire, for instance, insists that knotless mesh only must be used, to avoid damaging the fish's scales, etc. While this is commendable where coarse fish are concerned, because they are returned to the water, I cannot see the need when landing trout from a reservoir where the rules state that all trout caught must be killed. However, ignoring water company bye-laws only invites trouble.

RODS

Some people advocate 9½-foot, or even shorter, rods for reservoir work. Although these are light in weight, in the hands of the average caster they are unsuitable for the distance casting often required in bank-fishing. I do not believe that the physique of the user should play a major role in influencing the choice of a rod, so don't opt for a short rod just because you may feel that your arms aren't strong enough to handle anything longer.

Personally, I wouldn't consider anything under 10 feet in length for reservoir fishing, and certainly not in built-cane or fibreglass. Cane is far too heavy in the lengths required for reservoir work, and in any case it is ridiculously expensive nowadays. The few fibreglass models available in the early 1990s don't include anything I would recommend. Carbon fibre (called graphite by Americans) is the only choice in rod material, in my opinion, although this can be blended with either boron or Kevlar; in the cheaper carbon rods it is combined with quite a large proportion of fibreglass. There are also several types of carbon fibre, each having different strengths and stiffness (modulus); 'IM6' high-modulus carbon is a typical example. If a rod is designated a 'boron' rod, it is really made from carbon fibre to which has been added a small percentage of tungsten filaments on which boron particles have been deposited. Boron gives a rod increased power and sensitivity, but increases the weight very slightly. Kevlar, by comparison, gives a lighter rod with slimmer diameter for the same strength. Whatever the material, it is bonded in a basic resin matrix. It is high time that manufacturers were forced to declare the exact make-up of their blanks – some 'carbon' rods would hardly qualify for the description!

Good-quality carbon gives light rods with a better performance than any other material, so that you avoid fatigue in the arm and wrist. The quest for lightness can be carried too far, however; if the wall of the blanks is too thin, ovality will develop under stress, and breakage could easily occur. This was a failing in some early carbon rods. After several years of experience and research, such problems have been eliminated, and there are now very few bad rods on the market. The worst are those with a soft tip on a stiff butt, similar to the action of a match rod used in coarse-fishing, and designed by someone who doesn't know the requirements of a fly-rod. Not quite as bad are those which, also due to bad designing, continue to oscillate at the tip after completion of the forward-cast, thus reducing the energy put into the fly-line; the result is a rod which will not cast a long straight line. Tapers and wall-thicknesses are critical to good rod design. By altering these to controlled specifications, any action and power can be produced. Normark, for example, offer a range of 10-foot rods with line-ratings of 4 right through to 10. Generally speaking, stiff rods need heavy lines and good effort from the caster; they are the wrong choice for small flies and light leaders – too powerful – but are essential for use with deep-sunk lines, when their power is needed for hooking fish against the resistance of many feet of water. Conversely, soft rods need light lines and less effort by the caster; they are no good for lures or sunk lines.

Although I shall be dealing with fly-lines in a separate section, having mentioned the line-ratings of rods I must explain the connection between rod power and line-weights, because this also has a bearing on the action of a fly-rod. Basically, a fly-rod is a spring which throws a long thin weight, the fly-line. According to the power of the rod, a certain weight of fly-line can be cast. The 'size' of a fly-line is designated by an AFTM number related to the weight of the front ten yards of the line; the smaller the line-size number, the lighter the line. This AFTM number is marked on all modern fly-rods, telling you which line-size(s) the rod will comfortably cast. Many rods bear more than one number, e.g., 6/7, 7/8, or even 7/9. In these cases, the higher number refers to a forward-taper line profile, the lower number to a double-taper profile. (See the section on lines for more detail.)

Taken to extremes, rod rating is connected with size of fly and leader-tip strength. For example, a rod rated 8/9 is really too powerful for flies size 14 or 16, and a rod rated 4/5 isn't strong enough to use with size 6 or 8 lures. I would suggest that you use the following as a guide: a 6/7 rating for sizes 16 to 10; a 7/8 rating for sizes 14 to 8; an 8/9 rating for sizes 10 to 6. Similarly, using leaders of 4lb test, or less, is dangerous on a rod rated 8/9; a 6/7 rating would be more appropriate or, at most, a 7/8 rating. If fishing with finer or smaller-sized flies and leaders, some form of shock-absorber will need to be incorporated into the set-up (see section on leaders).

Assuming that the same material is used throughout a range of rods of the same length, those rated for light lines will have a softer (therefore slower) action than those rated for heavier lines, which will be stiffer (therefore faster) in action. To get the same action speed throughout the range of line ratings, different proportions of materials would have to be used. Don't confuse a soft slow action with a sloppy action. Sloppy action results from poor design, and such a rod should not be bought.

Rod actions are often referred to as tip, middle, or butt actions; these terms can be translated respectively into fast, medium, or slow. To find out the action of a rod in the shop without actually casting with it, don't just wobble it in one hand, as I've seen so many potential buyers do. All that does is to oscillate the rod, and gives no indication whatsoever of its performance. Instead, hold the rod-handle with both hands and flex the rod firmly from side to side in a horizontal plane. You will then see the action of the rod and get an idea of its power. If you next flex it sharply in a single-handed 'casting' simulation, you will not only be able to get the feeling of its power and action but you will also be testing its ability to damp any tendency to oscillate at the tip.

There is no need to put a lot of effort into casting with a soft slow-actioned rod; too much effort will, in fact, kill a lot of the power of the rod and the cast will be affected very adversely. Stiff fast-actioned rods will cast a longer distance but require more effort; they usually cast a tighter loop, and can also bully a fish to the net quickly (useful in fly-fishing competitions where time is precious, but guard against the hook pulling out!). I like to play a trout firmly but I never try to 'horse' one out, having lost too many in my early days through this. If a fish wants to 'go', I let it, under controlled finger-pressure on the line. I find that a medium-actioned rod, not too stiff and not too soft, suits my style of fishing and casting; I rarely fish big lures or sunk lines from the bank, and my main sunk-line fishing is loch-style from a boat.

My suggestions for consideration when choosing your rod(s) are:

Bank-fishing

10- or 10½-foot rod, rated for lines 7/8. For years, my preference was for a 10-foot Lamiglas carbon rod rated 6/7, but I found this a bit weak when casting in a strong side-wind. Otherwise, it was excellent for my usual method of small flies or nymphs on a floating line.

Now I use a 10½-foot boron rod rated 7/8 and although it takes a little more effort in casting I find this absolutely ideal. It will cast 30 yards accurately in all conditions, is very light, and plays a fish gently but firmly. It has enough power to hook fish on a sunk line if required, but will safely handle hooks from longshank 8 down to standard size 14. I wouldn't be too happy using it with size 16 flies or smaller; the inherent power in such a rod could easily pull out or straighten the hooks of these small flies. The 6/7 rod would suit them better.

Boat-fishing, loch-style

10½- or 11-foot rod, rated for lines 6/7 if used with floating or intermediate-density lines; 7/8 rating for use with sunk lines such as WetCel High-speed HiD. Modern loch-style fishing incorporates both long- and short-lining, and the 'dribbling' of the top dropper fly, with rod raised – the final stage in both methods – needs a light line to avoid too much 'line-droop'. Use a double-taper line one size lighter than the lower rating on the rod, e.g., DT5 on a 6/7 rod, if you find that the fish are coming to the surface flies. I find that even light rods longer than 11 foot put so much leverage on my wrist that I cannot fish with them all day without severe arm-ache. I use my 10½-foot (7/8) boron rod for all my 'over-the-front' boat-fishing, with either DT6F, WF8F, or WF8S lines as circumstances dictate.

Boat-fishing at anchor

Use the same rod as for bank work.

Boat-fishing, 'Northampton-style'

10-foot rod rated 9/11. I am using the description 'Northampton-style' to cover all methods which entail fishing behind a drifting boat. Because sunk lines are usually involved, often at some distance, we need a very powerful rod to drive the hook home when a trout takes. Many suitably powerful rods are too stiff for me to use comfortably, and I was delighted to find that when Steve Parton, an expert in this style, made me a present of a Shakespeare Worcester Boron 10-foot 9/11 rod, it suited me perfectly for the occasions when I had to resort to the sunk-line method. Although quite limber in action, it has the power to hook at depth, and is amazingly sensitive.

Three rods, therefore, are all I need for all my reservoir fishing. They each have a scroll-shaped cork handle, Fuji rings, Fuji reel seat, and sleeve joint. I don't like snake intermediate rings because they wear out comparatively quickly; I cannot say that Fujis have affected my line-shooting, despite what some people suggest. Theoretically, they shouldn't, because they are highly polished to lessen friction. The Fuji reel seat is superbly designed, and holds the reel in complete security. No modern carbon fly-rods now have ferrules, and few have spigot joints because these wear out in time and cause problems. The sleeve joint, where the top section fits over the butt section, doesn't seem to exhibit these drawbacks; at least, I haven't found any significant wear of the joints on my own rods.

Sleeve joints rely on friction to hold the sections firmly in place, and in my opinion it isn't enough just to push the sections together and hope that they stay fixed. In the course of a day's casting the joint can become loosened, and the stress point shifted to above the joint itself. I have seen so many customers' rods broken about three inches above the joint because of this. To overcome the problem, my trick is to align the rod-rings so that those on the top section are about 10° out of line with those on the butt section; push the sections together until just tight, then sharply push and twist the rings into line at the same time. The resultant friction grip means that the joint stays together firmly and safely. When you want to dismantle the rod, simply untwist the sections the opposite way from that in which you originally twisted them together; they come apart quite easily.

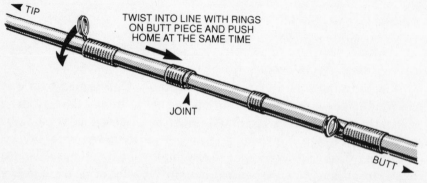

TIP

TWIST INTO LINE WITH RINGS
ON BUTT PIECE AND PUSH
HOME AT THE SAME TIME

JOINT

BUTT

Aligning rings in rod assembly

Carbon rods are no more likely to break than any others, but they must be treated with sensible care. If thrown down carelessly, for example, in a boat or on to rocks, slight nicks can later develop into serious weakness and ultimate breakage. No carbon rod-tip will withstand being bent into a U-shape too often, yet many anglers pull the fly-line down from the tip after threading it through the rings. This puts terrific strain on the rod-tip, and can break the rod. Always, when threading the line up the rod, put the butt on the floor, hold the rod near the tip, and finally pull the line up from the tip ring with the rod perfectly straight.

Casting

I cannot leave this section on rods without mentioning the subject of casting. I've no intention of trying to teach you to cast via the pages of this book, because my own experience has shown me that trying to cast properly from book instructions is doing things the hard way.

I strongly advise that you obtain tuition from a fully-qualified professional casting instructor, such as a member of the Association of Professional Game Angling Instructors (APGAI). This will give you basic expertise including information on how and why the fly-line reacts to your rod movements. For reservoir fishing, it is essential that you are able to cast 25–30 yards, even though this distance is not always required. Sometimes the fish are holding so far out that if you cannot cast this far you simply won't catch anything. Walk along the banks of any reservoir, and you will see examples of the most dreadful casting styles. I've seen the chap who, after dozens of false-casts, gets a final result of less than 15 yards, line bashing the water at each false-cast. Then there's the all-too-common style exhibiting great effort and loud swishings, forward-taper line extended 25 yards behind and dangerously low to the ground, with a superhuman final thrust more suited to an Olympic javelin-thrower, arms flailing the air. All obviously self-taught and all making far too much hard work of it. Casting should be enjoyable, not a chore. The double-haul technique is very necessary for getting distance easily and accurately with no great effort, and this is easily learned from a professional. A good roll-cast is also extremely useful in certain methods, both boat and bank, and this, too, you can learn quickly from a good tutor.

A casting instructor will not always teach you good *fishing* casting – you will sometimes have to adapt pure casting technique to suit actual fishing. For instance, constant positioning of the back-cast outside the plane of the forward-cast can cause the line to twist, resulting in severe tangles between reel and butt ring – the rod should move backward and forward in the same plane. A high back-cast is very necessary when bank-fishing; cultivate this, and dam walls or sloping banks will cause less concern. Too much power put into casting creates 'wind-knots' – nothing to do with the wind, but due to bad casting! Vigorous casting action wears out a fly-line quickly, and there's one particular common casting fault which wears out a forward-taper fly-line quicker than anything else. I'm referring to the habit of extending a WF line far beyond the tapered portion when false-casting in the air. This does very little to increase the load on the rod, but puts great strain on the junction between the tapered part and the thin level running-line as it 'hinges' back and forth, causing the coating to quickly crack and break down at that point. Always extend the tapered section no more than a foot or so outside the rod-tip, and shoot the running-line to obtain distance. You can't do this properly unless you have had the correct tuition. Weigh the cost of professional tuition against the cost of several fly-lines worn out before their time, and the answer is obvious.

Tips which I find helpful:

Always aim the back-cast high. When requiring maximum distance, turn your head and watch the back-cast unfold; you can then start the forward-cast at exactly the right moment (left foot forward for a right-handed caster). On the forward-cast, point the rod upwards at a 45°-angle – for some reason, this gives a much better shoot; lower the rod to the horizontal as the line falls, to give gentle presentation.

FLY-REELS

A lot of fly-fishers consider the reel as a very minor item of tackle. Functionally, for ninety-nine per cent of the time, it is. That odd one per cent is the time when you are playing a big trout, perhaps the fish of a lifetime, which is tearing off line from the reel as it heads for the other side of the reservoir. Funny, isn't it, how these big fish seem to take when you have retrieved no more than a foot of line? That's when you need to be sure that the reel is as reliable as possible, and in perfect working order. My own view is that the reel is quite a major item, and I always believe in using top-quality reels. Some materials used in reel manufacture, in what is to me a misguided striving for extreme lightness, wear badly; graphite and magnesium fail on that score.

Although the old idea of a reel having to 'balance' the fly-rod is currently out of fashion, belonging to the days when casting action was all wrist and 'a book under the elbow', the weight of a fly-reel is important when considered in relation to the longer lightweight rods used in reservoir fishing. A reel which is too light or too heavy will affect your casting comfort – too light, and the rod feels top-heavy (leading to arm fatigue), too heavy, and the whole feel of the rod is changed. I find that if the loaded reel balances the rod at a pivot point about 3 inches above the handle there's no problem.

My own preference is for medium-weight reels of the best possible quality: the Hardy Lightweight series, which are really well engineered and machined to very fine tolerances. Each comes in a zipped padded protective reel-case – good reels merit care. I keep them clean and free from internal grit, lubricate the spindle about twice a season, and they are as good as when I bought them in 1960. High priced, but weigh this against their longevity and they're a good buy: the Princess (3½-inch diameter) for lines DT5, DT6, or WF7, the St Aidan (3¾-inch diameter) for WF8 lines. These don't have an exposed rim, but it is not something I miss; the check control seems perfectly satisfactory at minimum setting. The lineguard does groove over a period of many years, but is easily replaced. The hub latch makes for quick and easy spool change, as conditions alter during the course of a day's fishing, and I have several spare spools for different lines. On the inside face of each spool I stick a small label telling me the size and type of line it carries; it's easy to forget their identity otherwise.

You may prefer a less expensive brand of reel – there are plenty to choose from. Probably the most popular model is the 3½-inch-diameter wide-drum type, which will take WF8S, WF8F or DT6F fly-lines plus plenty of backing line. Always make sure that the reel you choose will hold the required line; I advise no smaller than 3½-inch diameter, the standard-drum model of which will only take up to WF7F or DT5F lines. Sinking lines are thinner than floating lines, size for size, and so take up less room. Don't skimp on backing line! Once, at Grafham, I had a huge rainbow take out all my fly-line and 99.9 yards of backing, leaving only six

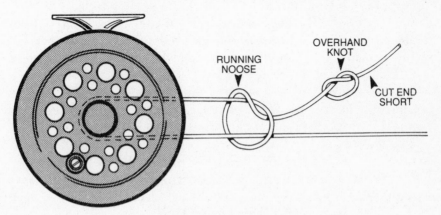

The backing-line-to-reel knot

turns on the reel before it stopped. I lost it at the net, but that's another story.

Make sure the check mechanism is reliable and that, if non-adjustable, it isn't too fierce. When playing that big fish, the drag of many yards of fly-line, plus a hard check, can be enough to break the leader or straighten the hook. I don't like geared multiplying fly-reels for this very reason – I feel that the gearing puts too much strain on a running fish. Automatic clockwork reels are much too heavy, hold insufficient line, and are quite unsuitable for reservoir fishing. Left-hand or right-hand winding? I don't think it matters. Use whichever you find most comfortable. Most reels are adaptable for either hand. Trout are usually played by hand-lining anyway; winding is only involved when reeling-in without a catch.

FLY-LINES

The basis on which fly-lines are categorised is that they are long thin *weights* thrown by the compatible power of the fly-rod. Two major profiles and one minor profile are involved, the majors being forward-taper and double-taper, the minor being single-taper or shooting-head. An important point to remember is that when you increase the length you cast of a double-taper line, you increase the load on the rod considerably, whereas doing so with a forward-taper line hardly alters it. This is important when choosing the size of a double-taper line because, when bank-fishing, you could need long-distance casting and must therefore choose a DT line of a lighter size than that designated on your rod. The first few yards will be hard to cast because the rod will be under-loaded, but as you increase the amount of line out beyond the rod-tip, the loading will become suitable for the rod and casting the full length of the line will be possible. For boat-fishing purposes, a DT line is normally only used for short-lining in front of the boat; here the lightest DT line your rod will handle is the best bet because you need to reduce line-droop from the rod-tip to a minimum. A soft rod will suit a lighter line than a stiff rod, of course.

All fly-lines taper at the 'business end' to give a nice turnover, due to the force put into the line by the rod reducing as it passes along the line yet acting on a reduced weight of line as the taper lessens the diameter.

Profiles, weights, and performance of fly-lines are designated by a system of letters and figures. Regarding profiles, DT = double-taper; WF = weight forward (also known as forward-taper); ST = single-taper (shooting-head). Level (L) lines used to be produced, but I know of none now available; they are useless anyway! There is a variation on forward-taper known as long-belly, having a forward tapered 'belly' section longer than the normal 10 yards. There is also a further rather unique long-belly variation designed by a well-known American fly-fisher, the Lee Wulff Triangle Taper, which has a very exaggerated quick taper down to a very thin running line. I have used this line, and it performs very well indeed, with excellent long-distance shooting power.

The relative weights of fly-lines (the AFTMA numbers) actually run from 2 to 15, but reservoir fishing normally encompasses only sizes 5 to 9. Remember, these weights refer only to the first 10 yards of the line.

Performance is defined by letters: F = floating; N = neutral density (extremely slow-sinking, virtually 'hanging' in the surface film); I = intermediate (actually a very slow sinker); S = sinking; F/S = sink-tip (in which a sinking tip is added to a floating line during manufacture). A floating line is probably the most important type of fly-line and your first priority; floaters are versatile because a reasonably wide range of depths can be fished by using longer leaders and weighted point flies. Because it lifts off the water easily, a floater is enjoyable to use. Sinking lines are available in various rates of sink, but these are not often evident from the letter/number title; the manufacturer usually states his sinking category on the packaging. Some makers designate very fast sinkers by the letters VFS. The faster a line sinks, the thinner is its diameter relative to others of the same AFTMA number (increased specific gravity) and it takes up less room on the reel. Resist the temptation to put these thinner lines on smaller reels; use your normal 3½-inch reel and load on more backing.

Although harder to cast long distances, being more difficult to shoot, a DT line gives the ability to cover a rising fish quickly. Assume your flies are 20 yards out, you are retrieving your line from a position straight ahead, and a fish rises 10 yards to your left. With one lift-off and back-cast you can immediately cover that fish with a forward-cast in its direction. Try this with a WF line, and you will find that it cannot be done with ease or accuracy; the weight of the line being concentrated at its far end, change of direction is only possible by a few degrees, and several false-casts are required for any major change of direction. By this time the fish is long gone! It is also impossible to roll-cast a WF line once the forward-tapered portion is outside the rod-tip; there isn't enough for the rod to 'get hold of' if you attempt to roll the thin running line. Long-belly WFs are 'rollable' if you keep some of the thick tapered section within the rod-rings.

For the majority of my own fishing, I use WF lines and find them quite satisfactory. I wish that all WF lines were 35 yards long, like the Cortland 444. I can cast more than 30 yards (and often need to) and I like to have a few turns of fly-line left on the reel; no one enjoys seeing the backing going up the rod without a big trout on the end of the line, and the normal

30-yard lines always seem too short to me because of this. Psychological, maybe, but I like to feel at ease. I only use DT lines in circumstances where I fish a rise from the bank, or short-line from a boat.

Shooting-heads have lost much of their erstwhile popularity. They are now used mostly by lure-strippers. The much-vaunted 40-yard distance was rarely attainable by any except the experienced tournament caster, and a good fishing caster can reach 32 yards or more with a WF line anyway. Heads are poor for nymphing; the backing doesn't give sufficient sensitivity and is difficult to handle in figure-of-eight retrieving. Many anglers are put off by the difficulties engendered by the backing line tangling, but much of this could be avoided if the backing was stretched before each fishing session.

Ninety per cent of both my boat- and bank-fishing is done with a floating line. When bank-fishing in a strong side-wind, a neutral-density line, which lies just under the water surface, helps to obviate side-drift and too great a bow in the line which can lead to difficulty in hooking fish; it adds little to the depth at which the flies are fishing. A neutral line is also handy for boat-fishing in strong winds, when you would otherwise use a floater; the neutral line holds better in the water, whereas the floater would be blown about. Strong bright sunshine or very cold conditions when loch-styling from a boat require a very fast-sinking line because the trout go deep; I use a WetCel High-speed HiD line, probably the fastest-sinking castable line on the market. It is very popular among the top competition fly-fishers, which is a recommendation in itself. Provided you cast virtually the whole line, it will get down to deep-lying fish before the boat overruns the flies.

There are odd occasions when a slow-sinking line is needed from a drifting boat – rainbows holding five or six feet down, for example. Takes can be felt well with a slow-sinker due to the direct contact with the flies. There may be times when a standard fast-sinker would be appropriate, but apart from certain instances related to Northampton-style boat-fishing, when the flies need to follow a natural retrieve path, I doubt if there are many. To have every possible type of line in one's kit can become confusing, not to mention the drain on finances!

Before I forget, there's an important point to mention relating to sinking lines. Never try to lift any length of sunk line out of the water; there is every danger that you will break your rod in the attempt to overcome such huge resistance. Always retrieve until you see the leader, then roll-cast off, and into a back-cast ready for the next delivery.

There has been argument about the colour of fly-lines for many years, particularly regarding floaters. Do brightly-coloured lines frighten the trout? Maybe they do in river fishing, where you are constantly false-casting over a limited area with static fish, but I am convinced that in reservoir fishing coloured lines cause no problem. A good reservoir fisher can get out 28–30 yards of line with two false-casts. The popularity of white, peach, and fluorescent green lines suggests that reservoir fly-fishers feel that line-visibility to the angler is more important than line-visibility to the trout, and I agree with them. In any event, the long leaders I recommend (at least 16 feet) mean that the flies are kept well away from the line. Perhaps those who criticise bright lines are those who use short leaders? Use whichever colour you can see best. You will then be able to pinpoint accurately the position of your flies, you will be able to gauge the exact speed at which your flies are moving and the effect the line is having on them, and by watching the movement of the fly-line (particularly that bit between the rod-tip and the water surface) you will be able to have visual indication of some takes. Slow or tentative takes can be missed if you rely solely on the feel of a pull from the trout. Sinking lines come in drab colours, usually dark greens, browns, or greys, so the question of scaring the trout does not arise.

I like my fly-lines to have a slick smooth surface, so that they shoot as easily as possible. I like them to be reasonably supple, especially at low temperatures, but beware of those which become like limp string in hot weather. There must, of course, be no permanent coil-memory (easily removed by stretching traditional PVC-coated lines). There are lines on offer with non-stretch cores coated with polyurethane loaded with PTFE (Teflon), advertised as giving increased sensitivity and non-crack dura-bility. Initially, these were guilty of severe coil-memory, but the makers tell me that this has been overcome. If you wear lines out quickly, you may like to consider a low-stretch line with a durable PTFE coating, from the Airflo range. My PVC-coated lines perform perfectly well for me, with no need for shock-absorbing braid insertions, and with the ability to accept needle-knotted Tynex; they last for years, so I see no reason to change.

For best performance, buy a top-quality line, spending as much as you can afford. Remember that a cheap 'mill-end' line is always faulty, and I don't advise one, even if you are worried about wearing out a costly line. Many reservoir anglers wear out their fly-lines very quickly, and this is perhaps due largely to casting faults and, to a lesser degree, careless treatment. One of the most common causes of wear in WF lines is due to extending too much line in the air and exerting far too much force in the final cast. Good casting technique gives comparatively silent casting and certainly lessens the wear on lines.

Exercise care when fishing sandy or rock-strewn banks. Sand is abrasive, easily picked up on wet lines; rocks have sharp edges which can cut into the line-coating. It may seem too obvious to need stating, but treading on a line doesn't do it much good! There's a lot to be said in favour of using a line-tray.

Keep your lines clean – washing in mild soapy water followed by application of a line cleaner after a couple of trips is advisable. Don't use detergent. Storage in hot sun should be avoided as this depletes the plasticiser in the line; plasticiser can be replaced by using Gherke's PZ or similar products, but this should not be overdone or you can ruin a line. If you know you have taken good care of your line, and the coating becomes stripped, cracked, or otherwise worn, check your rod-rings; one or more rings could be grooved or cracked, causing line-wear. If the rings are sound, return the line under guarantee – it could be a faulty one.

Few fly-fishers have knowledge of how fly-lines are actually made, so I asked Philip Tallents, chairman of Ryobi Masterline Ltd, for some information. Ryobi Masterline is a well-known British firm, highly experienced in the intricacies of fly-line manufacture. This is what he told me:

Most fly fishermen are fully aware of the qualities they seek in a fly-line. A wide spread of such qualities is involved and manufacturers find many of them mutually conflicting, in the present state of plastic technology. For instance, the resistance to wear of a very supple line may be less than that of a stiffer one. A line which shoots well will have a harder coating than one which does not, and hard coats usually come on stiff lines. There are many other such conflicts.

Since plastics – which meet most of these needs – are not sufficiently strong, it has become normal practice to use a core of braid or twist, which provides the strength, and to coat this with a plastic mixture which will provide the necessary density. Such cores are usually of nylon, Terylene, or Kevlar, and in the case of braid, manufacture must be of the highest quality. In fact, no plastic coating has yet been developed which completely meets the angler's requirement; all are, to a greater or lesser extent, mixtures that comprise the best formulas which individual manufacturers consider they can devise.

The plastics industry is spawning new materials by the hour, but only a relative few have any possible use to the line manufacturer. Because his consumption of plastics is minute, he usually ends up making his own mixtures. Over the last two years these have mainly been based on polyvinyl chloride (PVC) combined with a large selection of additives to give performance and colour. PVC has been used because it is a long-standing plastic equally capable of being made up in paste or in extruder chips. It has been well researched, has a very constant quality, and is readily available in the small quantities line makers require.

Many new chemicals have recently come on the market, making it possible to modify the physical qualities of PVC to such a degree that in the twenty-five years since I first interested myself in these matters the end product has been changed and improved beyond all recognition.

Ryobi Masterline have been working with alternative basic plastic materials, too. Some of these have shown great promise, to the degree that some are now used in our production formulations and doubtless will be used to a greater extent, but they will be used only when they have proved their suitability and superiority.

When it comes to manufacture, only three methods would appear to suggest themselves, because of the difficulty of producing tapers. First, and most popular until now, is the paste technique whereby the core is passed through a bath of plastic paste of the consistency of thick cream. The paste adheres to the core in excess of what may be required. The line then passes through scraper dies to remove the surplus, and these adjust themselves to the necessary diameter by one of two techniques.

The first type is a diaphragm similar to those used in cameras, where sickle-shaped pieces of sheet metal are swivelled on eccentric pins to form a hole of variable diameter. Another popular method is to scribe half the shape of the line on the periphery of each of twin rollers, or segments of roller; these are forced together so that an orifice is created at the point of contact and as the one arc rolls against the other the hole changes in diameter to give the line profile. In both cases, gearing is so provided that for each cycle of movement of the die, one full line is produced. After passing through the die, the line enters fusion ovens where its passage is monitored and its speed controlled. Lines are made in continuous lengths and later cut up into individual lines.

The second method might be to roll the plastic on to the core with heated rollers, but as far as I know no one is using this method. The third method is to extrude the plastic, which begins as a composite 'chip' containing all the ingredients. The line is both formed and fused on the core in the heated orifice of the extrusion press. Though initially the plant is expensive to purchase, this method is economical and we use it for our cheaper lines. At the present state of our technology, the paste process is reserved for our more expensive lines. One may well ask, 'Why include the line core if one is going to extrude the line anyway?' The answer is that, as yet, no plastic has been created which will fairly provide the other qualities required and at the same time possess the necessary strength. In fact, one American company made lines for a period by this method, but as far as I know, they no longer do so. Presumably they could not make them strong enough.

Lastly, there is the question of adjusting the density of the final product. In essence, this is achieved by adding things to the plastic. For floaters, the additive could be a so-called 'blowing agent' which fills the coating with minute bubbles and gives it its buoyancy, or it could be small glass balloons which achieve the same effect. When it comes to making sinkers, this additive takes the form of metal (or 'heavy earth') powders which are added to the mixture. All additives reduce the plastic content and, therefore, the tensile strength of the final coating, and this is the main reason why core lines have always been used (with the sole exception of the line referred to above).

A fly-line is a very complex and high-tech item, into which has gone a great deal of research and development. It is at their peril that newcomers to line-manufacture boast the excellence of their particular product – as a colleague of mine once said, 'Fly-line making is a very "unkindly" undertaking.'

BACKING LINE

There is a special secure knot to use for attaching the backing line to the reel hub. First, put an overhand knot in the end of the backing – this stops it pulling out of the actual knot itself. Take the backing round the reel hub and make a running noose around the line. Pull this tight and it will never come undone. (See diagram on page 61.)

Don't use nylon monofilament for backing; under tension, it can distort a reel drum. I use solid braided Terylene backing, and join it to the fly-line by a little plastic device sold as a 'cast connector'. For connecting cast (leader) to line these are quite unsuitable, in my opinion, but I have every confidence in them for backing connection. The only proviso is that your rod-rings are large enough for the connector to pass through; all but the smallest Fuji or Seymo rings are suitable in this respect. One tip regarding the holding knot for the fly-line – make it a double overhand, giving an end which doesn't stick out at an angle but sits nicely inside the connector.

I can't be bothered with hollow braided monofil and messing about with Superglue joins. My method works fine.

LEADERS

Good leader make-up is extremely important. A leader of unsuitable design can severely affect your chances of catching fish, so it is worth dealing with the subject in some detail. You will find knot-tying instruction in the Appendix. The junction between fly-line and leader must be one hundred per cent secure, and small enough to pass through the rod-rings without obstruction, bearing in mind that leaders are often twice the length of the rod. In recent years, tapered 'braided leaders' (or, more accurately, joining lengths) have been offered by the trade. Theoretically, these give smoother turnover of the final cast because they continue the taper of the fly-line down to the diameter of the leader itself. Whereas this feature can be of use to the inexpert river-angler fishing the dry fly, I cannot see any real advantage for the reservoir fisher in terms of better fly presentation. Those who use braided leaders say that the slight elasticity of the braid offers shock absorption for fine nylon. I have always found that 4 feet of 10- or 12-lb stiff Tynex nylon needle-knotted to the fly-line gives a perfect turnover to the longest leader, so I have never bothered to use braided leaders.

The needle knot is, in my opinion, the best to use for joining line to leader. The nail knot, though similar, provides obstruction because the end of the fly-line is jutting out alongside the nylon. Some advocate covering the needle knot with Vycoat but I have never found this to be essential. There are several types of nylon monofilament, varying in stiffness due to differing molecular structures. The limpest type, always used for bait-fishing and spinning, is also used by the majority for fly-fishing leaders, either 'off the spool' for knotted leaders or extruded in a tapered form for knotless leaders. It is available also in a pre-stretched condition (the so-called 'double strength') which gives the thinnest possible diameter for a given breaking-strain – until you knot it; in my experience, at the knot it then becomes weaker than any other nylon, so much so that the incorporation of stretchy High Power Gum and/or a braided joint becomes essential if fish are not to be lost through this and its lack of stretch.

Double-strength nylon needs very careful handling. Experts advise cutting the fly off after every fish caught, and tying it on again. They also advocate complete reconstruction of the leader after a few hours' fishing! Constant treatment with Fuller's Earth mixtures is also advised to combat the shiny appearance. All this trouble and risk, to get the probable advantage of a thinner diameter because it is perhaps less visible to the trout and gives more mobility to the flies! Many anglers use double-strength nylon, persuaded by certain experts. I haven't found it necessary. Maybe it *is* less noticeable – no nylon is actually invisible – but how do we know that the trout possesses enough intelligence to recognise what nylon is? They don't even realise the danger of a highly visible hook! Whether in prestretched or normal form, limp nylon has major faults when used for fly-fishing leaders, in my opinion. Droppers made from limp nylon tend to wrap themselves round the main leader, either during casting or during the retrieve, and the leader itself tangles easily if casting technique is not of an extremely high standard.

Therefore, for the past thirty-odd years I have used the stiffest nylon made, and this overcomes both the aforementioned problems. Marketed in the UK under the brand-name of Tynex, this stiff nylon enables level leaders of up to 24 feet in length, with three or four flies mounted, to be extended straight and untangled – an absolute boon for either boat- or bank-fishing. Tynex has two possible disadvantages, both of which are insignificant when set against its advantages. It is thicker than its equivalent strength in limp nylon, so is theoretically slightly more visible; it is, however, completely clear, and virtually disappears in water, so I discount its thickness as a drawback. Certainly it has never had an adverse effect on my catches, as far as I know, and I catch as many trout as most!

The second disadvantage is a more tangible one. Due to its molecular structure and the fact that it was not originally manufactured as a fishing-line, Tynex is not of a uniform constant strength, and occasionally you find a few yards which are not as strong as they should be. But this defect is easily accommodated. I always test (with a firm steady pull, *not* by a hard jerk!) the lengths I am going to use, before I tie up my leader; any suspect length is discarded (by winding round my fingers then cutting the coils so as not to leave any lengths dangerous to wildlife or grazing animals) and I am soon back on to nylon of satisfactory strength. Usually it is only a few yards which are unacceptable, a small price to pay for the superb presentation which Tynex offers. It has a slight coil-memory when first taken off the spool, but this is immediately removed by stretching; similarly, any kinks that result from undoing wind-knots or tangles are completely removed by stretching. Tynex doesn't 'pigtail' after pulling a Blood knot tight, as so many limp nylons do. Another big advantage of the stiffness of Tynex is the ease with which the rare wind-knots and tangles can be undone.

When forming droppers, the use of limp nylon necessitates Grinner or Cove (water) knots, which produce droppers at a 45°-angle to the main leader in an attempt to lessen the tendency of the droppers to wrap around the main leader on retrieve. A dropper fly wrapped round the leader simply isn't working. With Tynex, I always use a five-turn Blood knot, which produces a dropper standing out at 90° to the main leader, and the stiffness of the dropper means that every fly on the leader is able to work properly, and there are no 'passengers'. Using any other joining knot for Tynex reduces this feature. Several authors have slated the Blood knot, calling it insecure, unreliable, unsafe, etc. I bet they didn't make a good job of tying it. It never lets me down if properly tied. Don't use less than five turns when joining lengths of equal or near diameters. This five-turn version gives at least 85 per cent strength of the original nylon. If joining nylon of different diameters, use less turns of the thicker nylon to more turns of the thinner, thus equalising the tension on either side. Or you can double the thinner nylon and use an equal number of turns. In any case, you *must* lubricate the knot by moistening it with saliva before pulling tight slowly.

One important point regarding the tying of dropper knots: for the actual dropper, always use the end of the length of nylon which is nearest the fly-line. Then if a fish takes the dropper hard enough to break the knot, there is a chance that the dropper fly (and the trout!) will still remain attached.

The usual length of my dropper is 4–5 inches. If the dropper is longer, it may create its own half-hitch over the dropper knot during the course of casting, especially if a slim, heavy fly is attched to it. If a trout takes that dropper fly, there is every chance that it will break the dropper very easily indeed. I'm sure that many 'smash takes' are caused in this way. It's always worth while to check your droppers from time to time.

My usual leader make-up

My usual leader length is 16 feet – 8 feet to the top dropper, 4 feet from top dropper to middle dropper, and 4 feet between the middle dropper and point fly. Maximum length is about 22 feet – longer than that, and it becomes too tricky to net a fish which has taken the point fly (the top dropper won't go through the tip ring on the rod). For 99 per cent of the time, I use 5-lb Tynex straight through, with no need for tapering. If you choose to use limp nylon, you will have to taper the leader, probably using a 10-lb knotless tapered leader for the butt and joining to this whatever strength of nylon you feel is needed.

Don't be afraid of long leaders. Many people have said to me, 'Oh, I couldn't cast a 20-foot leader – I've "all on" to cast a 9-foot leader properly!' Yet, when I've made up a 16-foot Tynex leader for them, they have handled it perfectly well. Personally, I cannot understand why anglers continue to buy the old-fashioned commercial 9-foot leaders with two droppers, when longer leaders offer such considerable advantages. A 9-foot knotless tapered leader is fine for a lot of dry-fly river fishing, but for any kind of reservoir work I consider it essential to learn to tie the appropriate knots and to construct your own leaders. It is then possible to alter the make-up of your leaders to suit the prevailing conditions, and thereby get the best out of the day.

For example, an increase in wind velocity when casting into the wind will test even the most expert of anglers; the obvious solution to a better turnover of the leader is to shorten it and reduce the number of flies, avoiding tangles. In extreme cases, increase the breaking-strain also – in the stronger wave action, the trout won't notice a couple of thou extra in the diameter, and it will help the flies to beat the push of the wind. Short leaders are preferable when fishing sunk line; the flies move more attractively, and for boat-fishing the 'hang' technique is more easily performed.

A change in wind force when drifting loch-style will bring the need to alter both leader-length and the distance of the top dropper from the tip of the fly-line if the flies are going to work at their best. Altering the lengths of the droppers is often essential for perfect presentation.

These examples serve to prove my point. Others will be given when discussing different fishing techniques later in the book. I rarely tie up a leader prior to being either at, or on, the water. My leader is then tied to suit the conditions and the chosen method for the start of the fishing session.

I avoid complicated leaders formed from lots of short lengths of different diameters of nylon. Tom Ivens and Charles Ritz, both famous and excellent anglers in their day, devised such leaders supposedly to present the fly more perfectly. Full of knots and fiddly to tie, they appeal only to the crank. The fewer knots, the better, and with Tynex there's no need to taper anyway.

Don't have your droppers too close together. This invites tangles as the flies pass too close to each other during casting. It can also lead to foul-hooked fish; if a trout goes for a dropper fly and misses, it can easily hook itself on the lower fly as it turns down, if that fly is close enough. International fly-fishing competition rules give 20 inches as the minimum distance between droppers, and that is far too short in my opinion. Four feet is my minimum.

A word of caution about the labelling accuracy of some brands of nylon. Most nylon is spooled and labelled abroad, where there is no Trade Descriptions Act. It is easy to label a nylon as thinner and stronger than it really is, and unless you check the diameter with a micrometer and the breaking-strain on an accurate laboratory machine (both of which few of us have) you can easily be misled. French nylon is particularly suspect where strength is concerned.

Regarding colour of nylon, logic points to clear transparent nylon being preferable. Grey, pale green, or light brown are perhaps the next best choices. Any dark solid colour is obviously highly visible and perhaps more likely to make the trout wary of taking the fly?

Some people worry about glint and shine on nylon. I don't, because these features only show in air and in sunlight. Below the surface, they disappear. Removal of surface glint with abrasives leads to opaqueness and greater visibility.

The performance of a leader is affected by the flies you put on it. Bulky flies have air resistance, passing more slowly through the air. Obvious though it may appear in print, the size of a hook affects its weight, so it helps the leader to land straight if the point fly is the heaviest on the leader and the most bulky fly is on the top dropper. Remember, too, to cut the waste ends of any knot nice and close to the knot itself; untidy ends sticking out lead to tangles.

Always store your spools of nylon where sunlight cannot reach them, as the ultraviolet rays therein cause deterioration. Properly stored, nylon will last unaffected for several years.

FLIES

I'll deal with these in later chapters as we go fishing through the season. Listing them now would, I feel, be of little value.

ACCESSORIES

There are no gimmicky gadgets in my kit; every item has been found to be either completely essential or to make my fishing more trouble-free. I don't think I would be able to do without any of the following items:

Fly-boxes
We all collect flies in an attempt to find the 'answer'; many flies become 'desperation patterns' and after a while there are maybe more of these than the flies we normally use! To store all these flies, the choice is between several small boxes or one large box. I used to segregate my flies

in several small boxes, but have discarded these in favour of a large wooden fly-box, 15 × 9 × 3 inches, opening top and bottom to give four panels of Ethafoam to hold the flies. This box is used for everything except dry flies, which don't take kindly to being stuck in Ethafoam, and in any case it is best to keep reservoir dries permanently greased in a little pocket-sized tin.

Whether you choose one big box (which *is* awkward to cart around) or several small ones, it is important to arrange the flies in categories so that any pattern required is quickly and easily found. In my big box, two panels hold wet flies, Mini-Muddlers, and nymphs; the other two hold lures, fry flies, and 'daddies'. I find that having all my flies in the big box enables me to select a team of flies quickly because all the patterns are immediately on view when the box is opened. I can't forget a good pattern because there they all are. No time is wasted trying to find the right box from among several.

I arrange my flies neatly in rows, all individual patterns together. Every so often I have a sort-out and take out flies which have been superseded by better versions; in other words, I keep my collection up-to-date and orderly.

If you decide against the big box, I suggest you consider the plastic boxes available in various colours for identification of your various fly categories. Both Leeda and Fox have suitable boxes. Lovely though they are, I don't like the Wheatley aluminium fly-boxes with myriads of metal clips to hold the flies: I find the clips loth to release the flies and liable to spoil the hooks.

I hate fly wallets, finding it impossible to keep flies neat and pristine in them.

Bass

Don't keep your catch in a plastic bag; it's the worst container imaginable, resulting in semi-cooked trout on a hot day. Use a proper bass bag, either the traditional matting type (not easy to obtain nowadays) or the modern type with woven nylon mesh inside a canvas outer. Make sure the trout remain wet, as evaporation of the water helps to keep fish cool. It also slows down weight-loss. Some thrifty types use woven polypropylene vegetable bags. The one-upmanship boys sport cool-boxes!

All basses must be washed and dried after use if they are going to remain sanitary and last long.

Priest

Kill your trout immediately and humanely by 'administering the last rites' with a couple of firm blows on the head just behind the eyes. There are several versions on the market, all quite satisfactory. Some are combinations of priest and the following item.

Marrow spoon

As I've said already, it often helps to find out what a trout was feeding on before you caught it. It was a famous chalk-stream fly-fisher, the late great G. E. M. Skues, who first realised that the Victorian marrow spoon, originally used for extracting the marrow (considered a gourmet delicacy in those days) from big beef bones, could be used for this purpose. This long narrow spoon was ideally shaped for insertion into the trout's stomach. Modern versions are still based on the old design. After killing your fish, push the spoon well down its throat into the stomach, twist it and retrieve it. The spoon now holds examples of the stomach contents, which should be examined and identified in water in a plastic cup.

Scissor pliers

This is my favourite tool, one which I simply could not do without. Originally designed by Hardys, other manufacturers have improved on their model by enlarging it and providing nice big finger-holes. It is far better than ordinary scissors for cutting nylon, because it has a serrated blade which grips the nylon. The ends of the blades are formed into plier grips and these are a most useful alternative to artery forceps for taking the hooks out of trout; the ends are rounded, so there is no danger of spiking yourself should you, like me, keep the tool in a pocket instead of attached to your jacket or waistcoat by either a length of string or one of those 'pin-on retractor' gadgets. If you decide on the latter, make sure you buy a good-quality one; there are several cheap versions which don't last two minutes!

Thermometer

I have emphasised the importance of water temperature in an earlier chapter. Hardy's offer an accurate thermometer in a protective metal case.

Hook sharpener

The importance of extremely sharp hooks cannot be stressed too strongly. Although most fly-hooks seem sharp enough, it pays to make absolutely sure by adding a little personal treatment. The best hook sharpener is of American origin, the Ezelap, with a D-section hone incorporating diamond dust and a well-designed groove. It is so efficient that you have to take care not to remove too much metal when you first start to use one, but you soon get used to it. Another essential item!

Leader, line, and fly treatments

Keep all these in Minigrip plastic envelopes because most of them can leak out of their containers in hot weather, staining and impregnating the pocket if precautions are not taken. To make your leader sink immediately, rub it with Leadasink, a proprietary mixture of Fuller's Earth and detergent; this can dry out in its container, but can be reconstituted with a little water (glycerine is better).

It's amazing how much dirt and scum your line can pick up, even from what appears to be gin-clear water. Pull your line regularly through a pad of Cortland Line Cleaner; I know of none better.

To make flies or leaders float, often in the roughish waves of the average reservoir, takes more than the usual liquid flotants. Again we have to look to the USA for the best stuff – Gink. This is a gel which has found great popularity in recent years and it's very effective. Beware that it melts in very hot weather. To neutralise its flotation, should you later want the leader to sink, the same maker offers Xink; I also carry a dropper bottle containing liquid detergent, cheap and handy for washing hands, etc.

Fly-patch

In the heat of the moment, when time is running out, the fish are rising, and you are trying fly after fly to find out what they will take, there is never time to return rejected flies neatly to the fly-box. Don't stick them in your hat – make yourself a handy fly-patch by sticking self-adhesive Ethafoam on to a square of cloth of the appropriate size, and pin it to your jacket with a safety-pin. Some waistcoats come with a sheepskin fly-patch, but the Ethafoam is better.

Leader nylon spools

There are various ways of carrying your spools of nylon. I have told you about my waistcoat's internal pockets in each of which I keep a spool of Tynex, six different breaking-strains in all. I find this arrangement very handy. If yours doesn't have this feature, and few do, the best alternative is a plastic dispenser box. You can buy various models to hold two 100-yard spools – choose the size applicable to the spool size of the nylon you prefer. The ends of the nylon protrude through slits in the box. If you decide against this type of storage, keeping your spools loose, you need plastic clips on the spools to prevent the nylon unwinding, and I suggest a suitably-sized Minigrip envelope to keep them at least tidily.

Binoculars

It is often very helpful to be able to see what is happening on the far side of the reservoir, whether anyone is in your favourite spot, and so on. A good pair of binoculars is a useful item to carry, and the odd bit of wildlife study can add to the pleasure of the day.

Notebook

Every angler should keep a fishing diary. Throughout the average fishing day, there's an awful lot of information to remember, which will be helpful in future fishing, and it isn't a waste of time to break off occasionally and make a note which can later be entered in your diary.

FOOD AND DRINK

I'm often so busy fishing that I can't find time to eat much, but at least I take a snack with me. A Tupperware box keeps all fresh and attractive. I hate coffee or tea out of a flask, so I carry the 'makings' separately. Having broken many flasks over the years, I now have an unbreakable stainless-steel flask which I fill with boiling water; it's a bit heavy, but so what? Instant coffee and sugar are in two small Tupperware pots, and skimmed UHT milk (it keeps better) in a screw-top bottle. Together with a teaspoon, these all go into a plastic carrier-bag, which then goes into my big plastic sack if I'm banking, or my seat-box if I'm boating.

Boat-fishing requires the following additional pieces of equipment:

DROGUE

An underwater 'parachute' to slow down the speed of a drifting boat, the drogue is virtually indispensable if you're going to boat-fish properly. Most modern versions are the fold-up nylon type, in two sizes (1 metre square or 5 feet square), both of which can be needed: the larger one for very slow drift in normal winds, steady drift in stronger winds, or for bigger boats. The Datam brand comes with a cord which collapses the drogue for easy retrieval. Some drogues don't come complete with rope. Before you attach about 10 yards of ½-inch nylon or polypropylene rope to the swivel on the drogue, attach a couple of feet of light metal chain.

This will submerge the drogue quickly, ensuring that it works right away as it should do. Make a loop at the end of the rope; this attaches the drogue to the boat, usually to a rowlock. A G-clamp is a handy extra, to fit on to the gunwale in such a position that you can place the drogue rope round it so that the boat drifts as you want it to; not many boats drift straight.

It is important that the cords attached to each corner of the drogue do not get tangled, or it will not work at optimum efficiency. Always place the drogue carefully in the water and, with equal care, back into the boat; throwing it in any-old-how leads to tangling and associated problems.

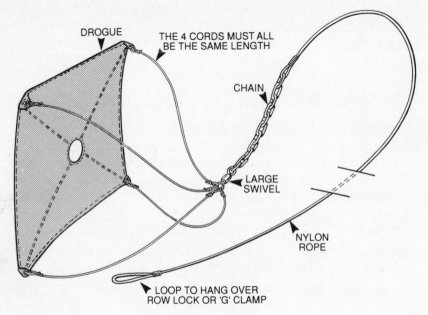

A typical drogue

ANCHOR

If there is an anchor already in the boat, provided by the reservoir management, rarely is it efficient enough. Some managers think that a lump of concrete attached to a length of rope is good enough! Best to take your own. Buy (or make) one which has three or four prongs which will dig into mud, clay, or rocky bottoms; it should weigh between 5 and 10lb. The anchor should be shackled to several feet of heavy chain, absolutely essential to create a horizontal pull on the anchor, which otherwise would not hold bottom. Knotted firmly to the chain should be up to 50 yards of ½-inch polypropylene rope with a loop at the end and several loops tied along its length so that the rope can be attached to the boat at various points. Polypropylene floats, so if by some chance you accidentally drop the anchor overboard, the rope is visible and you can pick it up again. Keep your anchor set-up in a strong canvas holdall – it's easier to carry.

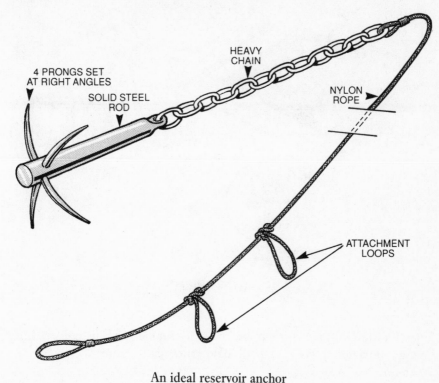

An ideal reservoir anchor

BOAT SEAT

Many boats have thwart seating which is far too low for day-long comfort, and in any case it is much better to be seated at gunwale level when fishing. The commercially-available Rutland Extending Boat Seat ledges on the gunwale and is adjustable to fit the width of the boat. You sit astride it, facing the way you are fishing. Most keen boat-fishers own one. If you're a practical DIY type, you can make your own out of wood, or

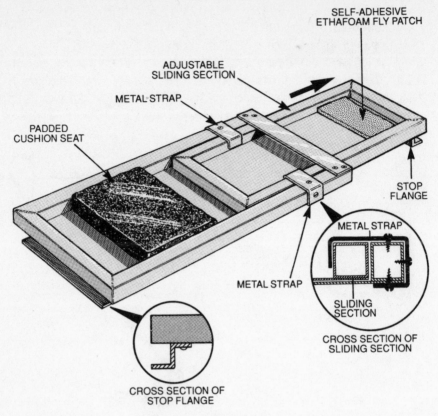

SELF-ADHESIVE
ETHAFOAM FLY PATCH

ADJUSTABLE
SLIDING SECTION

METAL STRAP

PADDED
CUSHION SEAT

STOP
FLANGE

METAL STRAP

METAL STRAP

SLIDING
SECTION

CROSS SECTION OF
SLIDING SECTION

CROSS SECTION OF
STOP FLANGE

Extending boat thwart seat

metal tubing. Make sure it includes a thick foam cushion! Sitting on an unyielding boat seat all day can create agony in the nether regions.

Right, I think we've finally got everything . . . let's go fishing! I'll take you bank-fishing first, month-by-month through the season, starting in April. The various styles of boat-fishing will be dealt with later in the book.

Chapter 5

Bank-Fishing in April

Most of the major reservoirs open for fishing on April 1 or Good Friday, whichever is the earlier. When I'm standing in icy-cold water, hands purple with cold, blustery showers spattering my specs, on an all-too-typical Opening Day, I reckon the epithet 'April Fool' is well merited, but it only needs that magic pull from the first trout of the season and any discomfort is immediately forgotten as excitement takes over and the adrenalin flows! If we are to make the best of the April fishing, we must be prepared to accept whatever the weather throws at us – after all, we can't throw it back! If your reservoir is situated so that westerly, south-westerly, or southerly winds give suitable wind directions for fishing the banks, you are indeed lucky. Luckier still if those winds prevail during April, bringing mild cloudy conditions. All too often, the reverse is the case, and raw north-easterlies create conditions where even newly introduced stockies are reluctant to take.

British weather being what it is, however, I've known several Opening Days when the sun beat down and jackets were discarded in air temperatures warmer than those of the following June. Even after one of the comparatively mild winters we've been experiencing during recent years, one thing is fairly certain – the main body of water will still be very cold. The big reservoirs take many weeks for the water to reach a comfortable temperature. It is only the shallower water round the banks which warms up more quickly and brings the trout into a situation where they become more active and need to feed more positively. The bank-fisher should therefore score over the boat-angler during this month because these more productive spots are not usually available to the boat-fisher. These bank shallows are out of bounds for boats, because reservoir rules usually prohibit them approaching within 50 metres of the bank, so anchoring-up near the bank is 'out'. Drifting boat methods are restricted to deep-sunk lures behind the boat, if allowed by the rules, or Highspeed HiD line over the front, with a very slow drift speed; loch-style fishing with floating line, covering as it does the upper layers, is usually unproductive.

Bank-fishers have the opportunity of enjoying the best of the action, fishing the most likely locations round the reservoir, places where fish are easily reached and where they are most likely to be feeding. Use your thermometer, and measure the temperature accurately. It's of little use just to dip your hand in the water. Look for readings above 45°F (7°C) if possible, at which trout will move quite well. You'll be amazed at the difference between one shore and another.

It is essential to remember that trout are cold-blooded creatures in the exact sense of the word, with their body temperature equalling that of the surrounding water. Body temperature controls metabolism and activity. In temperatures below 45°F (7°C) the trout will be quite lethargic. Within certain limits, the warmer the water, the more active are the fish and the more likely they are to feed. Discussing this point with Michael Leney, a trout farmer of very long experience, he told me that 55°F (13°C) is the optimum water temperature for trout. In stewponds, doubtless spurred on by competition from the other trout, they can take pellets in water which is only just above freezing, but conversion of the food into body weight is virtually nil at such temperatures. This is perhaps the equivalent of shoaling stockie rainbows taking lures on a cold opening day?

If recent and current weather conditions dictate that you fish into the wind, it isn't always the chore some think it is. Long-casting is rarely needed; often the trout are only a few yards out, beyond any band of coloured water which has been stirred up by the waves. Don't bother to fish really 'dirty' water, even though it may be the warmest in the reservoir; you can't expect trout to tolerate it, and even if they do, visibility is so poor it is doubtful if they can see your offerings. Fishing into the wind, remember to cut the rod-tip down through the wind to give the line that extra impetus, and keep the leader length to a minimum, with no more than two flies. A longer leader will just be blown back, and the flies won't fish properly until you have taken up the slack.

Whether it's allowed or not, don't wade shores into which a strong wind is blowing. Owing to the cloudy water, you often cannot see the bottom, and could easily step into a deep hole. A heavy wave can slop over the top of your waders, a mishap I try to avoid. By the way, if your waders do get wet inside, when you get home pack them with screwed-up newspaper, which will absorb much of the moisture overnight; after removing this, finish the drying process with prolonged use of a hair-dryer.

If your reservoir isn't stocked with triploids or female rainbows, and you want to avoid out-of-condition 'black' trout, steer clear of shallows with a hard stony bottom. Such places are often populated with male rainbows not worth catching. Similarly, stay away from any spots where feeder streams or drainage trickles enter the reservoir. Another 'no-go' area, though for a different reason, is anywhere which dried out completely during the previous season; all weed and insect-life will have been killed off and when the reservoir is refilled the barren bottom will not sustain any food items or offer shelter to hold trout there. The fish will tend to be found where last season's marginal weed remains, often 40 or 50 yards out, and at that distance they are out of range to even the expert shooting-head exponent. After a dry summer, and low water-levels, this means you should concentrate on the deeper parts where the bed slopes more sharply, and the weed is likely to be within reach. If there's a side-wind, so much the better.

If the water is no more than 8 feet deep, I like to use a floating line and long (say 20-foot) leader with a leaded point fly to get down quickly. Deeper than that, use a WF sinking line, the sinking rate of which is determined by the slope of the bed. A gradually shelving bank, giving water 10–12 feet deep at 25 yards out, could be tackled with a slow-sinker (sinking at around 2 inches per second); a fast-sinker would need too fast a retrieve to avoid snagging the bottom, and in cold water a very slow retrieve is essential. Trout won't chase after anything moving fast. Even lures should be moved slowly, so select those with mobile materials such as marabou.

Steeply-shelving bottoms or deep-water drop-offs require a fast-sinker (sink-rate about 3 inches per second); very deep water needs a very fast-sinking shooting-head, because you must cast a very long way to compensate for the greater depth to which the line must sink. Choice of shooting-head backing is then important; braided monofil backing is unsuitable because it is slightly buoyant and slows down the sinking rate of the set-up. I prefer 30-lb-test Stren monofil in the fluorescent yellow colour; this is thick enough to handle nicely and limp enough to resist tangles, provided you stretch it thoroughly before every fishing session. Join the monofil to the head with a needle knot finished with a few coats of Vycoat to facilitate passage through the rod-rings.

A brightly-coloured shooting-head backing enables you to use the portion between rod-tip and water surface as a take-indicator, in the same way as the coarse-fisherman uses a swing-tip when ledgering. Any deviation from its normal angle can mean that a trout has taken the fly – you don't need to wait for the pull before tightening. This visible indication of a take is equally important when fishing a floating line; when I'm figure-of-eight nymphing, there are many times when a slight lift of the line at the rod-tip tells me that a trout has my fly. Waiting for the pull might result in just a missed 'tweak'. Usually I do rely on a pull to indicate a take, however, and simply lift into it firmly; you will rarely hear a swish as I strike, because I don't strike with terrific force like some people do.

Lure-fishing at depth, using one lure only, requires a strong leader-point, say 8–10lb, and the leader need not be longer than 9 feet if a sinking line is used. The less-expert caster will find that a knotless-taper leader turns over well. If you prefer to fish nymphs or wet flies with a sinking line, you could increase the length to 15 feet, decrease the strength to 5 or 6lb, and have 4-inch droppers spaced at 4-foot intervals. Fishing into the wind, use no more than 10 feet of leader and no more than two flies.

With any type of sinking line, one warning applies to all. Do not attempt to back-cast until there are only a few feet of line remaining in the water. Trying to lift a longer length of sunk line could result in a broken rod, and at best makes life difficult. In any case, fish often follow the flies up from the depths and take as the fly is about to leave the water, so it pays not to lift off too soon. Hang the flies at the surface for a few seconds – yes, trout *will* take a static fly! If there is no take, roll-cast the line into the air, back-cast, and then false-cast to work outside the rod-tip the amount of line you need for the next cast; if using a shooting-head or WF line, this must only be a couple of feet longer than the head itself and the rest must be shot.

Even if there is no sign of surface activity and no hatch of insects, I like to start with nymphs if the wind isn't too strong. In winds of 10 knots or more I fish a lure at this time of the year. Any one method is rarely the complete answer, so although my preference is always towards the imitative approach I'm not against lures. Those who stick stubbornly to one method miss out sooner or later. Be prepared to alter your technique according to conditions.

Having chosen your specific location on the bank, and the method to be used, don't wade in straight away. Start fishing off the bank itself. Usually the water is very clear in April, with no development of suspended unicellular algae to give colour, so your approach to the water should be cautious in order not to scare any trout which may be close in. Cover the water with short casts at first, each cast at a different angle so that you fish a fan-shaped area. Lengthen the distance gradually until you are fishing at almost the full extent of your casting ability. Give your flies or lure time to sink to the appropriate depth before commencing the retrieve. Count off the seconds until the fly touches bottom or connects with weed on the retrieve, and knock off two or three seconds next time; you will then know that you are fishing just off the bottom, where the trout probably are.

Takes in cold water can be really quite gentle, often feeling almost as though you have hooked a bit of weed, so you must be sure that every slight stoppage is a fish and not weed. In any case, a fly festooned with weed or bits of bottom debris is most unlikely to be taken.

You may get takes as the fly is falling through the water ('on the drop' is the term used). If this happens, note the number of seconds' wait at which it occurred, and next time start the retrieve at that moment because the indication is that this is the depth at which the trout are moving. Retrieve slowly but not necessarily at a constant pace. 'Figure-of-eight' hand-gathering is preferable; I don't usually hold much retrieved line in my hand, but drop each handful as it comes straight from the butt ring. An erratic timing of little jerks mixed with steady 'figure-of-eight' movements can also prove attractive. Keep your rod-tip low, no more than a foot above the surface, and pointed at the line, so that you are in close contact with the fly. You don't want a lot of slack line hanging from the rod to be taken up before you feel a take. Don't worry – takes at this time of the year are rarely savage; usually it's a firm slow pull which just needs an equally firm tightening. If you are using a sinking line, tighten by moving the rod-tip sideways, not upwards; you will miss less fish that way.

At most reservoirs this month we will be mainly fishing for recently-stocked trout plus some over-wintered fish. Browns over-winter better than rainbows, because they are indigenous fish suited to our climate; rainbows, despite having been bred in this country, need a mild winter if an adequate number are to survive. Depending on the policy of the reservoir fishery management, 'stockies' can be very good or very bad fish. The bad ones have soft flabby flesh and their dorsal and tail fins bitten short through overcrowding in the stewponds or holding cages (many reservoirs now acclimatise their trout in floating net cages before releasing them – a good idea, provided there aren't too many in a cage); the rainbows turn 'black' a few minutes after being killed, a sign of previous prolonged stress. Usually, these poor fish have been purchased from breeders who produce mainly for the food market, where an eroded tail fin doesn't matter a lot, and, even worse, have been stocked for only a few days, if that. Good managers buy from trout farms specialising in fish for angling purposes, introduce their initial stocks long before Opening Day (weather permitting), and ensure that the rainbows are specially bred females or triploids.

Those I was catching at Rutland during April 1990 were lovely silver fish with full tails, averaging around 1¼lb in weight. Roger Thom, lessee of the fishing at 3,500-acre Rutland Water, told me that he had stocked 50,000 rainbows between January and the first week in March, and that these were fish reared specially for stocking, in earth-ponds to avoid any abrasion of the fins. His sources also make sure that their rearing ponds are not densely stocked, so that the fins of the fish don't get bitten. Roger acclimatises his trout in cages, continuing to feed them on pellets. His cages are 14 × 10 × 14 foot deep, and can hold 3,000 12-inch trout; he keeps only 2,000 in each cage, further ensuring that his fish remain in good condition, as they certainly were that April.

I had missed Opening Day, being away in Florida for the bonefish, and it was April 10 when I started fishing off the west side of one of the little bays on the Normanton shoreline. It was a cloudy afternoon with a cold moderate north-westerly wind giving left-to-right waves and slightly coloured water which was of a suitable temperature to offer the chance of some activity from the trout. Knowing that the water isn't more than 6 feet deep there, I chose to use my favourite WF8F floating line, with a 16-foot leader of 5-lb Tynex.

There were no insects evident, so what to put on? Try a lure. Black is a good early-season colour, and a slow retrieve means that a pattern with some mobility is required. I chose a black Concrete Bowl on a longshank 8 for the point. While tackling-up, another season-ticket holder passed by, and told me he had had a few fish on 'a big Dunkeld', so I stuck a Hairwing Dunkeld 8 on the top dropper. The grapevine had also told me that the fish were feeding on 'green buzzers', so I put an Olive Buzzer Nymph, size 12, on the middle dropper.

I dress my Concrete Bowl lures with some lead wire under the head, because this pattern is really only a variation on the Dog Nobbler theme, and the weighted head gives a nice undulating movement to the lure which activates the marabou tail in an attractive wiggle. To produce this movement needs a pull retrieve, so I cast a good long line, counted twenty slowly so that the flies were well down, and retrieved in short slow pulls. It wasn't long before the line went tight, and a lively rainbow of 1lb 5oz leapt into the air with the point fly in its jaw. During the next three hours another three fish took the Concrete Bowl and one took the Dunkeld. A couple of pulls were missed due to a big bow in the line (I really should have chosen an intermediate line!).

At about 5.30 p.m. a fish rose to my left, quite close in – the first rise I had seen – and I covered it immediately. Raising my rod slowly, as one does when short-lining from a boat, I loch-styled the flies, a favourite ploy of mine if the fish is near enough. There were a couple of splashes at the flies as they skimmed the waves, followed by a heavy boiling take on the middle dropper (the Olive Buzzer Nymph). A lovely over-wintered rainbow, 2lb 9oz in weight, like a bar of silver. Two casts later, there was a terrific pull and the leader broke at the top dropper. Probably the dropper had half-hitched round the leader in the strong wind, a situation where a break is quite likely. Funnily enough, I very rarely get broken, but if I do, it's always on the take.

By then, the weather had turned really cold and uncomfortable, so I decided to pack it in. When I examined the stomach contents at home, I discovered that the fish were full of bright green chironomid pupae, which they had obviously been taking just as they left the reservoir bottom. Yet most of my catch had taken a lure looking nothing like them. So much for exact imitation theories!

Mention of chironomid pupae reminds me that I must mention the main natural trout food items which are of interest to us at this time of the year – buzzers (chironomid midges), caddis grubs (sedge larvae), and hoglice (*Asellus*) – because despite the enigma I have just told you about, there are many occasions when it is essential that you fish fly patterns which represent trout food. So it's time for a little natural history. First, the buzzers, which are non-biting midges of the *Chironomus* family; this has 380 British species, of which (thank God!) only about 10 are of interest to us. The eggs are deposited in water and hatch into tiny larvae which live on the bottom, either in the mud or among bottom weed. The size and colour of the larva varies according to the species, but the most common are just under an inch long and bright red in colour – known to anglers as the bloodworm. The red colour is haemoglobin, necessary for absorption of what little oxygen is present in the mud. Other common midge larvae are pale olive in colour, often found in blanket-weed. The larvae can swim, and do so in a looping figure-of-eight motion, virtually impossible to imitate in an artificial fly, but the trout do eat them, and a bloodworm pattern can be very useful. I have caught fish on a very simple Bloodworm on a curved-shank Partridge K4A hook, the shank covered with fluorescent Glo-Brite floss (shade 4) and the same material left sticking out at the rear like a long 'tail'.

When it reaches full size, the larva changes into a pupa, which after a few days leaves the bottom and swims to the surface, provided that conditions are suitable. Heavy waves, strong winds, and very cold air temperatures prevent hatching. The pupa is by far the most important stage to the trout fisher, being probably the major item of trout food; it is very rarely that buzzer pupae are not found in the trout's stomach contents. As we have just seen, the pupae are taken by the trout on their way to the surface, and are also vulnerable as they hang vertically at the surface preparatory to hatching, breathing air through tracheal gills in the head which are seen as conspicuous white tufts of fine filaments. Trout rising to these hanging pupae usually do so with a slow head-and-tail rise. Shortly before the adult fly emerges from the pupal case or shuck, it adopts a horizontal position and wriggles quite positively. Gas forms just under the skin, giving the pupa a silvery appearance, and helps the insect to leave the shuck easily. It is at this stage that the pupa is mostly responsible for the enthusiastic determined rises we like to see. Particularly in calm conditions, and in scum-lanes (those smooth 'oily' areas which appear on the water after windy weather), the surface film is heavy and the pupae have difficulty in pushing their heads through. Having followed the pupae up from the bottom, the trout lose no time in taking advantage of an abundant easy meal. The importance of the buzzer nymph is reflected in the dozens of different patterns which keen fly-dressers have invented and continue to invent.

In those pupae which escape the attentions of the trout, the thorax splits, and the insect quickly emerges and after a few seconds flies off towards the land. In cold weather, especially in April, the hatched adults stay on the surface of the water for a long time. At Rutland, for example, the surface can be covered in flies, and not a single trout rises to them; the water is too cold for the trout to be interested in expending energy in collecting surface food. Even in warm weather, some species seem unwilling to leave the surface, and buzz around there for quite some time, providing further food for the trout. I have devised a couple of patterns which represent them. The popular name 'buzzer', however, does not originate to describe these species, but because of the sound the adult insects make as they fly in huge swarms, like smoke, to the shelter of waterside trees and hedges, for mating. Later, the females fly out and deposit their eggs, and the whole cycle starts again.

The second most important insect to reservoir anglers is the sedge-fly or caddis, but only one stage in the sedge's life-cycle is of interest to us this month. The adult sedges don't hatch until mid-June onwards. Sedges, of which there are almost two hundred British species, are moth-like insects having a typical insect life-cycle – egg, larva, pupa, adult. The larvae of most stillwater species of sedge are caterpillar-like grubs which cover themselves with a protective 'case' made of bits of stick, weed, sand, gravel, in fact almost any suitably-sized material lying on the bottom. The head and legs protrude from the front of the case, and the larva trundles along very slowly. From early June onwards, the larva seals the front of its case and pupates. During the next fortnight the pupa turns into the adult fly; just before hatching, it swims vigorously to either the water surface or the land, according to species. The skin of the pupa then splits at the head, and the fully-fledged sedge emerges; those which hatch at the surface make their way to bankside vegetation. In late evening they fly out on the water to mate and lay their eggs.

Like the buzzers, the sedge is eaten by trout at all stages during its life-history, but this month we concern ourselves only with the caddis grub in its case. The Stick Fly was probably the first imitation of the caddis grub to become popular, and it is still a good pattern to use, but Ken Smith and I devised a much more realistic Caddis Grub in the early 1960s which, by virtue of his promotion of it, has become associated with another Nottingham fly-dresser, Bob Carnill, who calls it the Cased Caddis. Let's say 'Great minds think alike'! In recent years, an American stone-fly nymph pattern, the Montana Nymph, has become popular here, and I'm sure this is because it is a very passable representation of a caddis grub peeking out of its case. All these patterns should be dressed on weighted 3X-longshank hooks, and fished with very slow figure-of-eight as close to the bottom as possible.

The hoglouse (*Asellus aquaticus*) is a freshwater aquatic crustacean which resembles the terrestrial woodlouse. It lives on the bottom and is a vegetarian scavenger, eating rotting weed, etc. Pull up a mat of blanket-weed from the bottom of most reservoirs, and you will find that it is swarming with hoglice; these are often found in trout stomach contents. In spring there's a lot of rotting vegetation, so the hoglouse population thrives. There isn't a commercially-tied hoglouse pattern, because the creature hasn't had the publicity it deserves. However, the success of the modern Gold-ribbed Hare's Ear Nymph with its picked-out straggly dubbing is, in my opinion, directly attributable to its similarity to this crustacean. Again, leaded versions fished slowly near the bottom are successful because this mimics the creature's mode of life.

Although I'm greatly attracted to the exact imitation approach, doubt-less due to my biological interest, the more I fish the more I realise that in many instances 'near enough is good enough' where flies are concerned. From a fly-dressing point of view, it is wonderful to tie a fly which in appearance is as near as humanly possible to the natural, and such creations catch a lot of trout, particularly when the fish are fussy and preoccupied with a certain food item. There are, however, even more occasions when patterns which can only be considered as caricatures of the real thing will take trout after trout. Much depends on that mysterious word 'presentation'; in other words, the way in which your flies are fished – depth, pace, and motion.

Some instances of success are inexplicable. Take April 1990, for example. I have already told you about my first day's fishing and the unaccountable attraction of the Black Concrete Bowl. Even more as-tounding is the fact that out of 33 trout caught during the month, 23 were taken on a special leaded Gold-ribbed Hare's Ear Nymph pattern on a 2X-longshank hook, size 12, which sported a bright orange fluorescent floss tail and the addition of 20 per cent of hot-orange Antron to the hare-fur dubbing. Fished deep, and slow enough for the trout to be able to examine the fly minutely, it was taken firmly, sometimes on the drop. There were also lots of plucks and tweaks, which might have meant that the fly was a bit too big. Okay, perhaps the Gold-ribbed Hare's Ear Nymph does resemble a hoglouse, but with an orange tinge and a fluorescent orange tail? A caricature indeed. The funny thing is, the stomachs were mostly full of large dark brown or olive buzzer pupae!

In addition to the flies I have mentioned so far, here are some more which I have caught fish on during April:

For buzzers
Pheasant Tail Nymph, Black Buzzer Nymph, Black Pennell, Black Quill, Ginger Quill, Olive Quill, Blae & Black, Connemara Black. Usually sizes 10 and 12.

General wet flies
Mallard & Claret, Hairwing Mallard & Claret, Purple Mallard & Claret, Wickham's Fancy, Black Mini-Muddler, Black & Peacock Spider. Again, sizes 10 or 12.

Lures
Sweeney Palmer, Viva, Black Tadpole, Juicy Lucy, Christmas Tree. On 3X-longshank 8 or 10.

Many of the above are standard patterns, but some are my own variations and the dressings of these are given in the Appendix.

Chapter 6

May: Buzzer Bonanza on the Bank

What an exciting month May can be for the reservoir fly-fisher! Especially for those who, like me, prefer the imitative approach rather than lure-fishing. The increase in natural food for the trout, which this month can bring, raises our hopes of some 'real' fishing. As with much of our reservoir trout fishing, the weather plays a very important part, controlling, as it does, the activity of the food organisms and of the trout themselves. Our enemies at this time of the year are east winds coupled with clear skies; this combination usually brings a chill to both air and water, keeping the trout down. If the water is still very cold at the beginning of the month, you can expect very little action. I've had quite a few blanks under such conditions.

I was checking my fishing diary entries for the month of May, preparatory to writing this chapter, and the least consistent factor that emerged was, of course, the weather. All four seasons in the course of a May week isn't stretching things beyond the bounds of possibility. Even so, the trend is generally towards a gradual rise in air temperatures, an increase in the numbers of rising trout, and certainly lengthening days which give more scope to the angler who can fish only after working hours or at weekends. By the end of the month it is quite possible to fish until almost 10.00 p.m., and assuming 'she-who-must-be-obeyed' allows, this is what you should aim to do, because there is often an excellent hatch of buzzers just before it goes dark.

Before I retired from business, I used to nip along to Rutland straight from work, just to fish for three hours or so, but these were probably the best part of the day. 'Nip along', did I say? More often than not, it was 'crawl along'. The road from Nottingham to Rutland, through Melton Mowbray, winds its way through village after village, and isn't there always a bus or a truck or a farm tractor to slow you down? So it was usually 6.30 p.m. at the earliest before I reached the water. By then, many of the hot-spots were well and truly occupied, and I had to fish other less-popular locations, some of which proved to be equally productive! Sometimes, a friend would move over a bit and let me in – friends with confidence in each other's abilities can fish ten yards apart without any problem. Don't try it with strangers though! Very rarely, even fifty yards between bank-anglers isn't enough, although I can only remember one incident of 'aggro' in this respect.

It was when Rutland first opened, and I had caught a few nice brownies at Spud Bay. Hoping to repeat the procedure, I went back one evening and found two anglers already there, but at least a hundred yards apart. Their Land-Rover was parked, quite against the rules, in the middle of the field. There was a gentle right-to-left breeze, and the odd fish rising. Just between the two anglers was the spot where I'd fished before, so I carefully bisected the distance and started to fish. I had made one cast when the younger of the two (apparently they were father and son) shouted in a rather upper-class accent, 'My father's fishing there!' The old lad was casting downwind, about twenty yards away, and he really had plenty of room, but this chap went on: 'Twenty-six miles of bank to choose from' (he'd read the publicity) 'and you have to push in here!' I nearly started an argument, beginning with 'You haven't bought the bloody bank, have you?', but after a hard day at work I needed peace and relaxation, so I said, 'If you want this spot so badly, gentlemen, you can have it.' I went round the corner to the other side of the spinney and got six lovely fish. A bailiff told me later that father and son had caught nothing, and because of the illegal parking he'd shifted them off. There *is* some justice left in the world. But usually people fishing the bank are helpful if you behave towards them in a polite manner.

Talking of help, my early fishing diaries were extremely helpful to me, and I frequently referred back to them (and still do) to look up what flies I fished, how I fished them, what the weather conditions were, and the successes and failures which resulted. Let me admit here and now that in those early days the failures were many and the successes few!

Lots of beginners are perhaps as confused as I was then, even though there is a great deal more information available nowadays. It really is amazing how much we reservoir fly-fishers have learned over the years – and there is still much to be learned. One of the attractions of trout fly-fishing is that we will never know it all. Much of the confusion for the beginner lies in the vast number of different flies, nymphs, and lures available today, and faced with this multitude of choices the tendency is to buy (or tie) haphazardly. Opening the fly-box, the same old question presents itself – 'What on earth do I put on?' – but for the next few weeks' fishing, this confusion is needless. There is only one main line of approach, because it is the buzzer that dominates the reservoir scene during May. By now, many of the early stockies are not so easily fooled with lures, and have long since started to feed naturally. Although trout will continue to be taken on lures, the imitative approach now comes into its own, and to my mind it's a much more satisfying way to catch trout.

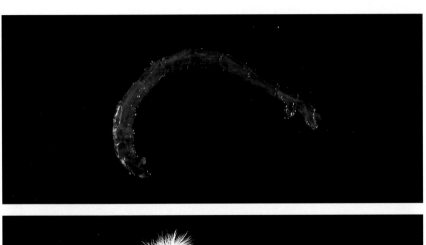

Top: The chironomid larva, the bloodworm
Centre: The chironomid pupa, the 'buzzer' nymph
Bottom: The marrow scoop shows that this trout ate chironomid pupae

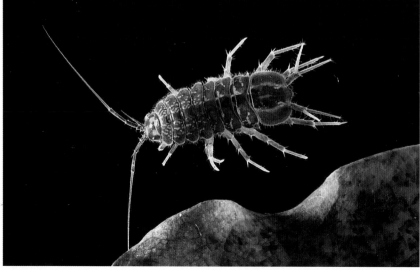

Top left: Adult 'buzzer'
(*Chironomus* species)

Centre left: Caddis larva.
This one made its case out
of sand grains.

Bottom left: Asellus, the hoglouse

Above: Lake Olive dun

Top right: Corixa, the
waterboatman

Centre right: Caenis dun, the
'fisherman's curse'

Bottom right: Gammarus, the
freshwater shrimp

Top: Sedge pupa   *Centre:* Adult cinnamon sedge
Bottom: A swarm of daphnia

Corixa (the 'lesser waterboatman') also become more active this month, and there are still the hoglice and caddis grubs I mentioned in the previous chapter. These are really of secondary importance, however, because early May very often produces massive hatches of dark buzzers which can preoccupy the trout. The bloodworm, too, seems to be less important in May, perhaps because the buzzer pupae are so obvious due to their numbers. The majority of pupae this month are large, dark brown or dark olive in colour, hatching into blacks, greys, olives, and later in the month, gingers.

A prolific buzzer hatch creates problems – your flies are a few among thousands of naturals. Try the larger sizes of buzzer nymphs – even up to size 8 – or patterns with a bit of added colour or sparkle, to make them stand out. You have the option of copying the colour as accurately as possible or adding some little attractive extras. This is when it pays you to be able to tie your own flies. You can add touches of fluorescence, for example, and I have also found that Crystal Hair or Lureflash Twinkle make highly attractive buzzer nymph bodies. If the outline and general appearance of your artificials are correct, these variations have the edge over standard shop-bought patterns, and stand a really good chance of being taken.

The amateur fly-dresser can spend time tying patterns which require precise, fiddly techniques which the professional cannot produce at an acceptable price. A typical example of this is a buzzer-pupa pattern which Ken Smith and I devised in the mid-1960s from a basic idea by the late Eric Hobson, a local chemist. Eric knew a lot of doctors, of course, and had access to medical supplies. He noted that the chironomid pupa had gas under the skin before it hatched, so why not make an artificial with exactly that feature? What material is translucent with air inside it? Answer: a nylon or polythene tube. Eric found a suitable type of very thin tubing which was used for delicate surgical purposes, just under 1mm in diameter; this was exactly right for buzzer nymph bodies.

He explained his idea to me, and I tried various ways of giving the tubed body the colour of the natural pupae without detracting from its basic advantages. After a lot of experiment, I came up with the idea of threading a transparent coloured material into the tubing. There are several effective choices of inserts, including horsehair and nylon monofil, both of which can be dyed and have the necessary shine and transparency. I also found that fluorescent single-strand floss or thread was good. Alternatively, you can dye the tubing itself: the tubed body gives segmentation, translucency, and internal colour plus the impression of gas (air) inside. Horsehair or nylon, being fairly rigid, can simply be pushed up the tubing, but floss or thread needs pulling through with a doubled length of very fine wire which is pushed in first. The floss or thread is then caught in the resulting loop and pulled through with the wire. Effective colours include ginger, brown, black, olive, lime green, and even neon magenta. The thorax material can be dark shades of herl, or dubbing. You can add imitation wing-stubs and white breathers if you wish.

We first used the tubed buzzer nymphs at Eyebrook and Grafham, and they were so good that they have had a permanent place in my list of essential flies ever since. They are tricky to tie, but well worth the effort: the more you tie, the easier it becomes. I class these as among the best patterns I have used for the ascending pupa. Tying instructions are given in the Appendix.

The tubed buzzer nymph is obviously one of the patterns in which we are trying to get close to imitating the natural pupa. Trout will also take patterns which are merely suggestions of the natural, and I must tell you about one which has taken a lot of trout for me since the late 1950s. It started life as a winged sea-trout fly, with a fluorescent neon-magenta DRF floss tail, silver tinsel body, peacock-herl thorax, black collar hackle and black wing. I found that without the wings it was a reasonable caricature of a chironomid pupa, and that killing variations could be created by altering the colour of the fluorescent tail and of the hackle.

This fly was the brain-child of an author who was featured frequently in the angling journals of that period. Fluorescents were just beginning to be the subject of much experiment by fly-dressers, and the acknowledged expert was Thomas Clegg, a brilliant professional fly-dresser, with whom this chap had had a lengthy correspondence. Much of what Clegg told him then appeared in print – a brain-picker if ever there was one! Clegg called him a 'Ned', a local Scots term for someone who walked along a railway-line picking up bits of coal which had fallen from the tender of a steam locomotive. So my nymph just cried out to be named Ned's Fancy! Like so many flies, after a while it ceased to be a constant choice, and for years a couple lay ignored in a corner of the fly-box. Then one morning I was fishing Chew and couldn't find anything the trout wanted – yes, we all get those days! Scanning the contents of the fly-box, I spied a size 14 Ned's Fancy, and decided to give it a chance. The very next cast (honestly!) it was grabbed savagely by a very fit 2-lb rainbow, and since then I've fished it many times, to great effect. Incidentally, this shows that it is not always necessary to dress buzzer patterns round the bend of the hook.

Many shop-tied buzzer nymphs have bodies of floss. Until recently, I didn't like these, feeling they were too opaque and lifeless. For the 'standard' style of dressing, I had a definite preference for bodies made of dyed turkey or goose herl or cock pheasant centre-tail (ribbed with fine wire to combat the destructive action of trout teeth). The herl body is combined with a slim thorax of cock pheasant centre-tail fibres, goose-biot wing-stubs, and the usual white tufts at head and tail. While I still have great faith in these, late May 1990 altered my opinion of floss as a body material. One or two outstandingly successful Rutland regulars reported good catches on very simple black buzzers with both body and thorax of black floss; the body ribbed with silver wire, and no white tufts anywhere! This rather confirmed a thought I'd had in the back of my mind for some time – that if you offered the trout something different but sufficiently like the prevalent food-form, they would take it.

My friend Bill Goodale, always experimenting at the vice, came up with a 'cracker' at about the same time. Dressed on 2X-longshank hooks, either size 12 or 14, this has a basic black floss body and thorax but the ribbing is pearl Lureflash; behind the thorax are short tufts of fluorescent Glo-Brite orange floss, and in front of the thorax are tufts of white Glo-Brite yarn. Bill had been catching fish on this pattern for quite some time before he showed it to me. The first time I used it, on the middle dropper, a limit of eight good rainbows took it in preference to anything else, each one on the drop. It had to have a name, so I call it the Pearl-rib Black Buzzer.

Whichever buzzer pupae patterns you choose, you must fish them at the right depth, of course. As a rough guide, when fishing deep with a floating line, on a 20-foot degreased leader your flies can reach 6 feet down. The 'right depth' is usually well sunk during the day and nearer the surface in the evening or when there is an obvious surface rise. At times, rising trout are cruising just below the surface, preoccupied with buzzer pupae hatching. Just then, the trout's field of vision (the 'window', as it is termed) is very narrow, and quick but accurate presentation is needed if the fish are to see your flies. Try not to 'line' a fish, i.e., let the line fall on top of, or very near, a cruising trout. This frightens the living daylights out of the fish, which bolts out of danger with a noisy splash. Panic spreads, and you could lose the shoal.

In a surface rise, it is critical that you keep your flies right in the top inch or so of water, and with nymphs the obvious answer to this is to grease the leader. It's important in all surface nymph fishing that your droppers are not too long, I would say no more than 2 inches, and that they are always degreased. Don't smear flotant along the whole of the leader; if you do, it is too obvious and could put the trout off. Just put a dab a few inches above the point and a few inches either side of each dropper. This should be enough. I use Gink or Permagrease, both of which stick well to nylon. With long leaders, it is sometimes necessary to grease a yard or so near the tip of the fly-line. If you then happen to get a trout on the point fly, you have to pull that greased part of the leader through your rod-rings, and this transfers grease to the rings. If you don't thoroughly remove this later with detergent and a toothbrush, it will transfer grease to your next leader whether you want it greased or not. This is why I don't like greasing-up except at dusk; at least I can degrease the rod-rings at home before the next trip.

If you do grease-up, don't move the flies. Let the breeze carry them round, and a take is usually signalled by the line tightening. If the line seems to be floating round too fast, copy the river fly-fisher and 'mend' the line upwind by moving the rod-tip through an arc. The ripple has to straighten the resulting upwind bow and this slows the flies down.

An alternative to greasing the leader when buzzer-nymph fishing is to put a well-greased Muddler on the point; this helps greatly in keeping your buzzers near the surface. In fact, you can carry out an extra little manoeuvre which sometimes triggers a take. Make sure the leader is fully degreased as this will help your dropper nymphs to sink an inch or two. Then tighten the line slowly, and the nymphs will rise, against the resistance of the bulky floating Muddler – the reservoir equivalent of the river angler's 'induced take'.

In recent years, imitation of the emerging chironomid has received a great deal of attention, and the so-called 'dry fly' (often more accurately the 'damp dry', because many are fished in, rather than on, the surface) has become very much in vogue. At one time, reservoir fishers would very rarely even think of putting a dry fly on the leader, and only then in a flat calm when trout were rising. Much of this reluctance stemmed from the inability of the typical 'river' dry fly to remain floating on the wave-tossed surface of a reservoir; there were no dries specifically designed for reservoir work. So dry-fly fishing was always considered a last-resort tactic, except perhaps when mayflies or crane-flies were on the water.

The modern reservoir 'dry' is the result of the constant search by competition boat-anglers for methods which will put them one up on their opponents, and it is fairly safe to say that it originated at Grafham, where Bob Wort and Dave Shipman did pioneer experimentation, and was developed further by the Bristol contingent at Chew. Although originally a boat method, it can be equally as effective from the bank. The amazing thing is that it is not necessary for fish to be showing at the surface for the dry-fly method to be successful. Particularly in clear-water conditions, good trout will come from nowhere and take the fly, and this happens a lot more frequently than you would think. Obviously, if the trout are rising to emerging or adult buzzers, you choose patterns which are reasonably close copies of the naturals in colour and shape, but at other times there are 'general' patterns which work very well. There are two things common to all good modern reservoir dries – strong lightweight hooks and dubbing bodies or thoraces.

A lightweight hook must obviously be made of thin wire, and this must be of the very highest quality and strength if the hook is not to open out when a big trout takes. The Partridge 'Captain Hamilton' dry-fly hook, code L3A, is a good choice. Where dubbing is concerned, seal fur is the number-one choice, but this material is fast becoming unobtainable due to pressure by fashionable conservationists who don't realise that seals must be culled for their own good. No one with a shred of compassion can condone the much-publicised brutal clubbing of seal pups, but there are alternative and humane ways of killing seals. I fear that, if left to their own devices, seals could increase in numbers to such an extent that they could devour every fish in their immediate habitat and then starve to death. The mysterious virus-attributed decimation of the European seal population in the late 1980s wasn't necessarily the result of pollution, in my opinion. Be that as it may, unless things change we will have to use other dubbings, and the material which approximates most closely to seal fur is Antron fibre, which has a similar texture, transparency, and shine.

The purpose of the dubbing is twofold: to give colour and to hold plenty of flotant. Therefore it should not be too tight, and the dubbing picked-out well. By far the best tool for picking-out dubbing is a little gadget called a teazle brush, obtainable at the haberdashery counters of department stores. The best flotant, by popular opinion, is Gink, and this should be applied long before you intend to use the flies, so that it soaks well into the dubbing – as soon as you tie or buy the fly, in fact. Since it is very 'gooey', warm a drop between finger and thumb to thin it, then work it into the fly. If you want to Gink the whole fly, warm the whole bottle, remove the cap, and dip the fly into the liquid. It is advisable to have a separate little fly-box solely for Ginked-up dries so that they don't 'contaminate' your other flies.

There are four basic types of dries – Shipman buzzers, emergers, hoppers, and floaters. The Shipman buzzers have a simple dubbed body ribbed with flat tinsel (often pearly) and a tuft of white at each end so that you can see them. Emergers have a dubbed thorax, and usually a herl body, hackle-point or better still white deer-hair wings, and a collar hackle; only the thorax and wings are Ginked, so that the body hangs below the surface. Hoppers are very similar to daddy-longlegs, but tend to be tied on smaller hooks; with dubbed bodies which are often blended mixtures of two or more colours, they have drooped-back 'legs' of pheasant-tail fibres, and several turns of hackle. Hoppers are Ginked completely, as are floaters, which can be either general 'impressionist' patterns usually consisting of a dubbed body and a white or badger hackle for visibility, or definite copies of adult flies.

You can fish a single dry, two dries, three dries, or put a dry on the top dropper, with wets or nymphs below it (if the dry is well-Ginked it will stay up). The leader must be thoroughly degreased, and must be as fine as possible within the bounds of safety. I favour a 20-foot leader with the first 10 feet in 5-lb Tynex, joined to 2 feet of 4-lb T-Line; the remainder of the leader is made of 4-lb T-Line with the flies 4 feet apart. I like the nylon to be clear, hence my choice. Some people will go down to 3-lb nylon, but you must use a soft rod if you do, to avoid losing fish. Leaving the dry flies static is the favoured technique; contain your impatience for as long as possible, merely taking up any slack line so that you keep in contact. If nothing happens, try a little twitch or, as a last resort, a slow figure-of-eight retrieve. A fast retrieve tends to swamp and sink all but the most buoyant dry, but a few false-casts and it will float again. In any case, you need to false-cast several times to dry the flies, as any river fly-fisher knows!

When covering a rising fish, you have to guess immediately the direction in which the trout is travelling, and the speed of travel. The question of direction is fairly easy to answer; trout usually move up against the wind and waves. In a flat calm, one side of the rise-form is 'pushed' more visibly, and that is the way the trout is going. The speed of travel is more difficult to gauge – it is very easy to underestimate how fast the trout is swimming, and by the time your fly arrives, the fish could be yards away. I once watched trout at Ladybower rising in a flat calm; my position, atop a high wall, with the sun behind me, gave excellent visibility. A tiny sipping surface rise was immediately followed by an amazingly fast dive and upward swoop which was efficiently braked at the last split-second by outspread pectoral fins. The nose was tipped up for the next gentle rise, at least ten yards away from the last rise in many instances. So, place your flies several yards in front of the fish.

Of course, the perverse nature of trout will sometimes mean that to get a take you have to place your flies in the centre of the rise (you can't win 'em all!). There are two 'always', though – always allow for any wind which will blow your flies off-course, and always aim your cast a yard above the surface so that the flies land gently. There is also one 'never' – never waste time in getting your flies on target; too many false-casts, and the fish will be long gone. Don't let the urgency of the situation spoil your casting; if you don't pause and let the line and leader straighten out behind you, the result will be a nasty heap of nylon landing with a fish-frightening splash.

The usual take to a dry should be given a couple of seconds before striking; in other words, let the trout take the fly down before tightening. Sometimes, however, the take is so quick and violent that the fish hooks itself. Once a dry has been taken by a trout it must be washed to remove any slime, and dried thoroughly by squeezing between folds of some highly-absorbent material (what a pity that amadou is no longer obtainable – I'm guarding my remaining piece against all comers!), and re-Ginked. Make sure you don't get Gink on the leader – it's essential that there's no floating nylon near the flies.

At any time between midday and late evening, female chironomids will return to the water for egg-laying, and this can be the cause of a good rise, albeit often very localised. Twenty yards away from the action, and you will catch nothing. These egg-laying females like to be helped by a breeze blowing off the land, and this gives a flat calm near the shore. Rises to the flies mostly occur at the far edge of this calm area, where the ripple starts. This is one time when long-casting ability scores. If you can cast your flies into the ripple you can get takes by a long-pull-and-pause retrieve which copies the female's intermittent flight path. Takes can be quite fierce, so don't grip the line too tightly, and don't actually strike – let the fish hook themselves. Palmered patterns give the impression of buzzing wings and these are my choice for this tactic.

If you want a change from buzzer fishing, some exciting moments can be had fishing the corixa. Most reservoirs have a corixa population in the weedy marginal shallows. The corixa is a small beetle-like aquatic insect, a member of the water-bug family, with legs in front for gripping and holding on to weeds, etc., and a pair of long fringed paddles amidships. It needs to breathe atmospheric air, and to obtain this it has to stick its tail-end above the water surface, after which it swims jerkily down, trying desperately to overcome the buoyancy of the air which is trapped in tiny hairs covering the body. All it has to do to regain the surface in order to renew its air supply, is to let go of the weed to which it is clinging, and float up.

It is this upward movement which we can best imitate, and which induces a take from the trout. After letting the fly sink, just lift the rod-tip steadily until the corixa reaches the surface, and with a bit of luck a trout will stop it getting there! I had an unforgettable session of corixa-fishing at Chew some years ago. The water-level was quite low, and it was possible to wade out from the North Shore on to Denny Island. When I got to the water at first light, four anglers had already beaten me to it and I could hear their chatter. It was almost flat calm. Threading my line through the rod-rings, and watching the water, I saw a series of quiet rings no more than six feet from the water's edge. I guessed 'corixa' and tied a special leaded corixa pattern on the point. I had devised this pattern specially for early-morning use, incorporating a silver-ribbed fluorescent phosphor-yellow chenille body, a good colour for dawn fishing. I had tried to make the fly fairly lifelike in shape, and had included two fibre-tips of dark green condor herl to imitate the paddles; the back was also of this material, and I had added a ginger hen hackle to give a bit of movement.

The water was so calm, and the fish so close in, it could easily have been scared off. I remembered the Red Indian stalking tactics I had used all those years ago on the little Bentley Brook in Derbyshire. Luckily I already had my waders on, because in order to get near enough to the water for a cast without spooking the trout I had had to crawl through grass which was sodden with dew. Still on my knees about six yards from the edge, I flicked the fly six feet in front of the last leisurely swirl, gave it a couple of seconds to sink, and raised the rod slowly. The trout bow-waved after the fly like a dog after a ball, and grabbed it hard. A few minutes later, still on my knees, I netted a superb rainbow which weighed exactly 3lb.

Trout continued to patrol the margins, feeding on corixa, and during the next hour, the process was repeated three times before the sun came up in a cloudless sky and the fish retired to the depths. Each time, I cast to a rising fish from a kneeling position well away from the edge, and each time the fly was taken enthusiastically on the lift. Together, the four fish weighed just over 10lb. Carrying them back to the car-park later, one of the four who had been fishing off the island (all fishless) rushed after me. 'You've done well!' he gasped. 'We've not had a pull. What did you get those on?' 'Corixa,' I said – I don't believe in pulling the legs of people who ask me that question – 'it's still on the leader.' Peering at it carefully (it did look a bit garish in the bright sunshine), his face was a picture of astonishment and hardly disguised envy. 'Bloody hell!' he said, 'you'll be using radar next!' and stomped off to his car, shaking his head.

He could have learned quite a few lessons from that encounter if he had also been watching me fishing. One, examine the water carefully for trout activity, at a safe distance, before starting to fish. Two, don't wade in as a matter of course. Three, conceal yourself as much as possible if the trout are active near the bank. Four, try a reasonably close imitation of what the trout are feeding on. Five, make it behave in a natural manner. Six, don't be afraid to use flies with plenty of suitable fluorescence. Seven, keep an open mind and be prepared to learn from other anglers.

There is just one more insect to mention while I am telling you about the possibilities for this month – the lake olive, which should start to appear around the third week of May. Beware, though, when other anglers tell you they have seen trout taking 'olives'; in many instances they are talking about olive buzzers. The lake olive is an upwinged fly of the same family as river fly-fishers' beloved Iron Blue, March Brown, and mayfly – the *Ephemeroptera.* If you watch the surface of shallow bays which are well furnished with weed-beds, you will see brownish-olive flies with upright wings, like little yacht sails. These are the 'dun' stage of the lake olive. Upwinged flies have two stages in the adult form. The dun, which emerges straight from the nymph (there is no pupa stage), later becomes the spinner, which is the final breeding insect. There is a similar species, which entomologically-inclined anglers refer to as the pond olive, but for practical purposes they are both the same.

Trout take these olive duns with a typical splashy rise, and respond quite well to a suitably-coloured winged wet fly on the top dropper. Greenwell's Glory, Olive Quill, or Medium Olive are acceptable standard patterns, but I think it pays to be fussy about the colour of Lake Olive patterns. It seems to make a difference to the response from the trout. The colour 'olive' covers a wide range of shades, and the most natural one has a brownish tinge about it. The nearer you can get to that subtle colour, the more confidently the trout will take. I like a blend of cinnamon and olive dubbing for the body, and, for the hackle, one which has been dyed with Veniard's Medium Olive dye, but at a cooler dye-bath temperature so that the resultant colour is brownish.

The trout can also be interested in the nymphs of the lake olive. A Pheasant Tail Nymph dressed with fibres from a tail which has been dyed olive is worth a try.

Here are some recommended flies for May, sizes 10, 12, or 14:

For buzzers
Tubed buzzer nymphs in black, brown, olive, or ginger; herl buzzer nymphs in black, olive, or pheasant tail; Pearl-rib Black Buzzer; Pheasant Tail Nymph, also with yellow thorax; Ned's Fancy with Glo-Brite Pink floss tail (shade 2), Ginger Quill, Black Quill, Olive Quill, Honey Buzzer. Dry floaters in black or hot orange.

For corixa
Cream or yellow-bodied corixa patterns, weighted.

For lake olives
Lake Olive, Greenwell's Glory, Olive Quill. Dry floaters in olive.

General
Stick Fly (weighted), Wickham's Fancy, Gold-ribbed Hare's Ear Nymph.

Chapter 7

June: Bank on a Bonus of Sedges

Traditionally, the month of June was always dry and sunny, so much so that it used to be known as 'flaming June'. For whatever reason, during the last few years June weather has been very mixed, with winds of varying strength from breeze to gale, and in every direction. Temperatures have ranged from downright cold to heatwave (and every possible stage between), and skies in every condition from cloudless to thunderstorm. So be prepared for anything, and don't ever forget to take your water-proofs! One great advantage is that June includes the longest day, and gives opportunities for weekday evening fishing to those who have to work an eight-hour day. The hours between 6.00 p.m. and dark can provide first-class sport, with every chance of attaining the magical limit bag by the imitative fishing methods which I prefer. The food chain has reached its most abundant stage of the year, and the water temperature has warmed to a nice level, even in the larger reservoirs. Trout are now in top condition, feeding heavily on a wealth of food items, but to make the most of the possibilities you must, as always, choose the right tackle. The floating line reigns supreme, with the neutral-density line a close second for use in flat calms or strong side-winds. The sinking line is quite unnecessary for June bank-fishing.

Much as I dislike using a shooting-head, with the added encumbrance of a line-tray, there are occasions when the trout are feeding well out, the nearest rises 40 yards from the bank. Despite the angler abstaining from wading, and being as quiet and unobtrusive as possible, the trout simply will not come closer. The only way to reach them is by skilful long-distance casting of a floating or neutral shooting-head combined with braided monofil backing. The imitative approach shouldn't always be restricted to standard DT or WF lines. However, if your rod has snake- or bridge-rings, watch out for severe wear, even though they are in hard chrome. The ability of the slightly rough surface of braided monofil to groove these rings has to be seen to be believed. Fuji or Seymo intermedi-ates are advisable, with the super-durable Fuji SiC rings well worth their extra cost.

The banquet on offer to the trout in June includes some interesting new courses. This makes life a little difficult because you should try to distinguish what they are feeding on, and the choice is so wide. The marrow spoon is really an essential item of equipment now. The first trout you catch must be spooned at once so that you have an indication of which food item(s) it has been eating over the past few hours. Sometimes it's one particular type of buzzer pupa and nothing else, and there's no problem. More often, it's a mixture – a little fish (possibly half-digested), plus a few buzzer pupae, a shrimp, and a sprinkling of daphnia. The knowledge gained from the marrow spoon, when combined with what you have seen in the way of rising fish or otherwise, builds up gradually to the stage where you have a pretty good idea of what to offer as a likely imitation at any given time. Not only that, but close study of the individual organisms in the stomach contents can help the enthusiastic fly-dresser to create better representations of the various food-forms.

Many of the pupae, etc., which have been most recently swallowed may be still alive when removed from the stomach, and the important features of colour, size, and action can be observed quite easily in a small amount of water. It was the study of buzzer pupae from the marrow spoon which helped me design my version of the Pheasant Tail Nymph and my series of buzzer nymphs, for example. Never underestimate the importance of the marrow spoon at any time of the season, but it is indispensable during the summer months of plenty, and in June there is certainly a wealth of choice.

Daphnia and several other species of tiny crustaceans (collectively known as 'water-fleas') are becoming increasingly abundant, and rainbows especially are mopping them up and piling on weight. Buzzers are still a major part of the trout diet, and are present in a wide range of sizes and colours; they can hatch at various times from dawn till dusk. There are numbers of *Asellus* and lake olives still about. *Gammarus*, the freshwater shrimp, is thriving now, particularly around the bottom of thick weed-beds where the plants have become so packed that their lower leaves are rotting and providing food. Also around the weed-beds at many reservoirs are myriads of tiny coarse-fish 'pin-fry' which have hatched from eggs laid on the weeds, and some of the trout will already be sampling them. Some waters have a population of sticklebacks, whose sharp dorsal spines don't seem to deter the trout from eating them.

Other important items of food which appear in June are two types of insect which are impossible to ignore. One I welcome – the sedges, the other I hate. The hated one is the infamous little ephemerid fly *Caenis*, the well-nicknamed 'Fisherman's Curse', and the main reason for my dislike of it is the extreme discomfort which a big hatch of *Caenis* causes. The tiny duns treat your person as an ideal place on which to carry out their amazingly quick change into spinners, and land in their hundreds on

face, hands, clothing and everywhere they can. If, like me, you wear
spectacles (or if, as you should, you have your polarised sunglasses on)
they have a nasty habit of crawling on to both the inside and outside of the
lenses, and can obscure vision by 50 per cent or more. And keep your
mouth shut – they taste horrible! One man I know used to fish in a bee-
keeper's veil when *Caenis* were about.

Caenis usually hatch in the early evening, particularly in conditions of
calm or a gentle breeze. Luckily the hatch rarely lasts long. The trout
certainly enjoy *Caenis* at each stage – nymph, dun, and spinner – but I
would suggest that the very start of the hatch is your only real chance of
tempting a fish with a *Caenis* imitation. When a *Caenis* hatch reaches its
peak, there are far too many for your flies to stand much chance of being
noticed. A size 16 or 18 Caenis Nymph could succeed, or the same size of
dry fly with cream-coloured tail, body, and hackle. Because of the small
size of the flies, you cannot use a leader point stronger than 3lb, and you
really need to use a soft-actioned rod, or at least Power Gum shock-
absorber, to avoid leader breaks or hooks pulling out. Maybe the best
place to be during a *Caenis* hatch is somewhere else!

To be honest, I don't bother trying to fish a hatch of *Caenis*. It is too
difficult, and the cavalry usually comes to the rescue midway through in
the form of our friends the sedges, to which the trout soon turn their
attention. There are almost two hundred British species of caddis- or
sedge-flies, in various sizes and shades of brown, fawn, or grey. Luckily
for the fly-fisher, they can be imitated by a fairly limited range of
artificials.

I have seen plenty of sedges as early as June 8 when the weather was
cloudy and the breeze warm, but usually they don't appear in significant
numbers until the third or fourth week in June, when you will often see
swarms of darkish moth-like insects, each with two prominent 'horns'
(antennae), dancing over clumps of waterside vegetation during early
evening. Should the wind strengthen, they disappear back on to the
foliage, but recommence their dancing flight as soon as there is a lull.
These are silverhorns or perhaps grouse-wing sedges, daytime-hatching
species which don't seem to be relished by the trout in the adult stage.

Much more attractive are the types which appear later in the evening –
the fairly common cinnamon sedges, gingery-fawn in colour, and the less
common large reddish-brown murragh or red sedge; there are one or two
small greyish species which can also be of interest, and your local water
could be the habitat of other species. Body colour can be green, fawn,
grey, brown, orange, or even yellow; check those which hatch on your
water, and choose your imitation accordingly. Many of the old traditional
wet flies are in reality suggestions of various sedges. Woodcock & Green,

Woodcock & Orange, Woodcock & Hare's Ear, Grouse & Green, Mallard & Claret, Fiery Brown, Invicta – all have something in common with natural sedges. The Invicta is probably the first choice of 'Mr Average Bank-fisher' when he notices the presence of sedge-flies, and it catches a lot of trout, but the choice should never be restricted to one pattern.

I have already told you in a previous chapter about the larval stage in the life-history of the sedge – the caddis grub crawling on the bottom in its protective case. Although this creature is still of interest to us, and imitations like the Stick Fly will take fish, the next stage – the sedge pupa – now becomes of much greater importance to the reservoir bank-fisher. After biting its way out of the now unwanted case, in which it has spent the last fortnight developing from the larva, the pupa swims quite strongly up through the water, using one pair of fringed legs as paddles. To release the adult fly, the pupal skin becomes inflated with gas and splits at the thorax. Some species hatch into the adult fly at the surface, even quite far out, whereas others must swim to the shore, climb up bankside rocks or rushes, and hatch there. I imagine that the common name 'sedge-fly' came about because early naturalists saw them clinging to the leaves of sedge plants.

In the same way that trout will take buzzer pupae both before and after they reach the surface, so they will feed on the sedge pupae as they swim and also as they rest at the surface. A late-afternoon rise is often attributed to buzzers but could really be caused by hatching sedges. As long ago as the mid-1920s, Dr Howard Bell recognised the importance of sedge pupae, and devised his famous Amber Nymph to use at Blagdon, but there are still many reservoir anglers who fail to take advantage of the opportunities which the appearance of the sedge pupa offers. From talking with other bank-fishers, I'm sure this is because they don't know much about it.

The sedge pupa is an untidy-looking creature. The fully-formed wings are tucked away in bulges protruding from the body, and the legs and antennae a mass (I nearly wrote 'mess') of jumbled filaments. In the act of hatching it is even more unkempt. Your own 'custom-built' artificials should reflect that untidiness – a 'legs-all-over-the-place' appearance. Shop-bought, commercially-tied examples are almost always too neat. Dubbing should be straggly and well picked-out; hackles should be soft and long-fibred. Some gamebird body plumage can be a better choice than hen hackles. Bodies, however, should not be too bulky. Luckily, it isn't necessary to have too many colours of sedge pupa in the fly-box; amber (or orange) and olive will usually suffice, unless your water has an obvious preponderance of something different. One of the bays at

Rutland, for example, has sedge pupae sporting yellow bodies with a row of black spots along the back.

If they fish sedge-pupa patterns at all, most people choose the Amber Nymph, Dick Walker's Longhorns or John Goddard's Sedge Pupa. A Wormfly dressed on a single longshank hook, with the front hackle nice and long, could be mistaken for a sedge pupa by an eager trout, as could a suitably-proportioned Mini-Muddler. Peter Gathercole has created an excellent imitation, probably the best to date, but there is room for further development in sedge-pupa patterns. I've been using one in both olive and amber, with dubbed Antron body and the legs represented by fibres of grouse body-feather, using the curved-shank Partridge K4A hook; the full dressing is given, along with many others, in the Appendix.

When you see swirly rise-forms – 'boils' and flats in the ripple in the late afternoon – fish sedge-pupa patterns on a long leader, using a medium-paced figure-of-eight retrieve interspersed with pauses. You can mount a Wickham's Fancy or Silver Invicta on the middle dropper, and on the top dropper one of the winged wet flies I mentioned earlier, to represent the just-hatched insect. You may have to cast a very long line to get amongst the fish, but the effort will be worth while.

You can have some good sport when the trout are taking the newly-hatched adult sedge as it skitters across the surface towards the bank (how on earth do they know which direction to take?). The rises then are unmistakable – noisy excited splashes. Use flies like Wickham's Fancy, Invicta, Murragh, or my variation of a Hatching Sedge pattern originally devised by C. F. Walker (which you can also use static on the top dropper of a sedge-pupa team). Use a very fast figure-of-eight retrieve rather than pulling (if your fingers are a blur, that's about right!). You will get exciting 'follows', many of which end up as solid takes, especially to the point fly. This technique also brings about one of my favourite reactions from the trout – a curving leap out of the water and down on to the fly. It is essential then to stop retrieving and wait about three seconds before tightening, to allow the fish to take the fly down properly. Quite an effort of will-power required! If you tighten too soon, the trout will only be pricked.

The sedge-flies which manage to reach the waterside rest among the vegetation for several hours, preparatory to flying out for mating and egg-laying. They usually fly over the water quite close to the surface, and this brings great activity on the part of the trout. The fish often jump out to try and catch the flying insects (usually missing them!). When the sedges finally land on the water, they are easy meat for the fish. The bigger females sit on the surface, surrounded by a swarm of attendant males. Now is the time for a realistic dry fly, and I have just the one. Let me tell you how I found it.

In 1965 I paid my first visit to the River Traun in Austria, my enthusiasm fired after reading Charles Ritz's book *A Flyfisher's Life* in which he told marvellous tales of the big trout and grayling he caught there. I stayed in the little town of Gmunden which straddles the lower end of the Traunsee lake. The river runs down from the mountains, a typical mountain stream often carrying suspensions of colour when in flood. It enters the lake, which acts as a huge settling basin, and at the outflow at the Gmunden end of the lake it is a fully-fledged river, a hundred yards wide, fast-running and as clear as crystal no matter what its level. Some years later, a hydroelectric dam was built downstream, just below Ritz's favourite Marienbrucke Hotel, and this spoiled the fishing at Gmunden, but that first evening in 1965 I stood on the boardwalk just below the town bridge, and watched huge brown trout and grayling rising to the hordes of big sedges fluttering over the river. It was obvious what was needed to match the hatch, but my dry sedge-flies were more suited to the placid Derbyshire brooks, and soon sank in the ripples and cross-currents of the mighty Traun.

The local hardware store had a fishing-tackle department, so the following morning I paid them a visit. Gmunden wasn't on the English tourist route, so no one in the shop spoke English. In my halting German (we didn't learn German at school) I asked, 'Fleigen fur Traunflüsse, bitte?' and was shown several drawers full of boxes of flies. These included some of the best dry-fly representations of sedges I had ever seen. They really looked like the real thing, even down to a pair of antennae at the head. Dressed locally, and designed specially for use on the Traun by famous river-keeper Hans Gebetsroither, every pattern had flat wings made from whole small feathers, selected from the body plumage of various birds, varnished to make them slim and stiff. These trapped air, and aided by excellent palmered cock hackles, ensured that the flies floated despite the weirpools and turbulent surface of the Traun.

Because of the clarity of the water, the fish were very selective, but I caught lots of superb grayling averaging 2lb in weight, and two 3-lb trout, all on these dry sedges. If they stay afloat on the Traun, they will float on a reservoir, I thought, and this was proved at Grafham when I returned to England. I made up three patterns to represent cinnamon, dark brown, and silver sedges, and called them my 'Super Sedges'. A good dose of flotant, and they sit up beautifully, even in a good wave. The first time I tried the Super Cinnamon Sedge, male cinnamons fluttered round it, under the impression that it was a female. I reckon when that happens, a fly-dresser has 'cracked it'!

Even after the adult sedges have disappeared, late in the evening, it is worth fishing wet-fly sedge patterns. The trout could still be looking for stragglers to mop up, provided there isn't a late hatch of buzzers to divert their attention. Whether the last-minute buzzer hatch occurs or not, depends on the air temperature. If cloud cover keeps the air temperature up, buzzers can hatch just before darkness sets in, but if the sky clears, causing a swift drop in temperature, or the breeze strengthens to a strong cold wind, rarely will buzzers appear. You would then be well advised either to continue with the wet sedges, or switch to a slowly fished Black Poodle lure, a trick which can be very productive indeed during the last minutes of dusk.

If trout continue to rise, and there are no sedges evident, you can bet that the late buzzer hatch has started. The occasional high-pitched whine in your ear should prompt you to glance up at the sky where you will see buzzers hovering in typical pose, like commas, above your head. You *must* change flies! There are only a few minutes of daylight left, so waste no time in mounting a team of dark buzzer patterns which, if you are wise, you will have previously tied on a 10-foot leader which you have wound on a cast-carrier. No way can you see well enough to tie flies on the leader you are already using. A suitable set-up would be Pheasant Tail Nymph on the point, Pearl-rib Black Buzzer Nymph on the middle dropper, and palmered Grey Buzzer or Blae & Black (with neon magenta floss tail) on the top dropper. A few dabs of Gink on the leader will keep the flies up where they are needed – you must grease-up, despite the problems it may cause. Whoever invents a floating monofil for leaders will make a fortune! It is most important that your flies are not too deep; even a few inches will make the difference beween success and failure. The trout are concentrating their attention at the surface, and will ignore any flies below their level. Don't retrieve fast, either! Dick Walker's humorous instruction 'An inch an hour' points the way. Often, it's best not to retrieve at all.

Don't bother with a longer leader. It will be almost dark by now, and there is no need to worry about the flies being too near the fly-line, provided you cast carefully without splashing. Another point – it's always more difficult to cast accurately when you can't see too well, and the short leader helps avoid tangles which can be disastrous with a greased-up leader. The trout at this moment in time are usually mad keen on feeding, lacking in caution, and eagerly looking for every scrap of food, so you should get at least a couple of fish.

Evening fishing can virtually be restricted to sedge-flies and buzzers, but a full day's fishing in June can be very varied. There will, of course, be periods during the day when no surface activity will be evident. The trout are busy below, perhaps rooting out freshwater shrimps (*Gammarus* species) from the weeds. It's always worth trying a shrimp pattern. *Gammarus* is usually a translucent greyish-olive in colour, but occasionally you will find orange specimens. There is a great deal of confusion about whether orange shrimps occur or not, but Arthur Cove told me that he had conclusive scientific proof that the orange-coloured shrimps are in fact individuals infected with a minute parasite rejoicing in the name of *Pomphorhyncus laevis*, and this causes the colour-change. Nothing to do with mating colours, as some have suggested, but those who have jumped to the conclusion that the shrimp changes colour just before it dies are near enough to the truth, because the parasite is lethal. Shrimp patterns are best if weighted; olive or orange dressings should be tried, in sizes 10 and 12. The retrieve, after waiting for the fly to sink, should be slow figure-of-eight with the odd foot-long pull, imitating the erratic behaviour of these little crustaceans.

Prolonged flat calms and sunny weather (yes, it can happen!) create conditions in which you may see lumps of 'gunge' floating up quite speedily from the bottom, sometimes causing a little boil as they surface. These blobs are composed of decayed algae, diatoms, and other debris which have formed a thick scum on the reservoir bed. Mixed in with this is live filamentous algae, which produces oxygen by photosynthesis under sunny conditions; the buoyancy of this oxygen makes the blobs rise to the surface. There is plenty of trout food living in the bottom scum, and as it breaks up, these creatures – bloodworms, *Asellus*, shrimps, and so on – are liberated into the water. The trout are often attracted to the area where this is occurring. Don't be put off by the presence of even quite a lot of these scummy blobs; careful fishing can produce fish despite the difficult conditions. The static nymph technique can bring takes on the drop, for example. If there is a slight side-breeze at this time, the blobs can become concentrated in narrow scum-lanes. Using a neutral-density line, cast your flies into the scum-lane and let them drift around. Don't be surprised when you get a determined pull!

To many anglers, flat calms make casting difficult, and I am no exception. Timing and power input have to be well-nigh perfect. There is no breeze to help the line and leader straighten. To make the leader turn over better, sacrifice a few feet of distance by giving the line a sharp tug just before the leader extends on the final forward-cast. This tends to flick the point fly out, and can help to avoid leader and flies falling in a heap.

I have just mentioned one cause of scum-lanes. Daphnia could perhaps be another cause. This tiny crustacean can be termed 'freshwater plankton', congregating in huge clouds in the water, feeding on suspensions of microscopic unicellular algae (the sort that turn the water into 'pea soup'). Summer conditions suit daphnia very well, because warm water encourages its prolific reproduction, as long as there is enough algae to feed on. In cold conditions or when food runs out, daphnia produces tiny eggs which are resistant to extreme environmental conditions such as freezing or drying-out; these eggs hatch when conditions improve.

Daphnia is very nutritious, full of good protein and oily material which often creates surface slicks. Trout, especially rainbows (and even big ones at that), gorge themselves on the tiny daphnia, which are no more than 2mm in size. There are several species of daphnia, the commonest of which is *Daphnia pulex*. 'Pulex' is Latin for 'flea', which the little creature resembles, hence the common name 'water-flea'. It even moves in the water in a flea-like hopping manner, swimming jerkily by using branched antennae near the head. This swimming action is quite feeble, so the swarms are at the mercy of drift currents which can concentrate them into very localised areas of the reservoir. An interesting point is that daphnia can change colour according to the amount of dissolved oxygen in the water; reduced oxygen increases the amount of haemoglobin in the blood, so the daphnia becomes reddish instead of the pale green it exhibits in well-aerated water.

The important fact to remember about daphnia is that it actively moves away from bright light, which it does not like. Scientists describe it as being 'negatively phototropic'. The latter word is derived from Greek – 'photo' referring to light and 'tropic' relating to tropism or movement. When the sun is shining on the water, the daphnia sink deep, and in dull cloudy conditions they rise to the upper levels. Don't forget that this change in depth can take place several times in a day if sun alternates with cloud. Naturally, the trout follow the daphnia, and in sunny weather are well down in the water unless attracted upwards by an abundance of some other food item, such as buzzer pupae rising from the bottom.

Being so tiny, daphnia is of course impossible to imitate in an artificial fly. The only way to catch trout which are feeding on daphnia is to attract their attention away from their preoccupation by using some form of lure which could perhaps induce curiosity or aggression – that's the theory, anyway. There's no place for imitative purism where daphnia is concerned! Lure-fishing for trout feeding on daphnia is often considered the sole province of the boat-angler, but this is not true. There are many times, particularly on dull days, when daphnia swarms are drifted near the bank by the prevailing breeze, probably causing a smooth slick which shouldn't be ignored, especially if you see trout swirling in it.

Orange is your first choice of colour in a lure for daphnia-feeders. I think my most successful patterns are the Orange Tadpole, Peach Doll, and a gold-bodied Orange Marabou Muddler with an orange deer-hair head. There are several others you can use – Whisky Fly, Old Nick, Jersey Herd, or Dunkeld, for example. If these don't work, try other colours –

white, black, or fluorescent green either on its own or combined with one of the other colours. As with all lure-fishing, there seems to be a 'colour of the day' and you have to experiment until you find it.

The lure doesn't always have to be a big one, although it pays to follow the loch-style boat-fishing maxim, 'The bigger the wave, the bigger the fly'. In a gentle ripple I have taken daphnia-feeders on Mini-Muddlers, dressed on size 10 Partridge 'Captain Hamilton' hooks. If orange isn't working, I try a Viva Mini-Muddler with a soft mobile hairwing of arctic fox dyed black. I like translucent dubbed bodies on a lot of my lures – seal fur or Antron, instead of chenille or floss, seems more attractive. Added sparkle is possible by using a pearl-flecked tinsel – Crystal Hair or Lureflash Twinkle – as ribbing; these are available in several colours and I have found them extremely good for bodies, tails or winging, as well as for ribbing. I have great faith in lures which incorporate mobile materials such as marabou or soft hair, both of which pulsate when pulled through the water. If the lure has a large 'head', as in a Muddler, this creates turbulence behind it which makes the mobile wings and/or tail wiggle, so that the lure appears more alive. The Tadpole design has a bulky head of chenille, either built up from the body chenille or made from chenille of wider diameter than the body, and I really like the action this produces, even at quite slow speeds. Feather-wings seem so rigid by comparison.

Bank-fishing for daphnia-feeding trout, I find the best technique is to fish a single lure on a tapered leader 15 feet long, tip-strength 7lb, on a weight-forward line; floater for dull days, slow-sinker for bright days. Either start the retrieve as soon as the line touches down, or wait until the lure has sunk (you must experiment until you find the correct depth), and strip back in fast foot-long pulls. The take is usually a firm stoppage, and the trout virtually hooks itself. Great fun! Which is what trout fishing should be all about.

You will find suitable special dressings in the Appendix, but here are some suggested standard-pattern flies for June:

For sedges
Larvae – Stick Fly, Montana Nymph.
Pupae – Amber Nymph, Olive Sedge Pupa, Longhorns.
Wet – Woodcock & Orange, Grouse & Green, Fiery Brown, Hatching
    Sedge, Woodcock & Hare's Ear, Invicta.
Dry – Super Sedges in cinnamon and dark brown.

For shrimps
Olive Chomper, Olive Shrimp, Orange Shrimp, Gold-ribbed Hare's Ear Nymph.

For daphnia

Muddlers, Mini-Muddlers, and lures, in orange, black, white, fluorescent green.

For fry and sticklebacks

Ethafoam Fry, Sinfoil Fry, Silver Invicta, small White Tadpole.

Chapter 8

The Bank in High Summer:
July and August

You will have noticed that I mention weather conditions frequently in this book. This is because our weather has a huge influence on reservoir fishing, controlling the activity of the trout and the natural trout-food creatures, and therefore the methods we must use. July and most of August can be warm and sunny, and this causes problems. The main difficulty is the high temperature of the water at the surface and round the banks. This interferes with the development pattern of insects, and trout are loth to enter water which is warmer than 65°F (18°C).

In heatwave weather, the best time to fish is at dawn. With a bit of luck, the water temperature cools down during the night, and it is possible that conditions are more normal first thing in the morning, perhaps helped by a cool breeze. Choose the upwind end of the reservoir, to avoid the warmer water.

If reservoir rules allow, to get the best out of these early-bird sessions you should reach the water before it gets light. You can virtually rely on buzzers being the main course of the trout's breakfast, and the fish are often feeding while it is still dark. Restrict yourself to one dropper unless you are confident of casting three flies successfully in the dark – timing seems to go haywire when you can't see what you are doing. Use buzzer representations in sizes 12 and 14, with the largest size on the point. Balanced distribution of flies on the leader is always important, but never more so than when casting solely by feel. Don't have the flies closer than 4 feet apart, and make sure there are no spurs of nylon sticking out from the knots. In other words, take all precautions against tangling.

You must waste no time fumbling about in the darkness, trying to set up your rod, line, flies, etc., so assemble your outfit in the comfort of your well-lit home the night before. If you do this just before going to bed, you can perhaps lean it against a wall in the hallway, out of harm's way. Invest in a pair of car rod-clips, and carry the rod complete with line, leader, and flies, on the car roof. There are some excellent types of rod-clips on the market. Most of them use the car guttering as a fixing point, but if your car has no gutter, there are magnetic models which are perfectly safe.

I usually carry my rod made up in this way. I hook the point fly into an intermediate rod-ring near the tip of the rod, and take the leader round the reel on the side away from the handle. Reel up until all is tight, without putting a bend in the tip, and it's ready to go anywhere.

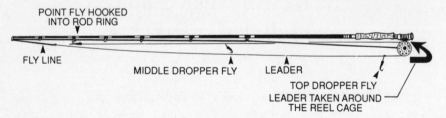

POINT FLY HOOKED
INTO ROD RING

FLY LINE

MIDDLE DROPPER FLY   LEADER

TOP DROPPER FLY
LEADER TAKEN AROUND
THE REEL CAGE

The 'transit position'

For this early-morning fishing, it's always best to fish a spot you know well, rather than one you haven't fished before. Take note of the previous late-night weather forecast, particularly with regard to wind direction and speed; this will help you in your choice of location. I have a weathervane at the bottom of my garden, and it is absolutely invaluable in helping me decide where to fish.

At the water, with just a breeze to give a nice ripple, you may hear the trout rising. Don't be too eager to wade! The fish can be quite close in, so first fish all the water you can cover from the bank. I remember arriving at Blagdon one such morning, a very faint lightening of the eastern sky just enabling me to distinguish land from water. Standing at the water's edge, I started to get line out. I had made the first cast, only 10 yards, and was about to pull more line off the reel when I heard a loud smacking kissing sound which seemed to come from the end of my rod. I'm never very alert at that time of the morning, and my thought process went something like this: 'What the hell was that? Sounded like a rise. Close in, too. It couldn't be to my fly, could it? Crikey, maybe it could. I'd better strike and find out!' All this took about three seconds. I struck, and found myself attached to a lively two pounds of rainbow trout. It had taken the static top dropper fly, a palmered Grey Buzzer, which must have been sitting there like a dry fly. Careless wading would have scared the trout away, I'm sure.

When you do decide to wade, do so very cautiously. You could easily step into an unseen dip in the bottom. At least investigate by prodding with a long-handled landing-net before taking each step. 'Fan' your casts so that you cover as wide an area as possible, from left to right. As you have just seen, the flies could be taken static, or you can move them quite slowly. With luck, you will have good sport for a couple of hours, but things usually slow down as soon as the sun appears. You can then try fishing the corixa, often a good bet at this time of the year. Look carefully into the water at your feet – you will perhaps see these little water-bugs paddling about. The air trapped in the tiny hairs on their bodies gives them a silvery appearance (bear this in mind when you choose a corixa pattern). Don't mistake a very similar bug, the waterboatman (*Notonecta*), for corixa; the waterboatman is larger, and swims on its back, whereas the true corixa swims 'right-way-up'. The waterboatman must taste nasty, because trout do not eat it.

There are several corixa patterns available commercially, the commonest having a cream floss body ribbed with silver, brown feather-fibre back, and a brown collar hackle. These do take their share of trout, if weighted so that the correct action can be given to the fly. I like to incorporate a representation of the prominent swimming legs, because I subscribe to the theory that an imitative artificial should suggest distinctive features of the natural. There is a commercial pattern with 'legs' of nylon monofil, but in my opinion this material is too stiff; the legs should flick and move as the fly is jerked, simulating a swimming motion. Fibres of goose or turkey can give this essential movement; condor is the strongest, but is unobtainable. If you have some in your collection of fly-tying materials, condor is the one to choose. All these feather fibres have a flue which gives the impression of the fringe on the insect's paddles. Although the standard of commercially-tied flies is now greatly improved, with many up-to-date ideas and patterns, tying your own is always so much better; creating a lifelike corixa is a perfect example of how the amateur fly-dresser can experiment.

As the hours pass, and the sun rises higher, fishing in high summer gets difficult. But not impossible. There are always the fry-bashers to fall back on. Bright sun rarely seems to prevent the trout from dashing into the shallows after the shoals of coarse-fish fry. On many a hot sunny afternoon, the only sign of trout activity is the occasional splash of a trout attacking fry. Each foray is preceded by a frantic scattering of the fry, many of which leap above the surface in their efforts to dodge the rush of the predator. When the fry are in tightly-packed shoals, several are stunned by the ferocious rush of the trout, and float to the surface. There's not much to beat the old Ethafoam Floating Stunned Fry to give you a chance of catching the trout when it returns to pick up these victims. This isn't always in the next few minutes. Fishing the fry is very much a waiting game, but there's always the chance of a really big trout. My little jokey reply to those who moan about how hard the fishing is, is 'Take your pal Percy with you – perseverance! And if his wife Patience comes along, all the better!'

These qualities not only apply to fishing the fry, but to all methods; if you add versatility, so much the better. Summer daytime fishing is rather opportunist and you should take advantage of every possibility. You must be prepared to try anything and everything (legal!). You cannot be versatile if you stick in one place. Roam the banks instead, searching for the odd feeding fish. During your travels on a warm summer day, you could see one very obvious flying insect – the strikingly beautiful blue damselfly, often mistakenly referred to as a dragonfly. Many reservoirs have a population of these. It is said that on some waters the trout will leap at the adult damselflies as they hover over the water, but personally I have never seen this. It is, however, an undisputed fact that trout feed underwater on the damselfly larvae, so if you see the adults flying in the heat of the day it is worth while fishing a Damselfly Nymph. The larvae swim quite actively, so there is no need for a very slow retrieve rate. They are capable of sudden darts of speed, by jetting water through holes in the tail – the original jet propulsion! Speed is needed to catch their prey – they feed on small larvae and nymphs, which they catch in pincer-like appendages. Again, there are several patterns of damselfly nymph tied commercially, including a tricky articulated version called the Damsel Wiggle Nymph, invented by John Goddard to suggest the wriggling motion of the swimming larva. The various species can be represented by browns and greens in several shades. Nottingham fly-dresser Mick Huffer has meticulously designed an excellent pattern which those readers who tie flies might like to try. The dressing is given in the Appendix.

The reservoir dam is always worth investigating. The film of algae which covers the concrete or rocks is food for water-snails, which in turn are food for trout. It is very rare for at least one part of the dam not to hold trout, often attracted there by numbers of snails grazing on the algae. One of the commonest water-snails eaten by trout is *Limnaea peregra*, the 'wandering snail', which is about the size of a fingernail, and brownish-olive in colour. Trout take one after another until their stomachs are bulging. This is one food-form which doesn't need the marrow spoon to discover it. All you have to do is squeeze the trout's abdomen, and you can feel the snails inside like so much gravel or pebbles.

Not much has been done about snail patterns. Most authors advise using a well-sunk weighted Black & Peacock Spider, and this does work sometimes. A sizeable Olive Chomper is perhaps a better fly to try. Fly-dressing readers might consider tying a more realistic impression with a bulky olive chenille body, two stubby olive goose biots extending in front to represent the tentacled eyes, and brown plastic raffia to imitate the shell. Remember to dampen the raffia and stretch it before tying in, or it will absorb water and come loose when you use the fly. Hooks should be sizes 10 and 12, and well weighted, of course. Fish these sunk snail patterns static or extremely slowly – you never see a speeding snail!

In summer, there is an aspect of this snail's behaviour which interests reservoir anglers even more than its algae-grazing. Myriads of snails release their grip on underwater stones and plants, and float to the surface, turning upside-down so that the foot clings to the underside of the surface film. They drift along on the ripple, literally migrating, though in a passive manner. As soon as the trout find these floating snails, they become completely preoccupied with them, and move steadily upwind, taking the snails off the top. The rise-forms are just like those to insects, and if you don't know about the migratory habits of our friend *L. peregra* you will fish the wrong flies and catch nothing. The fish simply will not look at anything but a floating snail pattern. In conditions of a gentle ripple, the rise-forms to snails are slow head-and-tailing; in a bigger wave, the trout make quite a splash.

I first discovered the problem of the floating snail one afternoon at Rutland a few years ago, fishing just west of the transformer near the top of the North Arm. A steady westerly wind gave a nice 'lop'. Marching up the waves came dozens of trout – maybe hundreds – feeding like mad. I threw everything at them and caught nothing. I never thought of looking closely at the surface; buzzers were uppermost in my mind. How wrong I was! Finally, purely by chance, I noticed snails at the surface, right at my feet, and the penny dropped.

I had nothing suitable in my box. The next day, I talked over the problem with John Clarkson, one of the bailiffs at that time, a very competent fly-dresser. I suggested that clipped deer hair would make a buoyant body, and plastic raffia or even polythene sheet could represent the shell of the snail. John lost no time in producing a few samples, and passed them around. Provided the deer hair has the correct bulk to exactly overcome the weight of the hook (which must be shortshank and wide-gape, or there will not be good hooking ability – Mustad 9479, size 10, is suitable), this answers the problem. It has become known at Rutland as 'John Clarkson's Snail', but John would be the first to acknowledge that it was I who gave him the idea!

The deer hair is spun on in the same way as making a Muddler-head, and clipped flat above the shank. Clip it to a convex shape below the shank, so that you now have a final shape like half an egg. Then tie in the material which suggests the shell. Again, if you use plastic raffia, it must be wetted and stretched before tying in and must not mask the point of the hook. All in all, this is quite a tricky pattern to tie. It is not enough just to hope that the amount of deer hair you use is sufficient. Ideally, each fly should be tested in a basin of water to see if it sinks or not. The natural snail is attached to the underside of the surface, and that is where your artificial must be. If it sinks, it is ignored by the trout. If it floats on the surface, it will be swirled at, nibbled, or splashed at, but rarely taken.

Smear the flat top of the deer hair with Gink or Permagrease, which will help to keep the thing from sinking. As with reservoir dry flies, you can fish one, two, or three, and the leader must be fully degreased. It is essential that there is no retrieve – drifting snails don't move! Simply let the line drift around, and with luck it will tighten and you're in business. It has been suggested by mischievous minds that the trout mistake the snail pattern for a pellet. What a naughty thought!

There are two summertime insects, the flying ant and the drone-fly, which bring about a complete preoccupation on the part of the trout; when they are on to either of these, there are no alternatives. Although in some years you may not encounter this situation, it is essential that your fly selection includes fairly close imitations of these two insects.

Huge numbers of large winged ants fly out from ant colonies on warm still summer afternoons on their mating flight, and often fall on nearby water. Once the trout find them, they continue rising until every one is eaten. Present a dry ant pattern, and I would almost bet on your success. I've seen boats drive right through a shoal of trout rising to ants, and the fish have continued to rise in the wake, so intense was their desire to feed. On my first encounter with the flying-ant rise, I mistook the insects for buzzers, and for over an hour I couldn't get a pull. One 'daft one' finally took a Blae & Black, but that was the only fish, and foolishly I didn't spoon it. It was only when the fish was gutted at home that I found the cause of the rise – the stomach was crammed solid with winged black ants. When I next found trout taking ants, on a lake in County Cork, Eire, there was no problem, even though it was a flat-calm/bright-sun situation. On went the dry ant, and out came the trout.

The drone-fly which anglers usually come across is really a hover-fly; the true drone-fly is similar to a honeybee, whereas the hover-fly has the yellow and black striping of a wasp. There are several species, some of which have orange replacing the yellow. None of them sting, incidentally. You can see them hovering motionless over flowers in your garden throughout the summer. Some years see quite a plague of hover-flies, but you can go through many a season without seeing one on the water. Even so, be sure to have a copy in your fly-box. On one day not too many years ago, four of us had double limits off the dam at Rutland when no one else made a catch, and every fish took a drone-fly pattern I had tied the night before. Top dropper, just dribbled along the surface, and it really was murder. Made up for some of the blanks!

If you want to be a hundred per cent prepared for any eventuality, you had better also include ladybird and greenfly imitations in your fly-box. Hot summers like we had in 1989 and 1990 can cause population explosions of these insects, and they do find their way on to the water. They are easy to imitate, but because of their very small size – the greenfly need to be on size 24 hooks or even smaller – you must fish them on very fine nylon and a soft light-line rod.

Around noon on any July or August day there could be a short hatch of buzzers, if conditions are right; not too much wind, high cloud or at least some haze to reduce the power of the sun. These buzzers will most probably be olives or gingers. Keep a close eye on any flies you see on the surface or in the air, and match the colour with your artificials. Palmered winged wets like my Honey Buzzer have brought good results for me. Mid-afternoon, you could see a buzzer hatch which I view with mixed feelings. The species in question is a small pale-olive buzzer which hatches from tiny olive pupae in vast numbers. Lots of trout come up for both pupae and adults, particularly in the slicks and scum-lanes, feeding in an almost continuous motion, heads, backs, and tails all half out of the water. I love to have trout to 'throw at', but how frustrating they can be when they are on to these midgets.

Even if you go down to size 16 or 18 hooks, the chance of a trout seeing your flies among the multitude of naturals is about the same odds as winning the treble chance.

The all-important question is whether to use a close copy of the buzzers, or patterns which stand out from the crowd by being more noticeable, or lures to break the trout's preoccupation. The first two alternatives certainly mean using small hooks, which in turn means the finest nylon you dare, plus Power Gum. Maybe the best choice is a team of small dries, perhaps one of which has a touch of signal-green or bright orange fluorescence, cast ahead of moving trout. If this fails, try going to the other extreme, and stick a large Muddler on the point. This should have a really big head, soaked in Gink, or even a head made from Plastazote, to give maximum surface disturbance. Rip the Muddler as fast as you can through the rising trout. Assuming they are rainbows, you may provoke a few follows, ten per cent of which might result in a take. Whatever method you try, a trout taken when the dreaded tiny olives are on the menu is well and truly earned.

Trying all these roaming tactics throughout the day can build up a steady catch of trout. The banks at this time of the year are not full of anglers – many people are away on family holidays, and those who fish for trout only up to June 16 are back at their coarse-fishing. There is plenty of room to move about. If you see an obvious shoal of rainbows travelling upwind, you can keep moving upwind with them and take several fish from the one shoal.

If the shoal is one of recently introduced stockies (and until you catch one, you can't know what they are), the snag with fishing more than one fly on the leader can become apparent. It's possible to get a trout on each fly simultaneously, three on at once, pulling in all directions and against each other. If not too big, they can be beached, but as you know, I don't like doing this, especially if the fish are going to be returned. Maybe there is another angler nearby whose net could help out? If so, make sure he (or it could be she) knows the safe and proper way to net a fish. The net must be submerged fully and held still. Your responsibility is to draw the trout, fully played out and on its side with its head abovewater, into the waiting net. Singly or collectively, the solution is to net the top fish first and the point fish last.

Sometimes the trout solve the problem for you by coming off! I must tell you one hard-luck tale. I was fishing the bank near Normanton Church at Rutland one evening. Buzzers hatching, and plenty of fish rising. I hooked a huge brownie on the top dropper – saw every inch of it because it leapt as I hooked it, and it was ten pounds if it was an ounce. The biggest trout I have ever had on. While I was playing it, a rainbow about 2lb in weight leapt in a strange manner near my line, and I realised that it had taken the point fly. About ten seconds after that, a little rainbow stockie jumped on to the middle dropper. Three on at once, and one the biggest I had ever seen! The first to come off was the big brownie – they have such hard mouths, and maybe the hook wasn't right in. The next to come off was the bigger rainbow – just my luck. I have never before or since been cruel to a trout, but I kicked that unfortunate little stockie up the bank! But I still fish more than one fly on the leader 99.9 per cent of the time.

Whatever the pleasures or difficulties of summer daytime fishing, the prime time during July and August (if the water isn't too warm) is definitely from early evening to dusk. Our friends the sedges are at the height of their activity at this time of the year, not to mention the almost certain pre-dark buzzer hatch. Summer days are long, and you need to be fit if you intend to fish from dawn till dusk. However, at the end of the day you should be the proud possessor of a limit bag of fine trout.

Here are some flies you can use:

Buzzers and sedge patterns as mentioned in previous chapters. Floating Snail, Damselfly Nymph, Damsel Wiggle Nymph, Floating Stunned Fry, Sinfoil Fry, Tom's Terror, Corixa, Black & Peacock Spider. Dry flies in olive, ginger, or orange.

Chapter 9

September Bank-Fishing: Sport to Remember

No matter how fickle the weather is – and it seems to have a will of its own from one day to the next in these modern times – there is a general trend towards cooler weather in September as the days grow shorter. This means that some of the problems associated with summer bank-fishing become less frustrating. Water temperatures in the shallows and at the surface usually begin to fall to a level more suitable to trout activity, and the chances of really hectic sport are now much better than during the hot midsummer weather. Trout are more likely to venture close to the bank instead of staying 'down and out', and often feed throughout the day on what is still a very varied menu. Buzzers particularly are more likely to hatch when the surface water is not too warm. Unless we experience an unseasonal heatwave, September promises such good sport that many anglers say it's the best month of the season. This month certainly offers great expectations for both imitative and lure-fishing techniques.

The changeable British weather dictates the methods we use, as always. Thankfully, conditions are often dull and humid, with reasonably warm westerly winds strong enough to give a good wave during the day and a nice ripple in the evenings. The days are shortening, and evening visits become quite restricted, with dusk at 8.00 p.m. towards the end of the month. During the last week of September, there is the possibility of very cold nights and even frost if the skies are clear. A couple of consecutive frosty nights soon send the fish down, and put a stop to surface insect activity. We must then forsake the floating line and resort to sinking or sink-tip lines and slow-moving lures. Almost back to the tactics of April, in fact.

Another September bonus is the absolutely splendid condition of the trout. The whole trout population is more likely to feed almost non-stop in the cooler conditions; even recently introduced stockies put on weight and regrow their fins. The larger brown trout feed well during September, giving improved catches of browns where these are stocked. Some writers put forward the opinion that the browns are feeding themselves up prior to spawning, as if the fish had a calendar to consult and an intelligence to anticipate the future! I would suggest that the browns are seen to feed more enthusiastically at this time of the year because they are able to enter the cooler water in the margins and can be caught from the bank, whereas during the summer they have been in the deeper water where only the lead-liners in their boats can reach them.

I'm not in favour of banning any legal method of fishing, but I do feel that in reservoirs which are stocked with a mixture of browns and rainbows there is a case for restricting the areas where lead-lining behind the boat is permitted (for example, the trolling areas), so as to give the browns a greater chance of survival for the benefit of bank-anglers. If left unmolested by the deep-dredging boat-anglers, the big browns come into the bank from September onwards, and the bank-fishers have the opportunity of catching more-or-less 'wild' specimens of 4lb and up-wards. Luckily for bank-anglers, few reservoirs now allow fishing behind a drifting boat.

In cold conditions, brown trout may give the lure a series of quite firm taps before taking it properly. You must be ready for these, and discipline yourself from striking at them, because all you will succeed in doing is pulling the lure away from the fish and frightening it. Follow the sage advice of the late Dick Shrive: 'Keep pulling – they don't know it's feathers!' Wait till you get a firm pull, and tighten sideways into it. If the pull doesn't come, a slow lift of the rod-tip at the end of the retrieve brings the lure to the surface and can induce the take.

Both rainbows and browns show a tendency to shoal at this time of the year, and it is important to locate the positions of these shoals. Very often, ten yards either side of a shoal, and you don't get a touch. Local season-ticket holders, many of whom almost live on the water, have the advantage of knowing where the fish are, thanks to highly-organised grapevines, jealously guarded. The occasional visitor must rely on helpful fishery staff pointing him in the right direction early enough to secure a favourable position. Whether regular or occasional visitor, you must be at the water early in time to secure your place. It's one of the disadvantages of fishing public waters, and you simply have to put up with it if you are to get the best of the late-season fishing. Your technique must be as good as you can make it, because you may have to accept a difficult wind direction or the need for very accurate casting, if you want to stay where the fish are. The trout don't position themselves with your comfort in mind! Versatility is also a major factor. Be prepared to fish imitative patterns or lures as conditions demand.

Lures will certainly be required if the trout are feeding on daphnia (which they still could be) or fry-bashing. It is not always necessary to fish huge weighted creations; often, longshank 10s are productive. The essentials for a successful lure are mobility of materials and the right colour. The 'colour of the day' can only be discovered by experiment, but here are a few pointers. Crystal-clear water usually means using black. White suits deep or cloudy water. Fluorescent pink is good, especially in the evening. Orange suits bright conditions. Fluorescent green, combined with black or white, is also very popular.

I would advise marabou for mobility in tails and wings – there are plenty of marabou lures stocked by tackle dealers. Fly-dressing anglers will be better off using soft hair, such as arctic fox, instead of marabou, giving greater durability without sacrificing action. A bulky head or thorax should be a feature of lures with these mobile tails and wings. The turbulence created by the large head makes the marabou or hair wiggle enticingly. Muddlers, Tadpoles, Froggies, Poodles, Concrete Bowls, Cat's Whiskers, or Dog Nobblers can all have the marabou replaced by soft hair. So can any featherwing lure be improved by substituting a wing of hair of similar colour to the feather used in the wing. There are some nicely-coloured squirrel tails which can be used – Parey squirrel for bronze mallard is a good example – and the modern technique of bleaching out the barring on the grey squirrel tail before dyeing it is perhaps one of the most useful developments in fly-tying. These 'plain-dyed' squirrel tails give you any single colour you want – dark brown, ginger, or any of the bright colours, including fluorescents. For black, of course, the pre-bleaching isn't necessary. For white, use the white portions of a ringcat (bassarisk) tail, which has a texture similar to squirrel.

It's very important to select the right texture of hair to suit the size of the lure. The shorter you have to cut the hair, to bring it into proportion with the hook-size, the stiffer it becomes. If a pattern is listed as requiring bucktail hair for the wing, for example, substitute the thinner squirrel-tail hair or fox or even rabbit when you tie the smaller sizes. You will have rightly guessed that if I have to fish lures, I like to keep them as small as possible. It is amazing how trout which have been feeding on big fry up to 4 inches long will sometimes take a size 10 longshank lure. Of course, there are times when a longshank tandem lure is required, but for me this is a last resort.

One type of lure I have a soft spot for is the Baby Doll, but not in its original wool material. There are more suitable modern fluorescent materials, in my opinion. I like to use Glow-Bug yarn for the body, and Glo-Brite Multi-Yarn for the back and tail. Both are made in a wide range of fluorescent colours, many not available in any other material. I make my version of the Peach Doll with Glow-Bug Apricot for the body and Glo-Brite Amber Multi-Yarn (shade 8) for the back and tail; it's the best Peach Doll of the lot. The Glow-Bug yarn is too thick in its original form, but you split it to a suitable thickness with a dubbing needle, and provided that you twist the yarn constantly as you wind it round the hook shank, it will hold together; if not twisted, it pulls apart. There is a nice sparkle to the Multi-Yarn.

Mention of 'sparkle' reminds me to tell you that the addition of a few strands of suitably-coloured Crystal Hair makes a fantastic difference to the attraction of virtually every lure. It makes excellent backs and tails on Baby Dolls, for example. Crystal Hair has tiny flecks of pearl along each fibre, and there is absolutely no doubt that the trout like it. There are several pearly tinsel materials on the market, and all of them seem to improve the attraction of a lure, often outclassing silver tinsel. Some tinsel-bodied wet flies have already had the benefit of 'pearling' – the Pearl Invicta is sometimes a better fly than its parent Silver Invicta, for example.

I gave some fry-suggesting lures in previous chapters, but if you come across perch fry in your water you need rather specific patterns. I've had good results with a gold Mylar-tubing-bodied lure with black and green hairwing. When perch were numerous at Grafham, the trout used to herd them into the shallows at dusk, and I had great catches on the Spuddler, a lure which I introduced from America a few years after I brought the first Muddlers to Britain. Whilst it has never attained the universal popularity of the Muddler Minnow, the Spuddler is well worth a place in the fly-box. The dressing is given in the Appendix.

By now, the fry will be a fair size, and it may pay you to fish big lures if you don't get a response to the smaller sizes. Remember, though, that big hooks need powerful rods to drive the barb in, and it's no use fishing big lures on a rod rated less than AFTM 9. Lures dressed on 3X-longshank hooks size 4 are not too big. Professional fly-dresser Chris Ingram makes a floating fry by adding an 'overcoat' of silver or pearl Mylar tubing into which Ethafoam is inserted, thereby producing a really attractive fish-like finish whilst ensuring good buoyancy. The tail end of the tubing is teased out around the forked Ethafoam tail. Strands of Crystal Hair would give a similar effect. I must stress the need to leave these floating fry patterns immobile. Patience is required! Leave well alone for several minutes if need be, before casting again. When fishing any of these big fry lures, don't use anything less than 7lb-test nylon leaders, or you could be broken. This sort of fishing can provide some exciting moments.

Equally exciting is the sport you can get when the trout turn their attention to the daddy-longlegs. In humid weather after rain, these flies hatch from the ground in huge numbers, and if the wind is strong enough they get blown on to the water. The trout soon get used to this new item of food, and can even become preoccupied on them. The natural flies stay

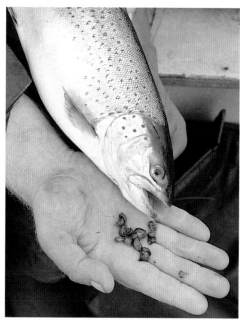

Freshwater snail

This trout was full of
freshwater snails

Hover fly, the angler's 'drone fly'

'Daddy-longlegs'

These rainbows had been feeding on 4-inch coarse fish 'fry'!

Stickleback (male); trout eat these, despite the sharp spines!

A nice tidy boat layout – everything to hand but not in the way

Loch-style, short-lining

Loch-style, long-lining

afloat for quite a long time, thanks to their long gangly spidery legs. Your artificial daddy should float for as long as possible, and this is quite a difficult requirement in a good wave. The best versions have detached bodies made from bundles of buoyant deer or elk hair. Some years ago, there were hollow soft plastic mayfly bodies available which were equally useful as daddy bodies, giving buoyancy. After being unavailable for some time, I see that these are now listed by some suppliers – excellent move! The legs are represented by long cock-pheasant centre-tail fibres with overhand knots tied in them to form bent joints (a really fiddly job). These don't have the ability to hold up the fly on the surface, but it isn't essential that the fly sits well up. In fact, in a good wave, the trout will take the artificial even though it is below the surface film. Doubtless the natural insect gets swamped when the wind is strong enough to create good waves, so a slightly-sunk daddy can be quite acceptable. The late Dick Walker used to insist that all the legs should point backwards, but I would say that his idea is completely wrong, except maybe for loch-style boat-fishing.

Any natural colour seems acceptable for the spent-tied wings, but I like blue-dun. A ginger saddle-hackle is ideal to give extra flotation. Anoint the fly liberally with Gink; liquid flotants are not good enough for reservoir work. One daddy on a tapered leader is enough, but you may prefer to live dangerously and mount two or even three on droppers.

Fish with the wind behind you, because this is the position where the most naturals will be found. Having cast to the edge of the ripple, pay out line slowly so that the fly drifts out on the wind. Don't pay out more than your full fly-line, because it is very difficult to hook fish further out. It doesn't really matter if you don't see fish rising; the trout are on the lookout for daddies, and it won't be long before your fly provokes a take. Give the fish two or three seconds to turn down before tightening into it.

There will still be buzzers and sedges around, plus many of the other food-forms mentioned in previous chapters. Use your eyes, recognise what is happening, and adapt your method to suit. Try not to drop into an automatic repeat of how you fished the last time you were out. It doesn't always work. Many nymph fishers use an unvarying dead-slow retrieve, but sometimes the fish want the flies moved faster. An outstanding example of this happened on two consecutive evenings at Rutland.

Trout were rising well to buzzers off the bank, east of Armley Wood; the breeze gave right-to-left waves. Eight rainbows took a size 12 Ned's Fancy moved in the usual slow figure-of-eight method after waiting twenty seconds for the flies to sink. Naturally, with exactly the same conditions prevailing the following evening, I made for the same spot. Sure enough, the trout were still there and taking buzzers. Using the same flies as on the previous evening, no takes came during twenty minutes of slow retrieving. I was baffled. Then, having made a cast, I suddenly decided that a change of fly might do the trick, and started to strip-in the line so that I could make the change. Bang! A nice 2-lb rainbow took solidly. I got six more fish, all on the Ned's Fancy, using fast foot-long pulls. Same conditions, probably the same shoal of fish, but needing a very different retrieve. Don't ask me why. But remember this incident, and don't drop into a rut.

Be ready to experiment with fly-size, speed, and depth, even when you have found the right pattern. Mindless 'chuck-and-chance' fishing doesn't get fish!

Here are some flies to try this month:

Honey Buzzer, Ned's Fancy, Pheasant Tail Nymph, Gold-ribbed Hare's Ear Nymph, Soldier Palmer, Wickham's Fancy, Silver or Pearl Invicta, Green Peter Mini-Muddler, Daddy-longlegs, Drone-fly, Peach Doll, White Tadpole, White Muddler, Spuddler, Viva, Floating Fry, Pheasant Tail Nymph with pearl thorax, dry Grenadier or Fiery Brown.

Chapter 10

Late-Season Bank-Fishing

Many reservoirs stay open until the end of October, and the modern trend is to remain open even until the end of the year, especially if the fishing is in private hands. Staff are still employed for reservoir maintenance and boat renovations, so whatever revenue can be drawn from keen bank-anglers is very welcome. 'Keen' is the right word – you have to be really keen to fish a reservoir on a cold blustery December day, but it's amazing what fish you can catch. Mild weather conditions improve chances, of course, encouraging the trout to feed.

Certainly, fishing in October or even later in the year gives the bank-fisher the best chance of catching the biggest trout of the season. Quality, not quantity, is the name of the game. Naturally, those people in charge of stocking our waters will not be pouring trout into the reservoirs at the end of the normal season, and the fish we are trying to catch will have been there for quite some time. These trout will not hurl themselves at any old fly or lure in wild abandon like the stockies of summer. They will have seen most of the artificials we are likely to present to them many times already, and to attract a take we may have to fish more thoughtfully than ever.

After the heavy feeding of the summer, the trout are in top condition, and weighty, although a proportion of the weight of the females will be spawn. Many of the fish will be well within casting-range, having been attracted to the margins over the past few weeks by the abundance of food, particularly coarse-fish fry and sticklebacks around the weed-beds. The spawning urge also helps to drive brownies into the shallows, especially where the reservoir bed is stony. So the opportunities are there for the bank-angler to end his season in a blaze of glory. It's up to us to make the most of them.

In general, weather conditions will be chilly, to say the least, unless an unseasonal Indian summer prolongs early autumn warmth into late October and beyond. Even with the chance of much milder weather resulting from the alleged global warming of the 'greenhouse effect', I doubt whether we will ever have 'June in January'. Early mornings and late evenings are now relegated to the 'not-so-good' category, with midday and early afternoon becoming the best times for fishing, especially if the weather is dull; the water temperature will be at its highest then. Cloud cover usually means a comfortable air temperature. Clear skies give night frosts and cold north-easterly winds. All these features normally become more severe as autumn approaches winter.

Cooler water means slower-and-deeper presentation of our flies, again similar to April tactics. Countdown is necessary for each cast, both to find the fish and to repeat the process. Near enough is rarely good enough! There is a tendency among the less-experienced anglers to assume that if the trout are not feeding at the surface they are feeding right on the bottom. This is not necessarily so; the fish could be hovering three feet down or at some other level, not showing but willing to take. Floating line and long leader with weighted point fly is the nicest way to fish, but you may need the intermediate or slow-sinker to give the acceptable retrieve path of the flies, or for some lure-fishing. Only over very deep holes will you need a fast-sinker. If you choose the floater and don't wish to fish dry fly, the weighted point fly is essential – unweighted flies sink quite slowly, and the long wait becomes tiresome and a waste of good fishing-time. A sinking braided leader is a useful addition for this style of fishing, turning your floating line into a sink-tip.

I mentioned dry fly just now. Don't smile – you would be surprised at the success of simple dubbed and hackled dries, even in December! Despite the scarcity of insect life, trout seem prepared to rise to them.

For this late-season sport, try to avoid fishing with the wind behind you – remember that this will mean you are fishing into the coldest water. Choose a location with a side-wind and a depth of between 6 and 10 feet. Weed-beds, submerged fences or hedgerows, tree-stumps, and rocks all attract fry, and therefore trout. Look out for these pointers and choose your location accordingly.

One difference between fishing in October rather than April is that now you can confidently fish some of the places which you would have avoided early in the season, such as hard-bottomed shallows, because there is no risk of out-of-condition 'black' rainbows. A very important point to remember is that brown trout must be returned unharmed once their close-season date arrives. Although it is disappointing to have to return a huge brownie, you must console yourself with the thought that with spawning imminent, its flesh would be virtually uneatable, and it's there to be caught another day.

Once you have had a pull, don't leave that spot, even though you may have to wait quite a long time for the next pull. The fish tend to frequent certain positions, and there is little point in wandering all over the reservoir. You may get a couple of fish in quick succession, then nothing for an hour or so, but remember one of the cardinal rules of reservoir fishing: 'Never leave fish'.

Bearing in mind the possibility of a really big trout, don't use too fine a leader. It's senseless to risk a break. A nylon point of 6lb is the absolute minimum, and 7lb is better, even with nymphs. For lures, 10lb is advisable. The water is usually crystal-clear at this time of the year, so I prefer a clear nylon for least visibility. We are fishing for trout which have been around for a while; they have survived due to their caution and wariness, and we have to reduce their chances to a minimum, so it is no use offering our artificials on highly visible leaders. You may feel tempted to use one of the 'super-strong' brands of nylon because of their thin diameter, but remember that their reduction in diameter is obtained by prestretching, which means there is no 'give', and any knots reduce the strength alarmingly. A wind-knot in this type of nylon would be disastrous if a big trout were to hit your fly.

From October onwards, even the ubiquitous buzzers are on the decrease. The type of buzzer we usually encounter at this time is the small dark species. If, like me, your preference is for imitative fishing, it's worth trying a team of buzzer patterns when you see evidence of their presence. These could include a Pheasant Tail Nymph dressed with dyed black cock pheasant centre-tail fibres. Remember to keep the thorax slim, and add a sparse beard hackle of black hen-hackle fibres. Rib with silver wire, or you could even incorporate some lead wire. Size 10 will be fine. The middle dropper fly could be a Black Buzzer Nymph, size 12. Ned's Fancy, size 12, on the top dropper could suggest the pupa on the point of hatching, or you could go mad and try my fluorescent Pink Nymph – don't ask me why, but this fly is especially productive late in the season. Maybe it's because they haven't seen anything quite like it before! Retrieve slowly, and some sizeable trout could be your reward.

A slow retrieve also suits the various Hare's Ear Nymph patterns. Again, try variations with fluorescent tails – white is good, so is crimson (Glo-Brite floss shades 16 and 3 respectively). I often add a small percentage of coloured seal fur or Antron to the basic hare fur. Hot orange, olive, crimson, or lime green are good colours. I don't use hare fur from the actual ear, finding it too short; fur from the back of the animal has a better length, colour, and texture. Shrimp and hoglice are now actively feeding on decaying weed, and these nymphs are fair caricatures of both. I like to fish them leaded on the point, often with an unleaded version on the middle dropper. To distinguish leaded from unleaded I use different colours of tying thread. Kamasan B830 hooks, size 10 or 12, suit these nymphs; they are 2X longshanks, just the right proportion. I wish Partridge made a 2X longshank hook!

Probably the major trout food item during these last months of the year is little fish. Coarse-fish fry or sticklebacks abound, and the trout are accustomed to feeding on them. By now, the trout will have seen a great many floating Ethafoam fry patterns, and only the most eager will have a go at them. I have given you some fry-suggesting lures in previous chapters, but it doesn't always follow that tinsel-bodied streamers are the only successful lures. Sometimes the sole requirement is a fish-like shape. Take the following experience, for example: When Rutland Water reopened in late October 1989 after the precautionary closure related to the toxic blue-green algae scare, two special patterns gave me two memorable days' bank-fishing. Saturday October 21 was a day of total cloud cover and a very strong blustery west wind. Normally, I wouldn't have bothered to go fishing in such conditions, but it was the first day's fishing available to me after a six-week lay-off. I braved the lousy weather, and arrived at the Normanton shore about 9.00 a.m. The grapevine had reported that fish had been caught there.

A point to the east of the little bay where the pontoon for disabled anglers is situated looked inviting and fishable, although I could have fished anywhere – not a soul was in sight. The wind was just about bearable, into the left cheek. I fished for quite some time without a pull, using only two flies on a 16-foot leader: White Tadpole on the point, Dunkeld on the dropper, both supposedly 'the killers' for other rods. Obviously nothing there, so I moved round the bay to the western point. I had cast only two or three times when I was joined by Bill Goodale, who reminded me that a good late-season pattern was his variation on the Viva theme. Bill's Viva has a basic 'fishy' outline and incorporates black and fluorescent green. I tied a size 8 longshank on the point.

Third cast, a firm pull, and the first fish on. Yes, on Bill's Viva. The marrow spoon showed a stomach stuffed with sticklebacks. During the next four hours I took another seven rainbows to give me a very satisfactory limit catch, all on Bill's Viva. The best two went 4lb and 3½lb.

After this success, what else could I do but give it another go the following day? Up reasonably early, at Normanton car-park by 8.30 a.m. You've already guessed it – 'my' point already had a couple of anglers in residence. Several other rods were dotted around the bay, so I just had to fit in where I could, straight down from the car-park. The weather was much better this time, still cloudy and showery but with just enough breeze to give a bit of a ripple.

In these conditions it was okay to use a 20-foot leader and three smaller flies. I put a size 10 longshank Bill's Viva on the middle dropper and a Silver Palmer pattern on the top. On the point went a size 10 Peetie, one of my own fry representations named after a favourite cat. Peetie has a

Mylar-tubing tinsel body, and prominent eyes. Eight fish came steadily during the next five hours, five to Peetie, three to Bill's Viva. Several taps and knocks, and two fish lost in play. I was home by 2.30. The blokes on the point of the bay only got one each – most of the fish had moved!

Black and flurorescent green also paid off at Rutland on November 5 1989. I had heard a whisper that some fish were being caught at the Three Trees location on Hambleton Peninsula. It was a cloudy day with a cold westerly wind. I fished the recommended spot from 10.00 to 11.00 a.m. without a pull; the water was really too dirty, stirred up by the waves. I moved round the reservoir to the Mound. Although the wind was right-to-left, the water was clear and it was fishable. Trout weren't exactly plentiful, but between 11.30 a.m. and 4.00 p.m. I had four strong-fighting rainbows for a total weight of 7lb, all on a size 10 Black Concrete Bowl on the point, pulled slowly after a twenty-second countdown. I lost another fish which took me unexpectedly on the drop. Not bad, for a bitter November day when, in order to keep some feeling in my fingers, it was essential to wear mittens and to dry my hands frequently on the towel in my coat pocket.

Sometimes, a multi-hook lure is the only thing the trout will take – it's the only format which is large enough to suggest a well-grown fry. Huge longshank hooks are impossible to use – even size 2 has a length of only 1½ inches. Stepping up the proportional shank-length to 6X gives too much leverage, in my opinion. Two or three size 8 longshank hooks, joined with 25lb stiff Tynex nylon (which at this strength is like wire) give a manageable big lure. These tandems and three-hook assemblies pass in and out of favour over the years, perhaps due to the supposed difficulty of tying them. Let me dispel that myth right away.

Mike Green, the superb fly-dresser from Corwen, North Wales, gave me this method. To link up two or three longshank hooks, cut a length of the suggested nylon equal to the total length of the hook shanks plus 1cm for each space between the hooks. You could use 40-lb-test ordinary nylon instead of Tynex. The stiffness is needed because it is essential to avoid sag between the hooks and throughout the overall length of the lure. With a flame, put a blob at each end of the length of nylon. Smear a layer of Evostik along the shank of each hook and, while the adhesive is still wet, bind the nylon to the upper side of the shanks with close turns of strong thread (Fly-Master Plus is good). Space the hooks along the nylon at 1-cm intervals. When the adhesive dries, they will never come apart.

Dress each hook in the vice in turn, starting with the rearmost, which is the only one which needs a tail. Similarly, the front hook is the only one which needs a hackle, Muddler-head, or eyed effect. All the hooks need bodies and wings, although in some tandem dressings the wing is restricted to the front hook only and is of sufficient length to cover both hooks. Goat hair is a nice long material for this; it is available in many dyed colours. Bucktail is too brittle. I don't like long single-feather or hackle wings on long lures – they tend to wrap around and under the shanks, resulting in an unattractive lure. Even long hair can do this, so I prefer to wing each hook. Marabou is a popular material for this, but remember that arctic fox is just as mobile yet more durable. Don't ignore the modern man-made fibres, especially the strands of Flashabou, Lureflash Mobile and Lureflash Twinkle, and Crystal Hair; a few strands of such material mixed with the hairwing can make all the difference between moderate success and a bonanza.

Multi-hook lure patterns are legion, but the most successful patterns at this time of the year seem to be those featuring a lot of white combined with pearl or silver tinsel. The pearl especially has proved its worth in recent years. If you are a fly-buyer and not a fly-tier, don't despair. Knowledgeable dealers stock a range of multi-hook lures, and there are individual professional fly-dressers who will tie them specially for you.

There is no need to rip these big lures through the water at breakneck speed. Some anglers seem to think that because a big lure is used, a-metre-a-second is the necessary speed. Not so. No trout will chase food in cold water; what attracts it is an easy-to-catch slow-moving lure which shimmers and moves like a sick little fish.

Some suggested patterns for your end-of-year fishing:

Black & Silver Tandem, White Marabou Tandem, 3-hook White Muddler, White Tadpole, Bill's Viva, Peetie, Black or White Concrete Bowl, Black Pheasant Tail Nymph, Black Buzzer Nymph, Ned's Fancy, hot orange dry fly.

I've taken you through a season's bank-fishing during the last few chapters. I sincerely hope that the experience I have passed on to you will help you to enjoy great success in your own fishing. I don't profess to 'know it all' – far from it. Thank God, we are all continually learning, no matter how long we have been fishing. Trout fishing is always a challenge – that's part of the enjoyment. Some people find enough pleasure restricting their activities to bank-fishing only. However, I would suggest that to enjoy reservoir trout fishing even more fully, you need to widen your horizons to include boat-fishing in at least one of its forms. Read on!

Chapter 11

Boat-Fishing:
Some Important Basics

It will have become obvious that I am a very enthusiastic bank-angler, but if the truth were known, I like my boat-fishing even more. In a boat, I'm much more mobile and able to engage the fish more directly. Every trout in the reservoir can be reached by one method or another, and there is no doubt that a boat increases your chances of catching fish by three or four times compared with average bank-fishing. Fishery managements recognise this and charge accordingly for boat hire, but usually it's money well spent. Before you rush to a phone and book a boat on the nearest reservoir, however, some words of advice and caution . . .

A good boat-fisher is not just a good bank-fisher afloat. Although boat and bank have certain things in common, most boat-fishing is really a different ball-game, and even an experienced bank-angler has to ignore much established bank-fishing technique and learn a whole new set of techniques when first out in a boat. In addition to these, there is – or should be – a unique code of discipline involved in boat-fishing. Following that code of behaviour means more enjoyable fishing for all, but in recent years many boat-anglers have exhibited an unthinking 'couldn't-care-less' tendency towards other anglers both in boats and on the bank. Whether that is due to 'don't know' or to 'don't care' is puzzling. I hope it's the former, and that the offenders will all read this book!

There are three basic types of boat-fishing – fishing in front of a drifting boat (certainly the most popular method), fishing behind a drifting boat (not allowed on many waters), and fishing static at anchor. The latter is the nearest thing to bank-fishing where techniques are concerned, the boat being merely a fishing platform which takes you to a location where you can reach fish you couldn't reach from the bank.

Many reservoirs have stretches of bank which are barred to bank-anglers, having been annexed by the bird-watching fraternity as 'nature reserves'. Luckily, boats are often allowed in these areas, provided that they do not approach nearer than 50 yards from the shore. The Nature Conservancy Council is a powerful body which can press for angling to be stopped in certain locations if a case can be presented which shows that angling is detrimental to the well-being of wildlife, so it pays all of us to beware of breaking any rules relating to access to nature reserve areas. The NCC have designated many of our reservoirs 'Sites of Special Scientific Interest' (SSSI) because of their populations of rare birds, etc., and in these places we must be even more careful about our actions.

Drifting or static methods of fishing have certain aspects in common, relating mainly to boat discipline and boat-handling – very important basics which play a highly significant part in influencing whether our day on the water is enjoyable, productive, and safe, or a disaster.

Let's start with a reminder of what we need:

First, things for personal comfort. Never go afloat without taking waterproofs, even on the sunniest day; it might rain later, and it's often a long trip back to the car, assuming you've brought them that far. PVC over-trousers are virtually essential in windy conditions when waves can easily slap over the gunwale and wet the inside of the boat and its occupants. Travelling diagonally across the waves creates splashes which can thoroughly wet the person handling the outboard motor if no waterproofs are being worn, and that includes a jacket. On days of strong blustery winds I wear my PVC coat with its hood up, whether it's raining or not. It's amazing how many times a fly hits the back of the hood like a pistol shot, blown off-course by a sudden gust. Much better than lodging in my neck! Polarised sunglasses protect the eyes from flying flies and prevent eyestrain; the glare off the surface of open water can be severe. Lipsalve is useful in preventing sunburnt or wind-chapped lips if you're not the weatherbeaten type – there's no shade in a boat. A breeze on the water can be more chilly than you think, and a jumper or cardigan can make all the difference between comfort and discomfort. A towel is advisable, to keep hands dry and to clear spectacle lenses of raindrops or wave-splashes, if, like me, you wear specs.

Any item you are not wearing should be stored in either a big plastic sack (with the top folded over to stop the contents getting wet) or a seat-box. An absolute essential is a thickly-padded cushion (preferably covered with waterproof PVC cloth) to sit on; there's nothing harder than a wooden boat seat after an hour or two! Even more preferable is a cushion which is part of a thwart seat, giving you a seating position high enough to fish more comfortably and more efficiently. Believe me, these seats are worth every penny.

Footwear for boating must have non-slip soles; don't underestimate how slippery the inside of some boats can be when wet. Studded soles are taboo, if only for their potential as noise-makers; thumps and vibrations travel fast and far through water, and scare fish. Derriboots are perhaps the most popular choice, but I often wear thigh waders, which I find handy if I have to hop over the side to beach the boat. Should you follow my example, take care to check the depth of water before you step into it; clear water especially is usually deeper than it looks! A probe with the net-handle will show you the depth and also tell you whether the bottom is firm enough to step on to. At some reservoirs. Rutland for example, beaching the boat is not permitted, so check the rules before you set out.

If allowed, it's pleasant sometimes to break for a relaxed lunch in the shade and shelter of a bankside hedge. Choose the upwind shore and approach the shallows slowly and cautiously, watching out for hazards like submerged rocks or tree-stumps. Near the shore, switch off the engine, raise the propeller, and use the oars for the last few yards. Pull the boat well up out of the water, and as a further precaution take the anchor and push it into the ground at the full extent of its rope. It has been known for the wind to change direction through 180° in the course of a few minutes! Never try to beach the boat on the downwind shore, even in a gentle breeze. A strong wind could spring up, and the resultant waves can damage the boat or the engine by banging on the bottom, when there will be the additional difficulty of getting the boat and yourselves afloat again.

I say 'yourselves' because I don't think it wise to try to beach a boat on your own. There's too much to do all at once, and many boats are too heavy for one person to haul about. In any case, many reservoir manage-ments do not allow less than two persons in a boat, for safety reasons. Regarding the number of boat occupants, three people fishing in a boat is one too many! The poor soul in the middle is very restricted, and those at each end cramped for casting space. It's tempting to share the cost of boat hire between three instead of two, but my advice is, 'Don't be tempted'.

Whilst on the subject of boat occupants, it's worth mentioning that if possible you should choose your boat partner with great care. A boat is a tiny area in which to share a day's fishing and friendships can be tested to the extreme. Ideally, both boat partners should be equal in ability and experience, and must be able to agree on the choice of method of fishing. If one of the partners is left-handed, it can be helpful; for all 'side-on' fishing, the left-handed caster is usually positioned at the left-hand end of the boat. If one of the partners is a better caster than the other, that partner should take the left-hand end. Some advise that the person on the left should cast over the left shoulder, even though right-handed, but an experienced caster shouldn't need to do this.

A good boat partner knows exactly what to do without being told, and is willing and able to share duties. The one in charge of the engine is fully occupied, and the other should handle the drogue, the oars, and the anchoring of the boat. Once a trout is hooked, the other partner should ideally reel in so as to avoid lines and flies tangling during the play of a lively fish. Only by common consent should the other continue to fish. It's quite possible for both to have a fish on at the same time (a situation my friends and I call 'doing a party piece') and mutual confidence in fish-handling ability is essential. Who nets whose fish must also be decided. Once you find a good boat partner, stick together; like a perfect marriage, a good boat partnership gets better and better! Assemble your tackle in the reservoir car-park, and tie at least the point fly on the leader. It's easier than trying to set up as the boat is travelling, and you lose no valuable fishing-time. You can always change flies when you start fishing. You may decide to take an additional rod on to the boat, in case you change methods. This too can be set up ready for action (except when competition fishing), and if so, should be laid flat on the seats along the boat, on the side which will be behind you in broadside drift fishing. Should extra rods be taken, both partners must always remember that they are there; it is all too easy to forget, and a broken rod can result. You need 'eyes in your backside' at all times on a boat. Sometimes it's better to keep spare rods in their cases . . . All spare tackle, along with food, drink, and clothing, should be stored in your seat-box, a zipped waterproof carry-all, or strong plastic sack(s). Place these out of the way in the middle of the boat. There is absolutely no place in a boat for 'clutter'. If there is anything at all for a fly-line to snag or flies to catch, it will happen all too soon and all too often; this causes great annoyance, concentration is broken, and your fishing suffers. Tidy the boat up before you start to fish, and keep it tidy.

The oars should be placed in the rowlocks and laid across the middle of the boat with the blades resting on the opposite gunwales. Either or both are then ready for immediate use, but are out of the way when fishing. If a drogue is not being used, a drifting boat can be repositioned to intercept an approaching fish, or to avoid a surface obstacle, by a few strokes on one or other of the oars.

Before leaving the boat moorings, don't forget to check that the oars and rowlocks are in the boat, and check the anchor. Some boats only have a lump of concrete provided as an 'anchor' and this is quite unsuitable. For peace of mind, you should both take your own anchors; in any case, two good ones are required if you intend to fish at anchor. With only one anchor in use, the boat will swing from side to side, even in a gentle breeze, and you'll be unable to fish properly. Similarly, although some boats have a drogue provided, it's always best to take your own. You should both include a G-clamp in your equipment; this is used for altering the gunwale position of the anchor or drogue-ropes, often critical in controlling the drift of the boat. Few boats drift perfectly straight. Whilst checking the boat equipment, make sure there are life-jackets and emergency flares provided. Normally, boat-fishing is not fraught with danger if simple common-sense safety precautions are taken, but 'better safe than sorry'. Check also that there is a bailer in the boat; even if not required for its primary purpose, it is often used to answer a certain 'call of nature'! A visit to the lodge's toilet facilities before boarding the boat is easily omitted in the excitement of it all.

You should both take a landing-net, which must be long-handled and wide-framed. A small short net is worse than useless. Lay each net across the gunwales towards the middle of the boat, out of the way yet ready to hand.

If your boat is provided with an outboard motor, an efficient management will have ensured that the motor is well maintained so that it starts at the first pull and runs smoothly. The fuel tank will be full. Careful staff will not have spilt fuel on the seat or on the floor, and will have wiped the fuel tank dry. Unfortunately, all staff are not careful, and there's nothing worse than outboard motor fuel for ruining the coating of a fly-line or staining your clothing. Apart from that, you don't want the smell of fuel on your flies – I'm sure it puts the fish off. So check the boat for cleanliness, and if things aren't right, complain.

Both partners should familiarise themselves with how to work the motor. Reservoir staff will gladly show you how. Start the motor in the presence of a staff member and satisfy yourself that it performs as it should. Make sure that any mooring-ropes are unclipped ('All gone for'ard, Cap'n!'), engage the gear, and off we go.

It's funny – no it isn't, it's bloody annoying – that apparently intelligent sensible people, once let loose in a boat on a reservoir, can forget how to behave properly. The outboard motor is at once the best and the worst thing to happen to boat-fishing. Best because it gives easy travelling over long distances, worst because in the wrong hands it can ruin the fishing both for its user and for other anglers. To some people, the motor has only one speed – flat out. Even in calm conditions, with other boats nearby, these people set off at full speed when they want to change position. The noise and disturbance can upset the fishing for a long time. Oars are used too infrequently by thoughtless anglers always over-eager to switch on the outboard motor. In conditions of calm, or a slight ripple, with rising fish about, or in shallow water, the motor should never be used because of the risk of frightening the trout. Careful and quiet use of the oars is quite sufficient to move the boat, and no real physical effort is entailed.

Years ago, I used to fish Lough Sheelin in Eire during the mayfly period, and it was essential that any rising fish should not be put down. If anyone dared to use the motor anywhere near other boats in calm conditions, he was loudly shouted at in language which could not be

misunderstood. Most boats on the lough being privately owned, per-
sistent offenders were liable to find the ultimate punishment of a hole in
their boat one morning!

Before Grafham opened in the mid-1960s, I used to boat-fish Eyebrook reservoir a lot. In those days, the trout there were free-rising,
thanks to an excellent insect population, but they were easy to put down.
No petrol-powered outboards were allowed on the lake, and you had to
have a doctor's certificate of infirmity to be allowed to use your own
electric outboard. So we had to row. I have known us row half a mile
upwind to start a new drift so as not to cross another boat's drift and
disturb water he would be covering. Gentlemanly behaviour like that is
almost unknown nowadays. People don't seem to realise what effect
thoughtless boat-handling can have.

When drifting, whether floating or sinking lines are being used, it is
stupid to motor back up your own drift, and selfishly thoughtless to motor
back up someone else's. Those fishing sunk lines can protest that it
doesn't matter because the trout are down anyway, but trout have a habit
of changing their depth and suddenly coming up. Why risk upsetting
them? At the end of a drift, make a wide detour back to the top of the drift,
trying at the same time to avoid spoiling other anglers' fishing by crossing
their drifts. Your boat should follow a D-shaped path.

Currently, there is the much-too-common habit of completely ignoring
other boats and what they are doing, blithely motoring (usually at top
speed) wherever the angler at the motor wants to go. I have experienced

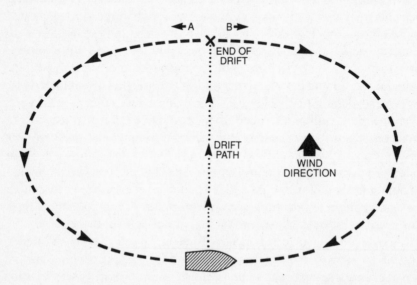

The D-shape drift pattern (take A or B as necessary)

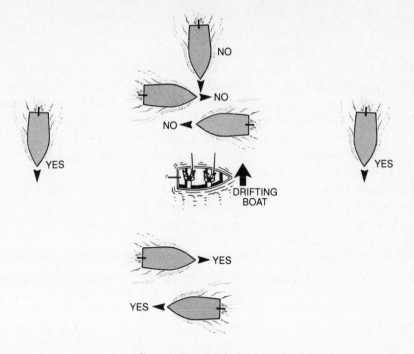

Correct boating behaviour

boats motoring flat out thirty yards in front of my boat when it was obvious that we were loch-styling with floating lines and that they were crossing our drift. I have had boats motoring flat out between my anchored boat and the bank towards which I was casting. I have seen boats motoring at full speed straight up my drift, the occupants chatting away quite oblivious of my presence, and even when finally aware of me, altering course only sufficiently to just miss a collision. When evening bank-fishing, I have had boats on their way back to the moorings motoring, always at top speed, less than twenty yards from my position, effectively scaring off any trout.

Now, all this is either due to ignorance, thoughtlessness, selfishness, or downright bloody-mindedness. The first shortcoming I could almost forgive, although anyone taking a boat out on a reservoir should make themselves aware of the correct way to behave. The other three are absolutely unforgivable, in my view. Swearing loudly at the offenders, even if they can hear you over the roar of the engine, brings either verbal abuse or surprised effrontery. In the case of the former, I class these people as the fishing equivalent of the yobbos who fling beer-cans and chip papers on the pavement next to a litter bin, products of the modern undisciplined 'couldn't-care-less' society. As to the latter, I can't believe that every one of them can plead, 'I didn't know I was doing wrong.'

My own code of good boating behaviour is simple: travel slowly when in the company of other boats, use your eyes and check what drifts other boats are doing, and don't motor up or across your own drift path or anyone else's. There's one more misdemeanour which has nothing to do with use of the outboard. I refer to the annoying practice of anchoring-up in the middle of what has been seen to be a productive drift. This is pure selfishness. You catch a couple of fish, and the next drift down you find a boat has moved in and anchored exactly where the fish are. If it had joined the drift and acted properly, both boats would have enjoyed good sport.

Yes, there is some unsociable behaviour by some boat-anglers, but thankfully it doesn't happen all the time, so don't be discouraged.

Now a few pointers on safe boating procedures:

In strong winds and heavy waves, travel upwind at a pace just sufficient to make steady headway. It is uncomfortable, particularly for the person not at the motor, if you travel too fast, so that the bow of the boat continually bangs up and down. The helmsman should take note of the size of the approaching waves, and as the boat meets particularly large waves, slow down at once until the wave has passed. It may help if the passenger sits on the middle thwart, but both should not sit in the stern, because this gives incorrect distribution of weight. It is best if the passenger sits in the bow, but up to the driver to provide a comfortable ride.

Travelling across heavy waves is dangerous at speed. The boat can start bucking to such an extent that an occupant could be thrown over the side. Travelling downwind, with large following waves, is another potentially dangerous situation; the stern of the boat will yaw about, so careful steering correction is needed, and in extreme conditions a bigger wave could break over the stern and swamp the boat. This is a time when speed can help, by beating the speed of the waves. By far the safest course is to seek the sheltered route, even if it means a long detour. Sometimes it will be impossible to return safely to the moorings, and the only solution then is to land on the upwind shore, pull the boat out of the water, and walk to the fishing lodge to report what you have done. Fishery staff can collect the boat when conditions improve. In all conditions of heavy waves, boat occupants must always sit centrally ('trim the ship') so that the boat does not dip to one side and present the opportunity for a wave to slop over the gunwale. Never stand up or move about the boat without holding firmly on to some support, and do not make any sudden movements which could rock the boat and throw its occupants off-balance.

Normally, reservoir managers will not allow boats out if the weather is too rough. A day which starts with calm conditions can suddenly turn rough, however, and it is best to know what to do if this should happen. In uncomfortably strong winds, it is impossible to fish properly anyway; with the line being blown all over the place, you can't even keep the flies in the water. Best to pack up and make for safety.

In addition to a code of practice relating to other boats, there is one for you and your partner to observe in your own boat. For side-on fishing, the boat and its surroundings should be divided in the middle by an 'invisible wall', and neither you nor any part of your tackle should pass through that barrier without first informing your partner of your intention, and getting agreement. Ideally, you should both cast alternately; this avoids lines and flies tangling in the air behind you (the wind can play nasty tricks with the line of even an excellent caster). If either of you needs to cast in a direction which will send your back-cast into the other's territory, perhaps to cover a fish rising off your end of the boat, a shout of 'Down!' should be enough to ensure that your partner's rod-tip is kept horizontal in front of the boat

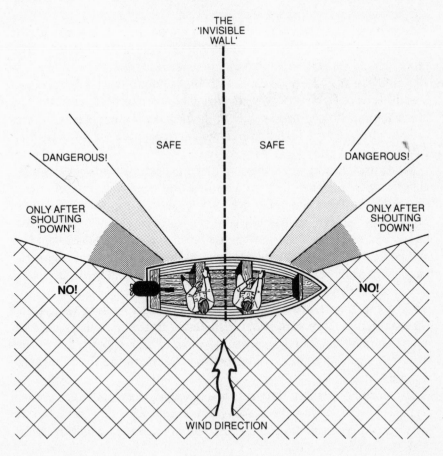

Where to cast

until you shout 'Okay'. Needless to say, neither should try to cover a fish seen in the other partner's half of the water.

When loch-styling or fishing at anchor, both partners should remain seated, so one of the first requirements of boat-fishing is that you learn to cast sitting down. Sit as far apart as possible. Standing up in a boat means that you present a more visible outline to any nearby trout, and this could easily scare them away. There is also the safety factor – if the boat is suddenly rocked by a quick movement on the part of the other occupant, anyone standing could be thrown off-balance. Even if they don't go over the side, they could fall and break a rod. The only excuse for standing up in a drifting boat is to change the angle of the drift when a drogue is not being used. To achieve this, the partner at the end of the boat opposite to the direction you want the boat to take, can stand up for a minute or so. The increased area of resistance presented to the wind will push that end of the boat forwards and change the drift. If you want to veer right, the left-hand partner stands up, and vice versa.

If both partners are right-handed, I like to do side-on fishing with the boat positioned so that the outboard motor is on the left and whoever is on the left-hand side isn't casting over the engine.

Not all anchored-up or drifting fishing is done from a boat placed broadside to the wind ('over the front', as it has been called). The Northampton style of fishing behind the boat, for example, is done with the boat drifting bow-first. Different positions for the occupants are then required.

When drift-fishing, it's important that, once having found fish, you are able to repeat the same drift. To do this, you need to position the boat accurately at the exact point where you started the successful drift. Sometimes there are surface markers, such as buoys, to make things easy, but otherwise you will need to line up four landmarks. If possible, these should be one ahead, one behind, one to the left, one to the right. Big trees, clumps of bushes, bird hides, church towers – all these are useful points of reference.

Of great importance is the need for both occupants to reel in and remove their flies from the water before motoring off to start a new drift. Apart from the fact that flies must not be trolled under power, there is the definite danger of wrapping an expensive fly-line round the propeller – not nice!

Boat-fishing requires extra care when netting fish. Make sure a fish is well played-out, with its head above water, before putting the net in the water. A dropper can easily get caught on the netting if a still-lively fish makes a sudden dive.

We have to share our water with yachts and wind-surfers. Thank

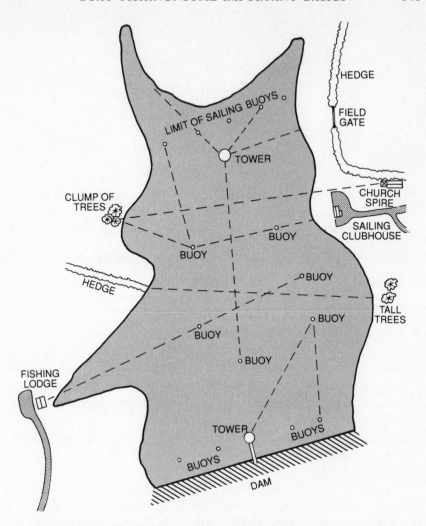

Lining up marks to repeat a drift

goodness they are only out between certain hours, because they can be a nuisance. Remember that 'Steam gives way to sail', and don't invite collisions. Report any stupid or dangerous sailing to the sailing club committee without delay. Most yachts at least have an identity number on the sail.

Despite the difficulties I have mentioned, and the rather disciplined approach required, boat-fishing can be very enjoyable and productive. I'll tell you how in the next chapter.

Chapter 12

Boat-Fishing Tactics

FISHING AT ANCHOR

This is probably the easiest boat-fishing technique for the bank-fisher to attempt. As I said in the last chapter, an anchored boat is really only a casting platform for bank-fishing techniques. The boat can take you to positions which you can't cover from the bank, and only from an anchored boat can you fish the flies slowly enough, especially where nymphs are concerned.

Boats should be anchored no nearer than 50 yards from the bank, and certainly not close to where bank-anglers are fishing. Please don't anchor in the middle of a drift being fished by another boat; instead, join the drift at least a hundred yards behind, and there will be sport for both boats. Ideally, anchor in water which is 6–12 feet deep – the sort of water-depths you would fish from the bank. If you're not sure of the depth over which you are anchored, push your rod vertically down into the water. If a 10-foot rod touches bottom, you're just about right.

In strong winds, avoid anchoring near the downwind shore; the waves will be too rough for comfort, and you would need very heavy anchors to hold there anyway.

You will note I said 'anchors', in the plural. Although many people use only one anchor for side-on fishing, it's a great deal better with two, for the reasons given in the previous chapter. If you are attempting to fish nymphs slowly in a boat that is drifting from side to side, the resulting bow in the line spoils your efforts. An anchor at each end of the boat prevents this problem. Here's how you carry out the anchoring procedure:

Have both anchors ready, long before you get to where you will be anchoring, and fix G-clamps on the gunwale at the bow and the starboard (right-hand to the landlubber!) corner of the stern. Approach your chosen spot slowly and quietly, detouring wide so as not to disturb the water you will be fishing. When the boat reaches a position about 15 yards upwind of your anchoring location, put the motor into reverse gear to stop any further forward movement, then cut the engine. Both anchors must simultaneously be lowered as silently as possible into the water on the upwind side of the boat. There's not much wrong with 'one–two–three–

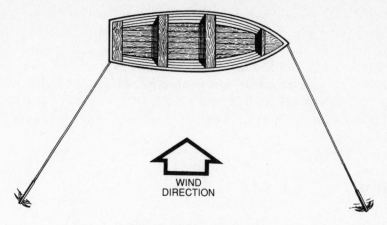

WIND
DIRECTION

Anchoring with two anchors

Go!' to make sure that both go in at the same time. Both anglers pay out the same length of rope (between 10 and 15 yards is about right). It helps if both ropes are marked with a black waterproof marker pen at 5-yard intervals. Fasten the ropes to the G-clamps, and the boat will soon stabilise.

If you have only one anchor, fasten the rope to a G-clamp mid-way along the upwind gunwale. Any slight adjustments in the position(s) of the clamps can be made after a few minutes' fishing.

The only problem with using two anchors is if the wind veers or suddenly changes direction. Some juggling with the rope-lengths is then required to reset the boat's position. Remember to avoid any banging and clattering which might scare the fish. Cultivate the high back-cast and as few false-casts as possible. Beware of the habitual bank-fisher-turned-boat-fisher who casts with lots of body-movement – talk about 'rocking the boat'! Remember too that heavy sinking lines, if you decide to use them, are harder than floaters to manage, especially in a good wind, and the angler on the left should try hard not to hit the other in the back of the head! Use the 'Down!' code when one partner wants to cast in any other direction than straight ahead.

There is another type of anchoring apart from the side-on position; using this method, a single anchor is attached to the stern of the boat. In a gentle breeze, the rope is tied to the gunwale immediately beside the motor, i.e., centrally. In stronger winds, attach the rope to the port (left-hand) corner. It is absolutely essential that both partners are excellent casters, if stern-anchoring is done. One partner sits in the stern on the right-hand side of the boat, the other in the bow near the left-hand side, both facing towards the bow. The bow angler fishes water in front and to the left; the stern angler fishes water on the right. Casting must be done alternately, and with the other angler always kept in mind. It must be remembered that the angler in the stern is casting in a wind blowing over the right shoulder, which can be awkward. The angler in the bow must always cast a high back-cast. Only two very experienced and accomplished anglers should attempt to fish in this way.

Rod specifications, lines, flies and methods are exactly the same as for bank-fishing.

LOCH-STYLE FISHING

Fishing with a floating line in front of a broadside-drifting boat is my favourite method. Fishing with a fast-sinking line in front of a broadside-drifting boat is probably my least-liked fishing method, but sometimes it has to be done if fish are to be caught. Nowadays, I usually reserve sunk-line loch-style for competition fishing, when every trout counts and one feels duty-bound to explore every angle and do one's best for the team. When fishing purely for pleasure, I've reached the stage where I would really rather fish the method I like, and perhaps catch less fish if conditions aren't a hundred per cent right for that method. A lot depends on the frame of mind I'm in.

One thing is certain: whatever the method, I constantly fish hard when I'm boat-fishing, concentrating all the time. Often, if I eat at all, it's sandwich in one hand, rod in the other. I have to force myself to take a break for refreshments. I admit to the underlying psychological stimulus of getting value-for-money relative to the cost of hiring the boat, but I'm sure that the main reason for my keen concentration isn't mercenary! I fish with the attitude that every next cast could bring a take, and great concentration is needed because there are so many ways in which a trout can take your fly when loch-styling, and you must be ready to identify each one immediately in order to react correctly. I'll describe a few of them later in this chapter, but first I must give you some basic advice which will help you to become a successful loch-style fly-fisher.

The rod can be from 10½–11½ feet in length, preferably rated from 5–7. A popular length is 11 feet 3 inches. Longer than that, and the leverage of even a lightweight rod becomes very tiring to the arm after an hour or so. The fact that you are constantly pushing a long rod against a back-wind adds to the fatigue. Funnily enough, a heavy reel helps, by providing a counterbalance to the leverage.

The reason for the long rod is quite simple. One of the most effective stages in fishing-out a loch-style cast is the 'dribbling' of the flies through the surface, stimulating the fish into taking what appears to be an escaping insect. This dribbling seems to be most effective when the line is at about 45° to the water; the rod is then almost vertical. If you think back to your schoolday geometry, and the right-angled triangle diagram, you will find that the horizontal line represents the water surface, the vertical line the approximate rod position, and the sloping line represents the fly-line. To keep the 45°-angles at which the sloping line joins the others, both vertical and horizontal lines have to be equal in length. Translating this into fishing terms, the longer the rod, the further away from the boat does the line assume that magic near-45° angle.

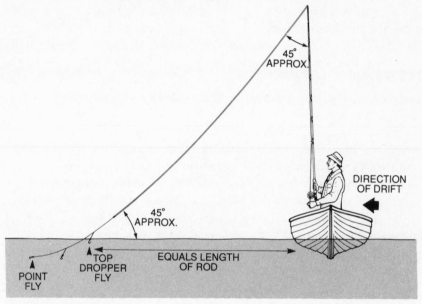

The case for the longer rod

The required specification of a long rod with a light line-rating tests the rod designer to the utmost. High-modulus carbon is essential. If incorrectly designed, the rod will be too soft and sloppy to cast accurately and to have much control over a fish during play, a very serious practical fault. A trout which can do as it likes will usually go under the boat and wrap your leader round the propeller or the drogue rope or both! By the way, if a trout does go under the boat, push your rod vertically down into the water so that the tip is below the level of the keel, then move the rod through the water round your end of the boat. You can then raise the rod and play the fish properly.

The reason for the light line-rating is to avoid line-droop as the rod is raised. Although the wind reduces this to some degree as it acts on the line, the actual weight of the amount of line hanging from the rod-tip creates a downward belly. This has to be taken up before the hook can be set in a trout which takes during the dribble, and the less drooping belly there is, the more direct and the quicker will be your contact with the fish.

One of the difficulties experienced by people trying loch-style fishing for the first time is in remembering that the boat is in fact drifting, and in gauging the speed of drift. Except when using the dry fly, your flies must be moved in order to attract the fish, and to effect that movement they have to be moved faster than the speed at which the boat is drifting. It is easy to fall into the trap of simply retrieving line at such a slow pace that the flies are left static. In a decent wind, quite a fast retrieve will hardly move the flies. As with all techniques, expertise comes with practice, so that choice of retrieve rate becomes instinctive. Meanwhile, the beginner must give this a lot of attention. A drogue helps, in slowing down the speed of the drift so that the angler doesn't have to retrieve so fast. Incidentally, the drogue also ensures that the boat drifts over a productive area for a longer time, meaning more chances of offers from the fish.

There are two alternatives in loch-style fishing – short-lining or long-lining, referring to the relative casting distances involved. Short-lining is really only effective when the trout are in the upper layers of water or in water no more than around 8 feet deep, because the flies are not in the water long enough for the fish to come to them from a distance. However, it can be very productive when insects bring the trout up.

I was first introduced to the style by Lawrie Williamson, the well-liked Head Warden at Blagdon during the late 1950s. I was out in a boat one wet and windy day, and at that time I knew very little about fishing in boats. All I could do was to make sure the flies were in the water, and it would have been a very daft trout which went anywhere near them. So when we returned to the 'Hut' for a dry-out and some lunch, the score was nil in reply to Lawrie's 'How have you done, gentlemen?' I told him I knew nothing about boat-fishing, and his advice described short-lining in a nutshell: 'Cast no more than three rod-lengths out, then raise the rod and skitter the flies back along the surface, making a wake.' When we went back out later, I followed his advice and took four nice rainbows, after I had missed a few through striking too soon. It was thanks to Lawrie that my love for loch-style fishing originated.

Although short-lining is done mostly with a floating line, it can also be done with sinkers, but then the line doesn't have time to sink very far. In strong winds, the sinking line enables the flies to be fished better because the grip of the water stops the line and flies being blown off. As no distance is involved, the lightest double-tapered line your rod will cast is the best choice.

In traditional short-lining, about 10 yards of line are cast. I make sure the rod-tip is near the surface at the end of the delivery; this gives the maximum retrieve distance and more control over the line. After a couple of seconds' wait to allow the flies to settle, the retrieve is commenced. I find the best method of retrieve is to figure-of-eight whilst raising the rod-tip. I think this is better than the strip retrieve because it gives a steady draw of the flies instead of a jerky one. By varying the speed of both rod and line movement, a wide variation of behaviour can be given to your flies. One of my old friends, the late Eric Hobson – a game-fisher of great experience – used to wiggle his rod-tip from side to side as he dabbled the top dropper fly in the surface. The erratic movement this gave to the fly often resulted in an offer. Some traditionalists make the fly travel in spurts by jerking the rod-tip vertically.

As the rod approaches the vertical, raise your arm to give a longer dribble of the flies. When you 'run out of arm', don't be in too much of a hurry to lift off the flies. Hold them steady in the water for a few seconds. It's amazing how often a trout will come up and take one of your flies only a yard from the boat. If this happens, let the fish turn down with the fly, and strike by pulling on the line with the left hand (if you're casting right-handed).

I'll never forget the first time I took one particular friend loch-styling. Jim was a very experienced lead-liner, but had never done any short-lining over the front. He asked me to show him how it was done. We took an evening boat on Rutland; it was early July, and we had several hours' fishing to look forward to. Knowing that there were some good fish at the top of the South Arm, we made the long trip up to the Bunds. There were plenty of sedges flying, and a few walloping rises showed that the trout were getting interested. I mounted a trio of sedge patterns on the leader. A breeze was blowing out of Hideaway Bay, so I started the drift from the corner, giving a running commentary of what I was doing, while Jim watched.

'Cast about ten yards, let the flies settle, raise the rod and figure-of-eight at the same time, nice steady draw, make the top dropper dribble along the top . . .' The top dropper had just dribbled to within six feet from the boat when a beautiful 4-lb brown leapt from the water and down on to it! I counted one, two, slowly, and set the hook. '. . . and that's all there is to it.' You should have seen his face! First cast – we hadn't drifted more than three or four yards – and a textbook example of what short-lining can produce. He's a keen loch-styler now. If a take doesn't occur, roll-cast the flies off the water, one back-cast, and off we go again. Short-lining is essentially a continuous sequence of cast and retrieve – until it's interrupted by a trout taking the fly. Fan your casts to cover as much water as possible, but always with your partner's position in mind.

Long-lining is a modern form of loch-styling, well suited to fishing for rainbows, which are more likely to follow the flies for a distance before taking. Like short-lining, it is done from a boat drifting broadside to the wind. It will also take browns and, much to the surprise of traditionally-minded ghillies on the natural lakes of Scotland and Eire, sea-trout. Of late, the Bristol fly-fishers have been laying claim to having originated long-lining, but this style in fact emerged on the Midland reservoirs, particularly at Grafham in the mid-1960s.

As the term suggests, as long a line as possible is cast, so it pays to use a forward-tapered line. The following advice refers only to the use of floating, neutral-density, or intermediate lines. The line is retrieved by stripping at a suitable speed to give an attractive movement to the flies. Stripping back is best done with the rod-tip held low over the water so as to keep in close touch with the line and flies, assuming you are not fishing dry flies. It need not always be fast, or in long pulls; it can be slow or jerky. You have to experiment to find out how the fish want the flies. If you're fishing dry, then you don't retrieve, but just gather in line at the same speed as the boat is drifting, to take up the slack.

Stripping is done by hooking the line from the butt ring under the first two fingers of the rod hand and trapping the line against the rod-handle when you let go of it with the other hand to pull in the next length. The line is thus held at all times by one hand or the other, and when a take is seen or felt, immediate response can be made. Retrieve until you have about 10 yards of line out, then, if no take has occurred, switch to an exact copy of the short-lining technique, raising the rod and dribbling the top dropper.

In these surface-layer methods of loch-styling, construction of the leader is critical. Variations in make-up are determined by the strength of the wind. To get the best out of this style of fishing, it is imperative that you are able to tie up your own leaders. Standard commercially-tied leaders are useless in comparison. Aim for as long a leader as conditions permit. The distance between the end of the fly-line and the top dropper must be varied so that the 'bob-fly' (the fly on the top dropper) works for the longest possible time. The stronger the wind, the further from the line the dropper should be. Similarly, the actual lengths of the droppers should be varied, according to the height of the waves; high waves mean long droppers. The top dropper should always be longer than the middle dropper. Remember, however, that long droppers have a greater tendency to wrap around the main leader, so there is a maximum practical limit of about 8 inches, even with stiff Tynex nylon. The distances between the droppers should also be varied to suit the wind conditions, until each fly is working at its optimum. Time spent making these alterations is not time wasted.

The above style of long-lining suits the times when the trout are fairly high in the water, on a nice dull day with a steady wind. I hate blustery winds and squalls, and so do the fish, by the way.

There will be times when the trout are not in the upper layers, such as early or late in the season when the water is cold, or when the sun shines out of a cloudless sky, or when trout are feeding at a lower level. Loch-styling then means long-lining with sinking lines, the sinking-rate being determined by the depth at which the trout are (discovered by logical trial-and-error). For this method, it is essential that the boat be slowed down by a drogue, or even two drogues in very strong winds or when the fish are very deep. The slower the boat drifts, the deeper the line can sink.

It is only since the late 1980s that this method has come into prominence, popularised mainly by the experts who fish in competitions, when every trout in the net is a contribution to a possible winning catch. They had to find a method of reaching deep-dwelling trout while restricted to rules which stated that 'flies must not be weighted' and 'flies must not be fished behind the boat'. The flies must reach the trout before the boat overruns the line.

Sinking lines must be fished on a powerful rod rated at least 7/8 to enable fish to be hooked against the resistance of the sunk line. Probably the most popular choices of sinking lines for this method are the fast-sinker such as WetCel 2, and the WetCel High-speed HiD which is a very fast sinker indeed. These two will cover most depths. If you are a long-leader devotee when fishing the floating line, forget it! A 10-foot leader is plenty long enough, with the top dropper no more than 4 feet from the tip of the fly-line. Anything longer, and you can't hook a fish which takes as you lift the flies to the surface, because you 'run out of arm' on the lift.

Briefly, the method is to cast as far as possible (a WF profile is essential) and merely take up the slack as the boat drifts along. This allows the line to sink to the required depth, after which it is retrieved by hand-lining. The retrieve needn't be at breakneck speed. I fished Chew one day with John Horsey, an expert competition fisher. In conditions of just a gentle breeze, John showed me that nymphs could be effectively fished on the HiD using a slow figure-of-eight. He had four trout in the boat before I tumbled to what he was doing and slowed down. A countdown is necessary so that the productive depth, when found, can be repeated. The take is simply a stoppage and pull of the line. If no take occurs, the last few feet of line are lifted from the water by raising the rod-tip; this sometimes induces a take. If not, don't be in too great a hurry to lift off and cast again.

As the top dropper reaches the surface, hang it there for several seconds. A trout which has followed the flies up from below will often be tempted into taking. You can also try lowering the flies again – watch the leader closely and if it moves, strike.

For deep fishing with HiD, the top dropper fly is the most productive, fishing deepest due to the curve in the line. Normally, a steady retrieve will suffice, but if this produces no takes, alter the speed. If you get numerous plucks but no solid takes, try the 'jig' method; impart an up-and-down movement to the rod-tip whilst retrieving line.

Fishing the sunk line isn't as enjoyable as fishing the floater, but neither is a blank day!

As the boat drifts, keep a sharp lookout for rising fish. It's worth pointing out that not many rises take the form of audible splashes. Some people never seem to be able to spot a rise. Here's how simple it is:

Every wind creates a regular pattern of waves, and any break or change in that pattern could mean that a trout has risen and created a disturbance. All you do is watch for ripples going 'the other way'. Okay, it may be a false alarm, but 'When in doubt, still cast out', because most times, it points to a fish. It's imperative that a rise is covered without delay, and to do this you have to be a good caster, able to deliver the flies to the fish immediately. False-casting is out; it has to be 'lift off and straight there', or the trout will be far away. Usually, trout move up against the waves, and it's amazing how fast they can do so. When covering a rise, you must take into account where you think the trout will be when your flies land – usually several feet upwind of the rise. You must also remember that the wind will blow your line downwind, so aim further upwind than ever in order to accommodate this.

Resist the temptation to cover rises behind the boat. Casting three flies into the wind after a sudden violent change in direction usually results in an almighty tangle. When I do it, I usually wish I hadn't!

Don't restrict your casting to a straight downwind direction. Presenting your flies diagonally across the waves can often mean that more trout see them than would otherwise be the case. You must, however, be always mindful of the fact that your partner is present, as neither of you will enjoy unravelling two tangled leaders.

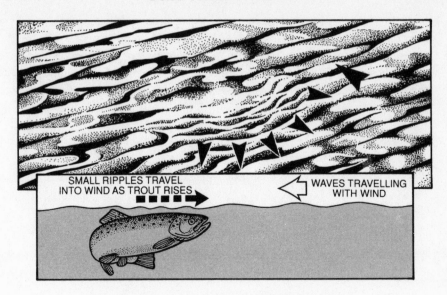

SMALL RIPPLES TRAVEL
INTO WIND AS TROUT RISES

WAVES TRAVELLING
WITH WIND

The alteration in wave-pattern made by a trout

I mentioned earlier in this chapter the different kinds of takes which you can experience when loch-styling. The principal form of take to the sunk fly (usually the point fly) is the 'stop', which is similar to the pull you get when bank-fishing. The line straightens, you feel a resistance, then the pull as the fish turns away with the fly. All you need to do is tighten by raising the rod, because the fish has virtually hooked itself. The further away this take occurs, the harder you need to tighten. Sometimes, the take is preceded by a series of taps; resist the temptation to strike – you won't

The 'stop' or 'pull' take

hook the fish. 'Wait until the fish pulls *you*, then pull the fish', is an old adage which is applicable in this case. There will be pulls which you don't connect with, just as in bank-fishing. There's little or nothing you can do about these, because so much depends on how the trout has actually taken the fly. As always in every kind of fly-fishing, don't let your attention

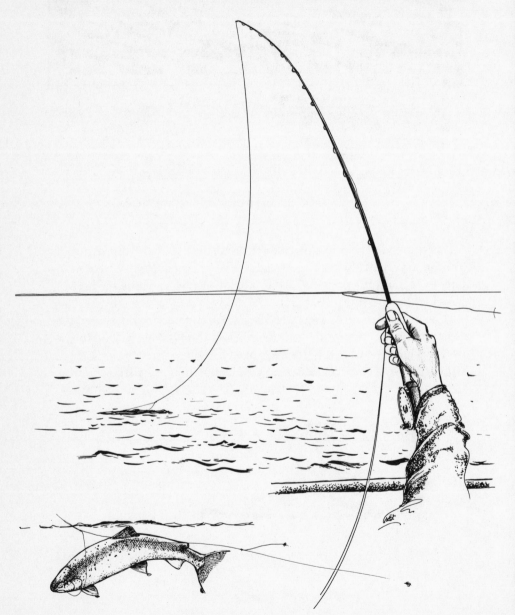

The 'swirl' take

wander – how is it that a trout invariably seems to take at the moment when you have glanced up at an overhead jet fighter plane?

On odd occasions a trout will take the fly in its mouth without giving a pull or any other obvious indication. As you try to lift off, you find you can't. Sometimes the fish is firmly hooked, but mostly you feel a couple of throbs and it's off. The general opinion is that these takes are by big browns, which makes the failure even more annoying!

A common take is the swirl or boil to a sub-surface fly, but this is one which is often not recognised as an actual take. The swirl is surface evidence created by the movement of the fish as it turns down after taking the fly. Many people see the swirl and think that the trout has only had a look at the fly. If you don't react by striking, you will just feel a pluck as the fly touches the trout's mouth. The strike should be timed a second or so after the swirl. Only sometimes will you be lucky enough for the fish to hook itself. Of course, there are swirls which are only the result of a fish taking a look at the fly and refusing it, but don't let that stop you striking each time you see them.

A common take to the dribbled dropper fly is the 'splash', in which the head or body of the trout breaks the surface. As this usually occurs close to the boat, it can startle the unwary into jerking the fly away from the fish. If you are fishing with constant concentration and expecting a trout every cast, you will be ready for this take, and will calmly wait the necessary second or so before tightening into the fish. Coarse-fishermen who take up trout fishing are so used to reacting immediately they see a float go down, that they are unable to hook 90 per cent of the trout which take their flies in this way because they whip the fly out of the trout's mouth.

As I've said, one of my favourite takes is the 'leap'. Usually to a pulled fly which is just below the surface, the actual take is preceded by the trout leaping from the water. The fly is taken as the trout enters the water, and you must then count a slow 'one–two–three' and tighten into it. Ninety-nine per cent of the time, this means a firm hooking right in the scissors of the jaw. If you strike too soon, you will only get a pluck. In rough waves, the fish may miss the fly entirely, and there's nothing you can do about it. I remember one very windy day on Rutland when I was on a drift past Normanton Church in very high waves. Big waves make good conditions for a 'wake' fly on the top dropper, and there's none better than a Popper. I was working the Popper back steadily, when a huge brownie – I'm not exaggerating when I tell you it was at least 12lb – leapt completely out of the water and down on to the Popper. I had the presence of mind to wait before I tightened – into nothing. The trout had missed the fly in the turbulence of the waves! We did the drift a few more times, but never saw the fish again.

Somehow, I rarely experience the take which none of us want – the 'smash' take. Probably because I don't use weak nylon, and I don't strip flies at supersonic speed. Very occasionally I get a break when I strike a trout which has taken the fly on a dropper accidentally looped in a half-hitch round the main leader. Normally, a smash take happens when a trout takes a fly at speed while it is being retrieved at speed.

Rainbows have a nasty habit of following the fly, often for many yards, without taking it. The nose of the fish seems attached to the fly by an invisible four-inch string! A bulging bow-wave shows the trout's position. I must tell you here and now that there is no perfect solution to this

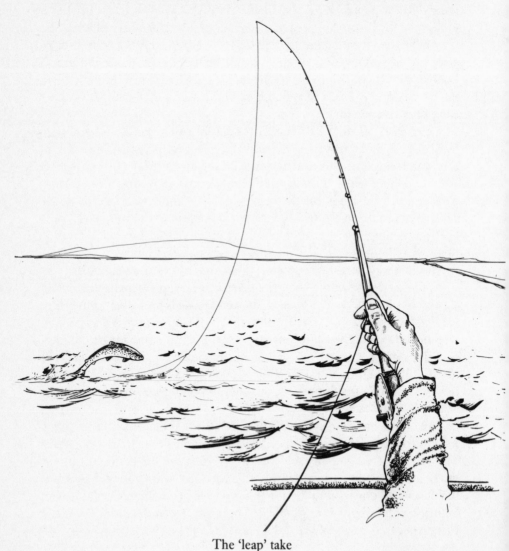

The 'leap' take

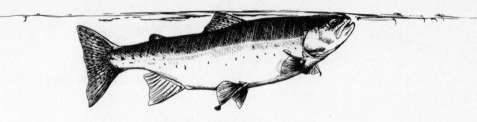

Takes to the dry fly: 1 The 'sip'.

problem. Speed up, slow down, stop – all work occasionally but mostly not at all. Sometimes it pays to lift off the flies in the middle of a 'follow', and immediately cast them back to the same spot. If the trout is eager enough, it will still be looking for the fly and will take it firmly. If the bow-wave disappears, wait a second or so, then strike, because this often means that the trout has turned down and taken one of the flies. If you continually get 'follows' which come to nothing, change to smaller flies. It's worth trying, although the change can mean that you get no interest whatsoever in the flies! Trout can be fickle creatures.

Dry-fly fishing has become a popular and productive method of fishing from a drifting boat, using flotant-treated flies which sit in or on the surface film. At one time, the dry fly was considered a desperation tactic, reserved for flat calms or hectic evening rises. It has been proved that it can be used at any time and in any conditions. It isn't necessary for fish to be rising. The main essentials are that the flies should be well-impregnated with a long-lasting flotant (the most popular being Gink) and that the leader should be treated so that it does not float. The 'static' retrieve is the most common, simply taking up the slack as the boat drifts; hesitant trout which swirl at the static dry can sometimes be tempted to take by a slow figure-of-eight movement.

Takes to the dry fly often come out of the blue, so constant vigilance is needed. They can be enthusiastic splashes, head-and-tail slow-motion rolls, or quiet sips. In each case, the rule is to wait a couple of seconds before lifting into the fish.

When trout are obviously rising to a particular species of insect, such as adult sedges or daddy-longlegs, it is logical to fish fairly realistic dry imitations, but loch-style dries usually fall into the 'emerging buzzer' class. Shipman-style buzzer nymphs have proved their worth, but the most popular type of dry seems to be the loosely-dubbed white-hackled pattern. The dubbing should be seal fur when possible, but Antron makes a good substitute. The body needs to hold as much flotant as possible, usually the popular Gink. Hot orange and ginger are two popular colours,

Takes to the dry fly: 2 The 'head-and-tail'

but fiery brown, olive, and black are always worth having. It is best to keep your dries ready-Ginked in a tin.

Choice of wet flies and lures for loch-styling is very wide, but it is fairly easy to put them into categories, e.g., lures, imitators, and attractors. It is important to remind you that you must distribute the various types of flies properly on your leader. The point fly should always be the heaviest and the top dropper fly the most air-resistant. Your leader will then extend nicely, and furthermore, the point fly will act as an 'anchor' against which the dropper flies can work. Unless the trout are obviously feeding right in the surface, I like to use a weighted point fly. The top dropper fly is usually a palmered or Muddler-headed pattern which will give a nice wake as it is dribbled along. The middle-dropper position is often viewed as an 'also-ran', but I consider it to be important, and a good number of my fish are taken by the middle dropper fly. It can be a slim winged pattern or similar to either the point or top dropper flies.

If there is a hatch of fly, or specific insects are perhaps being blown on to the water from the surrounding land, then it obviously pays to choose imitative patterns. Similarly, if coarse-fish fry are on the trout's menu, then it is wise to offer them white lures which mimic the appearance of little fish. Much of loch-style fishing relies, however, on attracting the trout by general impression and movement, and there are many such flies. Regarding sizes, a good rule-of-thumb is 'The bigger the wave, the larger the fly'. I would have lures in sizes 8 and 10; attractors in 10 and 12 (add size 8 for silver-bodied and gold-bodied patterns which can be used as point flies); sizes 10, 12 and 14 for imitators.

The following list gives all the loch-style fly patterns which have caught trout for me during recent years, month-by-month:

April
Lures: Viva.
Attractors: Silver Invicta Mini-Muddler, Dunkeld.
Imitators: Ned's Fancy (Glo-Brite Orange tail), Black Pheasant Tail Nymph, Orange Gold-ribbed Hare's Ear Nymph.

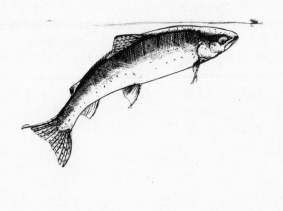

Takes to the dry fly: 3 The 'splash'
(from bottom left: observation, levitation, acceleration!)

May

Lures: Viva, Orange Tadpole.

Attractors: Dunkeld, Wingless Wickham Mini-Muddler, Wickham's Fancy, Silver Invicta.

Imitators: Black Quill, Soldier Palmer, Honey Buzzer, Grenadier Mini-Muddler, Ned's Fancy (signal-green tail), Mallard & Claret, Orange Gold-ribbed Hare's Ear Nymph.

June

Lures: Jersey Herd, Muddler Minnow, Viva, Susie, Whisky Muddler, Orange Muddler, Appetiser, White Muddler, Squirrel & Orange, Black Tadpole, Peach Doll.

Attractors: Silver Invicta, Wickham's Fancy, Claret Palmer (Glo-Brite shade 7 tail), Orange-bodied Muddler, Dunkeld, Wingless Wickham, Viva Mini-Muddler, Original Mini-Muddler, Red Palmer.

Imitators: Greenwell's Glory, Black Quill, Pheasant Tail Nymph, Ginger Quill, Soldier Palmer, Hatching Sedge, Woodcock & Green, Green Peter, Gold-ribbed Hare's Ear Nymph, Black Mini-Muddler, Claret & Black Mini-Muddler, Ned's Fancy (neon magenta tail), Grenadier Palmer, Honey Buzzer, Grenadier Mini-Muddler, dry Orange, dry Ginger.

July

Lures: Jersey Herd, Peppermint Doll, White Muddler, Susie, Muddler Minnow, Peetie, Whisky Muddler, White Tadpole, Viva, Orange Muddler, Orange Tadpole, Black Tadpole, Black Muddler, Peach Doll.

Attractors: Silver Invicta, Claret Palmer (Glo-Brite shade 4 tail), Wickham's Fancy, Original Mini-Muddler, Wingless Wickham, Viva Mini-Muddler, Peach Palmer.

Imitators: Soldier Palmer, Black Pennell, Pheasant Tail Nymph, Hatching Sedge, Fiery Brown, Murragh, Gold-ribbed Hare's Ear Nymph (Glo-Brite shade 7 tail), Gold-ribbed Hare's Ear, Ned's Fancy (Glo-Brite shade 2 tail), Grenadier, Honey Buzzer, Ginger Quill, Black Quill, Claret & Black Mini-Muddler, Grenadier Palmer (Glo-Brite shade 7 tail), Ned's Fancy (neon magenta tail), Olive Quill, Lake Olive, dry Olive, dry Hot Orange.

August

Lures: White Lure, White Muddler, Jersey Herd, Peetie, Orange Tadpole, Viva, White Tadpole, Orange Marabou Lure, Muddler Minnow.

Attractors: Wickham's Fancy, Wingless Wickham Mini-Muddler, Silver

Invicta, Fluebrush, Original Mini-Muddler, White Wickham's, Pearl
Invicta, Peach Mini-Muddler, Mallard & Claret.
Imitators: Daddy-longlegs, Hatching Sedge, Grenadier, Soldier Palmer,
Gold-ribbed Hare's Ear Nymph (Glo-Brite shade 7 tail), Drone-fly,
Connemara Black, Invicta, Bibio, Ned's Fancy (signal-green tail), Ned's
Fancy (Glo-Brite shade 2 tail), Grenadier Palmer, Claret & Black Mini-
Muddler, Grenadier Mini-Muddler, dry Ginger, dry Fiery Brown.

September

Lures: Appetiser, Jersey Herd, White Muddler, White Chenille Lure,
Muddler Minnow, Orange Tadpole, Tom's Terror, Black Tadpole, Viva.
Attractors: Original Mini-Muddler, Dunkeld, Kingfisher Butcher,
Wormfly, Fluebrush, Claret Palmer (Glo-Brite shade 7 tail), Mallard
& Silver, Orange Mini-Muddler, Peach Mini-Muddler, Wingless
Wickham Mini-Muddler, Silver Invicta.
Imitators: Fiery Brown, Ginger Quill, Gold-ribbed Hare's Ear, Daddy-
longlegs, Ned's Fancy (Glo-Brite shade 2 tail), Olive Quill, Stick Fly,
Mallard & Claret, Soldier Palmer, Claret & Black Mini-Muddler,
Grenadier, Honey Buzzer, Ned's Fancy (signal-green tail).

October

Lures: Muddler Minnow, White Marabou, Black Lure, Black Marabou
Lure, Whisky Fly, Black Tadpole.
Attractors: Silver Invicta, Pearl Invicta.
Imitators: Black Pennell, Connemara Black, Mallard & Claret, Pheasant
Tail Nymph, Soldier Palmer.

On checking this list, you will find that there are certain patterns
applicable to virtually every month, and you may care to make these the
basis of your fly collection. If you refer to the month-by-month chapters
on bank-fishing, you will be able to choose which imitative patterns to use
for loch-styling as the season progresses. The few nymphs included in the
list can be effective on very slow drifts.

Which drifts to choose? – that's the 64,000-dollar question! You just
have to find where the fish are at the time (says he, passing the buck firmly
to the reader!). I can give you a little help, however. Drifting over water
between 6 and 12 feet deep is usually worth while, and remember that
such shallow areas may be found in mid-water, where hillocks have been
submerged when the reservoir was built. Brown's Island at Rutland and
the Roman Shallows at Chew are well-known examples. Drifting around
weed-beds can be productive, but you have to be very careful when
playing the fish or you will lose them in the weeds.

Slicks and scum-lanes are always worth investigation, but are not guaranteed to hold fish, despite popular opinion. Drift along one side of a scum-lane, rather than down the middle of it. Because of the smooth surface, the trout have better visibility and are more easily scared than in the rippled water. Deep water must not be neglected – buzzers often hatch from water over 20 feet deep, and bring the trout up sufficiently for them to be caught by loch-styling methods. On dull days, daphnia might also concentrate the trout in the middle of the reservoir.

A little bird-watching can help in the choice of a productive drift. A flock of excited seagulls wheeling over an area can indicate the presence of fry. These birds are opportunists, and so should you be. Stick a set of fry-type lures on the leader, and be ready for action. As you approach the area, you should see trout splashing at the fry; at each splash, a seagull drops down to pick up a stunned fry – it's amazing how they learn that a trout's splash means an easy morsel. Drift through the activity time after time, and you should pick up a load of trout. A crowd of swallows, swifts, or martins skimming the waves usually means that a hatch of buzzers is taking place. Watch the terns, too – they like fry and buzzers. And don't ignore the ducks – why do you think the Irish call the black buzzer the 'duck fly'?

There are favourite drifts on every reservoir, for every wind direction. Visit a reservoir regularly, and you will discover them for yourself.

Fishing the 'boils'

Many reservoirs have aerators situated in the deeper parts, to circulate the water and prevent stagnation. When working, the powerful stream of air-bubbles creates massive boils at the surface. Trout are attracted to the boils because they provide highly-aerated water and perhaps a supply of food brought up from the depths. Although not strictly drift-fishing, fishing these boils is so popular, and often so productive, that some hints on the technique cannot be omitted from this chapter.

Approach a boil from upwind and set the boat so that it will hit the centre of the boil. The ideal situation then is that the strength of the wind will equal the push of the water current set up by the bubbles, so that the boat sits steady a few yards away from the turmoil. If the wind is only a gentle breeze, the chances are that the boat will be pushed away from the boil; if the wind is too strong, the boat will be pushed to one side and drift past the boil and you will have to make the approach run time and time again.

Don't be too eager to get back on to the boil if this happens. The slicks which form downwind of a boil often hold fish. Don't be tempted to anchor near a boil; it's very difficult, and in any case it's a selfish act.

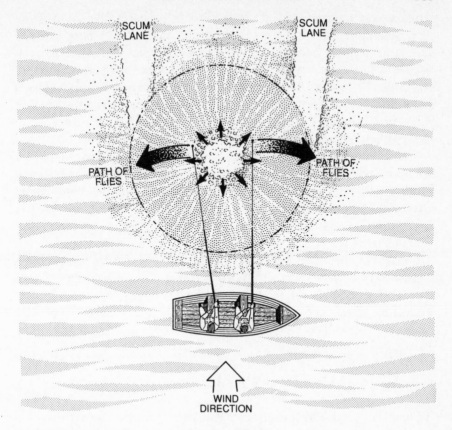

Fishing a 'boil'

To fish the boil itself, the left-hand rod must cast so that the flies land just to the left of the centre of the boil, and the right-hand rod just to the right. The flies are then pushed out to the side by the current, exactly like 'across-and-down' wet fly in a river. Try not to hit the centre of the boil, because your flies will then be pushed back towards you. The line becomes slack, and you have to strip in like a wild thing to keep in contact with the flies. You can use either floating or sinking lines on the boils.

Every boil doesn't necessarily hold fish. Perhaps only one out of several will be worth fishing, but when you find that one, stick to it – it can mean a lot of fish in the boat.

Competition fishing

Based on loch-style fishing, with several restrictive rules, competition fishing has become quite popular in recent years. There are now a large number of competitions held every year, both at club-member level and at national and international levels. Just as in times of war or in space exploration, the urge to win competitions has engendered many new and successful tactics, techniques, and pieces of equipment. Whether you become a keen competition fly-fisher depends on your personal nature and attitude to fishing. I have entered several competitions, and even won some, but I find the tension and hassle which are inevitably involved rather uncomfortable. There is enough competition from the trout, in my view, without competing with one's fellow anglers!

There is one great benefit to be gained by entering a competition. If you are drawn with a really expert boat partner, you can learn an awful lot by carefully watching his (or her – there are some excellent lady competitors around) techniques. Club matches are useful in this respect, because you are usually fishing with someone you know, and the stress of fishing with a complete stranger is eliminated. If you finally decide to venture into the national field, there is always the possibility that if you prove good enough you could end up by representing your country in the fly-fishing World Cup. As a start, I recommend that you read two books on the subject – *Competitive Fly-fishing* by Tony Pawson (Pelham Books) and *Competition Trout Fishing* by Chris Ogborne (Crowood Press).

NORTHAMPTON-STYLE

To many, this style of fishing from a boat drifting with its stern to the wind is synonymous with the lead-core line and fishing deep behind the boat; to others it is classed as 'no better than trawling, not proper fly-fishing'. Neither opinion is strictly true. The skilful practitioner of Northampton-style often casts to the side of the boat and retrieves the flies before they have sunk very far – the 'side-swiping' technique. Lines of various sinking-rates are used, dictated by the depth at which the trout are holding. Admittedly, it is almost 100-per-cent lure-fishing, but many bank-fishers use nothing but lures.

Done properly in all its forms, this style is in fact a very skilful exercise, and extremely productive in terms of numbers and size of fish caught, and that in itself is one reason for its bad reputation. It has been said that if every boat-fisher fished only the Northampton style, and fished it expertly, they could practically empty a reservoir of trout in a season, and no reservoir management could afford to restock a sufficient number of fish to keep up with the extraction. It is significant that on many reservoirs, fishing behind the boat is prohibited. Unfortunately, boat etiquette among many who fish Northampton-style is almost non-existent. Because they are mostly fishing for deep-lying trout, they pay little attention to the need not to scare surface-feeding fish, and tear along at full speed up loch-styling drifts. It is no wonder that these people are not popular among loch-stylers. In my opinion, the two styles simply do not mix, if only because each gets in the other's way.

Personally, I don't enjoy fishing Northampton-style. I have done it on occasions, in the company of such experts as Steve Parton, Jim Clements and Max Hill, from all of whom I learned a lot about the skills involved. I did it because when I was in business I had to be able to sell my customers the correct tackle for the style, and to tell them the basics of the technique. Nowadays, I don't fish Northampton-style, from choice, and as this book is about fishing 'the Tom Saville way' I must refer anyone who wishes to take up the style to Steve Parton's book *Boatfishing for Trout* (Allen & Unwin). It contains all you will wish to know.

Chapter 13

Fly-Tying, the Indispensable Skill

It is my belief that no one can get the maximum enjoyment out of fly-fishing until a reasonable standard of fly-tying ability is accomplished. Using standard patterns of flies is fine, up to a point, but a fly-dresser with the ability to devise and tie new variations and patterns of flies, based on practical fishing experience, can only improve chances. Not only that, but there is great enjoyment and fulfilment to be had in the actual act of creating a successful new fly. If you don't tie flies, and you have ever walked out of a tackle shop disappointed that they hadn't got exactly the pattern of fly you had in mind, I urge you to take up fly-tying as a hobby. It isn't as difficult as you may imagine, and even if you have hands like hams and fingers like bananas, that's no excuse. Fly-tying uses tools which make things easy for you.

Today's keen reservoir fly-fisher should be an enthusiastic fly-dresser through necessity. The average tackle shop simply does not stock any but the well-established standard patterns. Of course, many of these standards are very successful and catch lots of trout. Examples of such standard patterns are Soldier Palmer, Invicta, Butcher, Mallard & Claret, Greenwell, Zulu, Black Pennell. Some of the flies and lures we think of as 'modern' have been around long enough to be included in the category of 'standard' – after all, it is almost 25 years since I first imported the Muddler Minnow into Britain!

The more successful is a fly or lure, the quicker it becomes accepted as a standard pattern. Baby Doll, Muddler, Black & Peacock Spider, Pheasant Tail Nymph, and Stick Fly – all are of comparatively recent origin, but are 'household words' to reservoir fly-fishers. The most obvious recent meteoric rise to fame is that of the Dog Nobbler; ten years ago it was unknown. Only the Muddler had a quicker trip into popularity.

If there is one thing that distinguishes the modern reservoir fly-fisher, it is the constant search for the ultimate fly. Unhampered by old-fashioned traditions, therefore with a free imagination, today's reservoir fisher is not afraid to use plastics, man-made fibres, or metal beads, for example, and is completely uninhibited where colours are concerned.

No sooner has a fly become an established 'standard' than the keenest among us start to try to improve it. Even the Dog Nobbler soon had a host of offspring – palmered, goggle-eyed, fluorescent, and even luminous versions abound. But very few of these are possible contenders for the Hall of Fame. Many will sink into oblivion as quickly as they appeared, because they are just products of some professional fly-dresser jumping on the bandwagon and virtually perming eight-from-ten with insufficient practical field-testing or logical thought controlling their development. Only by chance will a winning combination come up.

In complete contrast to this hit-and-miss approach are the improvements thought out by the best of our fly-fisher/fly-dressers – people who fish almost daily, who live, sleep, eat, and breathe fly-fishing, and who develop new flies or variations by constant painstaking practical experiment based on educated observation of how trout behave. Fame sometimes comes more slowly to their creations, but it lasts a lot longer. Often closely guarded secrets known only to the angler and his friends, some of these flies never get the universal recognition they deserve.

No matter how good a pattern is, it needs the publicity of print to provide the wider arena in which it can extend its reputation. Once publicised, its final wide acceptance depends on how readily available are the materials used in its make-up, and, to a lesser degree, by the ease (or otherwise) with which these materials are manipulated. The only thing that slowed down the Muddler's climb to popularity was the inability of UK fly-dressers to construct the clipped deer-hair heads. Nowadays this technique is well known, but at the time of the Muddler's introduction it was quite a stumbling-block. The present-day fly-fishing magazines provide the ideal distribution centres for bringing new patterns to the attention of the fly-fishing public.

It's all too often that the trout seem to prefer 'something a little bit different' from standard flies. A lot of my most successful flies are 'specials' or variations on standard patterns. I'm a great believer in the effectiveness of fluorescence in flies, and many of my patterns incorporate fluorescent materials. I like hairwings for their mobility. I like the added attraction of pearly tinsel, especially in the form of Crystal Hair. I like the translucent sparkle of Antron dubbing. As a fly-dresser, I can incorporate any of these materials into my flies, and I can alter shape and proportion of any pattern to suit my own ideas of what should be attractive to the trout. I can add whatever amount of lead I wish, to change the depth at which the fly fishes.

Fly-tying is acknowledged as a marvellous close-season pastime, and it certainly is a very pleasant way of passing winter evenings, but the really keen fly-dressers tie right through the season, when new patterns can be tested and re-designed almost within hours of their conception.

Although fly-tying can be learned from a book or video cassette, there is really no substitute for personal tuition. So enrol in one of the series of winter fly-tying classes, join the local branch of the Fly Dressers' Guild, and I guarantee you will enjoy your fishing all the more.

You don't need a terrifying amount of stuff to start with. Get the basic set of tools plus a small selection of materials for practising the various techniques. In the old days, many fly-tyers dressed the hooks by holding them in the fingers, but it's so much easier, and better, to hold the hook in a specially designed fly-tying vice. There are lots of these on the market, many of which are Indian copies of American designs; the best of these are very good, but many are rubbish. American vices are high-priced but extremely well designed. There are really good British vices available, particularly those marketed by John Weaver as his 'Ultimate' models. Most popular are those in which the jaws are opened and closed by means of a lever.

Other essential tools include a spigot bobbin-holder (the first of which I introduced to the UK in 1969), which holds the spool of tying thread and enables accurate placing of the thread without wastage. You need a superb pair of small scissors, with large finger-holes and with blades that cut right to the tips. Guard these from other members of the household; they must not be used for cutting paper, string, fingernails or anything else! A second pair, about 4 inches long, are handy for slightly more heavy-duty use, such as snipping wire tinsel and clipping deer hair. You also need two pairs of hackle pliers, one medium size and one small, for winding hackles. I find very little use for a dubbing needle, traditionally used for picking out strands of dubbing; instead I use a little gadget called a 'teazle brush', sold at the haberdashery counters of large department stores. A few strokes with this and a dubbing body becomes nicely straggly.

You may like to buy a whip-finish tool to enable you to make secure heads on the flies. This gadget is rather fiddly to use, but once you have learned how to use it, it is quick and efficient. However, I learned to do a good whip-finish with my fingers, from photographs in an American fly-tying book, and I have never felt the need of a whip-finish tool.

These, then, are the basic tools. You will need in addition some ready-waxed thread (I like Danville's Monocord) in black, orange, and olive, to start with, plus a piece of white resinous wax to add more adhesion when dubbing. Cellulose varnish in black and clear, for a 'professional' finish to the fly heads, and two Varnish Applicators, wonderful little gadgets marketed by Lureflash Products to make accurate varnishing so very easy.

The most important items are, of course, the hooks. Some of the best in the world are hand-made by Partridge of Redditch, under the caring and dedicated direction of Alan Bramley. Partridge hooks are characterised by top-quality material and sharp points; very rarely does one break or open up. The designs are excellent, but unfortunately, at the time of writing this book, some useful designs are not made by Partridge, so we have to look to other manufacturers for these. The Japanese Kamasan brand are good (they also make the hooks sold under the Drennan brand name), and Mustad from Norway are among the best of the machine-made hooks.

Having tested many hooks during my time in the tackle trade, I choose the following as the most reliable and the best designs for the types of flies I use:

For Lures: Mustad 9672 (3X-longshank, round-bend, forged).
For Wet Flies and Nymphs: Partridge L2A or GRS2A 'Capt. Hamilton' also Partridge CS7 'International' Capt. Hamilton (wide-gape, round-bend, forged).
For Weighted Nymphs: Kamasan B830 (2X-longshank, round-bend, forged).
For Special Nymphs: Partridge K4A or GRS6A (curved shank).
For Dry Flies: Partridge L3A 'Capt. Hamilton' (lightweight wire, wide-gape, round-bend, forged).

You will note that I prefer the round-bend profile, which is the widest practical gape possible, and that I like a forged hook because this gives the greatest strength at the bend.

Good visibility is important when tying flies, not only to avoid eye-strain, but to manipulate materials neatly and accurately. Invest in a good lamp, such as an Anglepoise, which will illuminate the tying area without the light glaring into your eyes. Use a sheet of white Formica, or Conti-board, as a base over which to tie, so that details of the fly are easily seen against the light background. At one edge of the sheet, paint an area of black; light-coloured materials stand out better against that.

When it comes to buying materials, be warned that there is quite a lot of poor-quality stuff about. Go to a specialist supplier of fly-tying materials, who should have sorted out and discarded all the rubbish. Be prepared to pay a good price for quality – there's rarely a cheap 'bargain' that is worth buying. If you shoot, or have a friend who shoots, you are in an ideal situation to get excellent game-bird feathers straight off the bird, with all the natural oils still present, for the cost of a few cartridges. Watch out for centre tail feathers from old cock pheasants, both normal, melanistic, and albino varieties; these have nice long fibres not present on those from young birds. The small speckled brown feathers from the back of a partridge are worth their weight in gold – small enough feathers are seldom included in commercially available packets. Bronze mallard flank

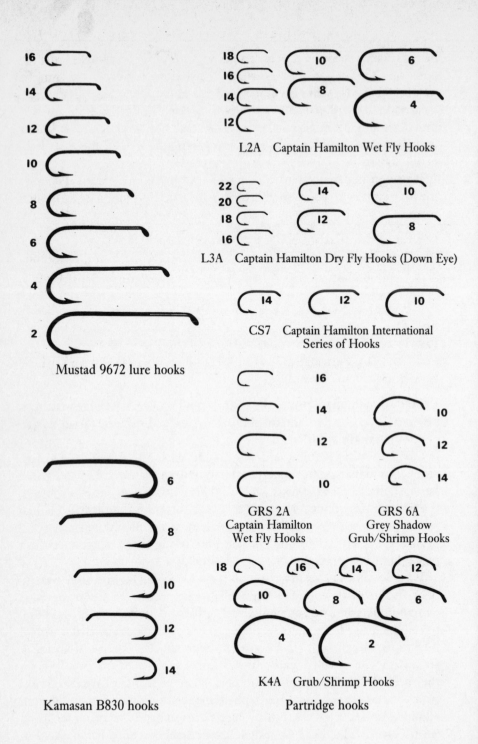

16

14

12

10

8

6

4

2

Mustad 9672 lure hooks

18
16
14
12

L2A   Captain Hamilton Wet Fly Hooks

10   6

8   4

22
20
18
16

L3A   Captain Hamilton Dry Fly Hooks (Down Eye)

14   10

12   8

CS7   Captain Hamilton International
Series of Hooks

14   12   10

16

14

12

10

GRS 2A
Captain Hamilton
Wet Fly Hooks

GRS 6A
Grey Shadow
Grub/Shrimp Hooks

10

12

14

6

8

10

12

14

Kamasan B830 hooks

18   16   14   12

10   8   6

4   2

K4A   Grub/Shrimp Hooks

Partridge hooks

Hooks used by the author (actual size)

feathers and barred teal or widgeon feathers should be plucked and sorted into various sizes of lefts and rights. Cut the wings off mallard and teal, provided the feathers aren't split and blood-stained; the grey feathers are excellent winging material. Similarly with cock and hen pheasant and woodcock wings. Jay wings are useful for more than the blue 'Invicta' feathers, and while we're thinking of creatures that are a nuisance on the shoot, remember the grey squirrel's tail. Leave all these wings and tails for several weeks to dry slowly, making sure that flies can't get to them and deposit eggs.

Rough shoots provide hare and rabbit skins, and these are easily preserved by scraping away any fat, pinning the stretched skin fur-downwards on a board, and rubbing tannic acid powder into it. Local farmers can be primed to save you the bodies of bantam cocks which die of old age; the skins, or at least the capes, can be cured in the same way as the hare skins. Don't bother with ordinary poultry cocks; the hackles are not good enough. Hens are a better proposition, especially whites, blacks, gingers, and furnace; unfortunately, those that have been kept with cocks often have mutilated feathers, so examine them carefully.

Whether you are a shooter or not, most of the materials you need will have to be bought. At the start, buy only those items you need for practising the various techniques of fly-tying. Don't worry about tying flies to actually fish with until you have become sufficiently competent at dubbing, winging, hackling, ribbing, etc. Fly-tying really *is* an example of 'Practice makes perfect'. Keep tying until every technique becomes second nature. Then you can really go to town on tying both standards and specials.

When you are fishing, observe the characteristics of the various trout food forms, and think about how you can incorporate them into fly patterns. Let me give you two examples of how I devised successful specials:

Bank-fishing at Rutland one June evening, there was quite a rise going on. The rise-forms were rather splashy, and when I checked the water surface I saw pale gingery adult chironomids buzzing around on the surface. Unlike most buzzers, which fly off from the surface once they have quit the pupal shuck, these seemed unwilling to put more than an inch between themselves and the surface. In fact they spent most of the time flying erratically along the surface. The reason for the splashy rises was that the trout were having to chase the insects as they weaved their way along. I had nothing in my fly-box that the trout liked, and was lucky to get a fish on a winged wet Gold-ribbed Hare's Ear.

The following evening I set up my fly-tying gear with the sole intention of producing a pattern resembling the pale ginger buzzer. Black tying thread was obviously not appropriate, so I used light olive Monocord; later versions have been tied with orange Monocord, and they look even better. A size 12 Partridge GRS2A seemed the right size of hook; 14s have also been successful. The naturals were at first sight a jumble of buzzing wings and legs, and a palmered cock hackle was the obvious answer to the problem of suggesting those features. I used a mottled honey-coloured hackle which, when palmered, gave a colour fairly close to that of the flies I had seen. Later I used hackles from a pale ginger Metz genetic cock cape; despite the high price of these capes, they are so good that they are worth every penny. Stiff, full of sparkle, and perfectly short-fibred, one hackle palmered the fly exactly right. To increase the impression of movement, and to help keep the fly up in the water, I included fibres from a large hackle of the same colour as a tail. Merely as a 'bed' for the palmered hackle, I chose a body of pheasant tail fibres, using a pale gingerish cock centre tail feather (it's surprising how many shades of colour are available in pheasants). To reinforce the dressing, I ribbed the body and hackle with fine gold wire. A pair of wings seemed to be called for (although maybe the trout wouldn't have insisted). I chose grey secondary mallard wing feather slips, but any suitably sized grey wing feather would have been okay. The finished fly looked just right to my eyes, and not long afterwards the new fly had a chance to prove itself. Boat-fishing at Chew on June 13, with a steady hatch of ginger buzzers all day, eight trout took it (on the middle dropper) while drifting from Denny Island towards Wick Green. Since then, the fly has taken trout at several reservoirs whenever ginger buzzers were in evidence. It performs best when skimming the surface on a dropper. Needing a name, I called it the Honey Buzzer.

In August 1990 I heard that the trout were solidly 'on the fry' at Grafham, and that white lures were taking fish. Having booked a boat, I thought I would give them something they might not have seen before. I don't like lures, which are too big, so I used Mustad 9672 size 8. White . . . for fry . . . why not a white hairwing? White Monocord seemed appropriate for the tying thread. First, the tail. Orange is a good summer lure colour, so a few strands of orange Crystal Hair, flecked with bright pearl pinpoints, were tied in. Something pearly-cum-silvery for the body of a little fish – I built up a suitable girth of silver thread, and slipped a length of pearl Mylar tubing over it, securing both ends with the white Monocord. Fins needed to be suggested, so I added a 'beard hackle' of the same material as the tail; it looked attractive. A neighbour's dog provided some lovely lustrous white hair, having just been bathed! The Grafham trout loved it. The dog's name, and that of the lure – Susie. You could use white goat hair if you can't find a white dog!

A few useful tips relating to fly-tying materials:

You'll be surprised at the improvement a wash can make to what at first sight is a poor quality hackle cape or tail. When they arrive from the original source, capes, etc., are often dirty, and some wholesalers don't trouble to clean them. A ten-minute soaking in warm water and washing-up liquid will loosen the dirt. Next, gently rub the hackles whilst keeping the cape submerged, and rinse under a running tap. Squeeze the cape in a towel to remove most of the water, then dry off the hackles with a hairdrier. Bend the skin of the cape so that the hackles stand out, and start with the smallest hackles at the top of the cape. Shaking the cape vigorously as you dry it will quicken the drying. Pay special attention to the large hackles, which hold the most moisture. When you are certain that all the hackles are dry, you still need to dry the skin, which will have absorbed water during the soak. This is best done by placing the cape between layers of kitchen towel for a day or so. A heavy book will ensure that the cape comes out of the treatment nicely flat. You'll be amazed at how good it looks, compared with its previous condition.

Hackles and other feathers that have been crushed out of their original shape are easily renovated by steam treatment. You need an old-fashioned kettle, or an electric kettle that doesn't switch itself off as soon as the water is boiling. The feathers are held in the jet of steam which comes from the spout of the kettle; single feathers can be held in tweezers, or a handful of feathers can be placed in an aquarium net. Each feather miraculously springs back into shape as soon as the steam touches it.

If you decide to attempt dyeing feathers or other materials, use only enamelled pans; aluminium pans, for example, will be affected by the acid used in the dyeing process. Whereas bright colours such as red, yellow and orange are easy to dye, colours like olive, blue dun and ginger are much more difficult. This is because the dyestuffs are complex mixtures, each ingredient entering the material at a different speed. The temperature of the dye-bath is critical, so use a thermometer – don't guess the temperature. At 92°C, all the ingredients of the dye will go into the material at the same time, and the correct colour will result. At this temperature, the water will be bubbling, but not boiling, so the texture of the material will not be spoiled. Wait until the critical temperature has been reached before placing the material in the dye bath. If it is necessary to keep the material in the dye bath for some time (such as when dyeing black), it is important to keep the solution at 92°C throughout.

Hair, fur, and feather can become infested with mites, beetles, or moth grubs, all of which eat your precious materials. It is essential to keep these at bay, so package every item in a plastic bag. For preference, your materials should be stored in tins – biscuit tins are good – with lids to keep out unwanted insect visitors. There is an excellent bug-killer marketed by Vapona, in the form of a solid which emits insecticidal vapour; this is available in a suitable 'small space' pack, often sold at caravan supply stores. One pack in each tin will ensure that your materials are safe for at least six months, after which the pack should be replaced. If you have ever seen the damage a few moth grubs can do to a Metz cape, you would not ignore this particular hint!

Don't worry if the flies you tie are not perfect – many thousands of trout have been caught on rough-looking flies. As long as each ingredient is firmly tied in, and the head whip-finished so that it won't come undone, the main essential is that your flies are proportioned correctly. Body not too fat or too thin, wings at a nice streamlined angle, that sort of thing. I remember meeting an old chap in one of the car parks on Hambleton peninsula at Rutland Water. It was a rough, rainy day, with big waves running along the bank. He had just finished fishing, and had eight lovely trout in his bag. He kindly gave me the fly he had caught them all on. It was a huge 'Pheasant Tail Nymph', and the inverted commas are intentional, because I have never seen such a monstrosity. On a 6 longshank hook, it had bits of pheasant fibres sticking out all over the place, and a very straggly thorax crowned by a sort of bow-tie in white wool. However, if he could catch on it, so could I, so I tied it on the point. I caught four good rainbows on it and the fifth broke me and stole the fly. Try as I might, I didn't get another pull. That night I sat down at the vice and tried to make some copies. I never caught a fish on any of them – I couldn't tie them rough enough!

Tying flies for a fly-tying competition is one thing; tying flies to catch fish is another.

Appendix A

Knots

I use only five knots for my reservoir fishing. Two of these, the Blood knot and the half-Blood knot, I use each time I fish. The other three are used as required, which is very rarely; they are the needle knot, the nail knot, and the loop. None of these knots, when tied properly, have let me down, and I have found no need to even try to tie a Grinner or Cove knot! If I ever wanted to, I would have to look up the instructions in some other publication, and if you want to learn either of these knots, so must you – after all, this *is* about fishing the Tom Saville way!

The half-Blood knot

This is the knot I use for attaching the fly to the leader. I have never found it necessary to use the 'tucked' version of the half-Blood knot, which is reputed to be more secure. Many years ago, I was advised by the DuPont Company of America (one of the major manufacturers of nylon) that five turns was the optimum number for this knot and its big brother, the Blood knot, and I have found this to be absolutely correct. Sometimes, for flies size 14 or below, I reduce the turns to four because the five-turn knot maybe looks a bit big against the small hook. Ninety-nine per cent of the time, I am perfectly happy with the five turns.

So that the fly 'swims' properly, I think it's important to enter the nylon into the top of the eye of a TDE hook, so to start with I hold the fly upside-down. I use about 2 inches of nylon through the eye, to form the knot.

After inserting the nylon, I 'hide' the fly in a tight grip between thumb and first finger of the left hand. I keep the leader taut by gripping it between third and little fingers of the right hand, and make the five turns towards me by alternating the grip on the nylon between the thumb and first finger of the right hand and the second and third fingers of the left hand. Finally, keeping the nylon taut, I transfer the hold on the nylon to the thumb and first finger of the right hand, and expose the eye of the fly. I then push the end of the nylon up through the loop which has been formed immediately next to the eye, and grip the end firmly against the fly with the thumb and first finger of the left hand.

I moisten the nylon with saliva, and tighten the knot slowly by pulling the nylon in the right hand. I cut off the tip close to the knot, finding no need to leave more than 1mm sticking out. A longer spur invites tangles.

The above is how I tie the knot using Tynex nylon. If you use a limp type of nylon, you may get a 'corkscrew' next to the knot, made by the nylon having been pulled through its own coils. To avoid this, tighten the knot by pulling the tip of the nylon.

END OF NYLON IS PUSHED
THROUGH LOOP NEXT TO
THE EYE

The half-Blood knot

The Blood knot

Named after its inventor, and not because you sweat blood while learning to tie it! Five turns each side is the optimum number for this knot, and I only reduce the number when joining nylon of widely-differing diameters, in which case I reduce the turns of the thicker nylon to three.

For me, this is the ideal knot for joining nylon (a) because it doesn't let me down and (b) because the ends of the knot project at right-angles to the nylon, the best angle for use as droppers. I have not found it to be a weak knot; DuPont give the strength of the five-turn Blood knot as 85 per cent of the unknotted nylon. It's not an easy knot to tie, when you first attempt it, but improvement comes if you follow the advice given by a New York cop when asked by a dear old spinster, 'How do I get to Carnegie Hall, officer?' – 'You gotta practise, lady!'

Here's how I do it:

Cross the two pieces of nylon to be joined, one over the other, the piece in the left hand being the one which will form the dropper if required. This piece should be the one nearest the fly-line; let us call it **A**, and the other piece **B**. A goes under B at the crossover point. The lengths of the free ends should be 7 inches for **A**, 3 inches for **B**. The crossover is held firmly between thumb and first finger of the left hand, in just the same way as the fly is held when making the half-Blood knot described above.

The free end of **A** is turned five times towards me in exactly the same way as in the half-Blood knot; it is essential to keep the main length of **B** taut. Then, still keeping **B** taut, the free end of **A** is taken behind the free end of **B** which is held between thumb and first finger of the left hand.

The grip on the crossover point is transferred to thumb and first finger of the right hand, and the free end of **B** is taken behind the free end of **A** to make five turns away from me (anti-clockwise) round the main length of **A**, using the left hand. This will leave a gap next to the right-hand thumb; push the free end of **B** down through that gap, and open the grip of the right-hand thumb and first finger just enough to grip the tip of the free end of **B**.

Grip the free end of **A** between thumb and first finger of the left hand, the main length of **A** between second and third fingers of the left hand, the tip of **B** between thumb and first finger of the right hand, and the main length of **B** in the remaining fingers of the right hand. Moisten with saliva, and ease the knot tight slowly, pulling on the two main lengths rather than on the free ends.

Cut off the free ends closely, or leave the free end of **A** to form the dropper.

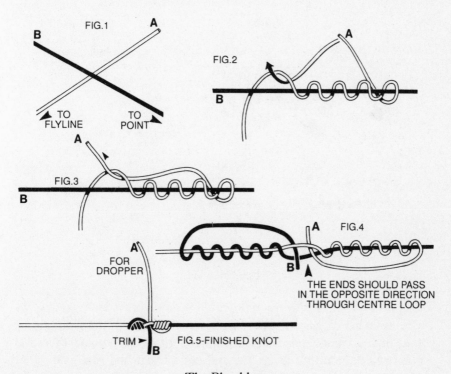

The Blood knot

The needle knot

This is the best knot of all for ensuring free passage through the rod-rings of the joint between fly-line and leader. It can only be used with PVC-coated fly-lines.

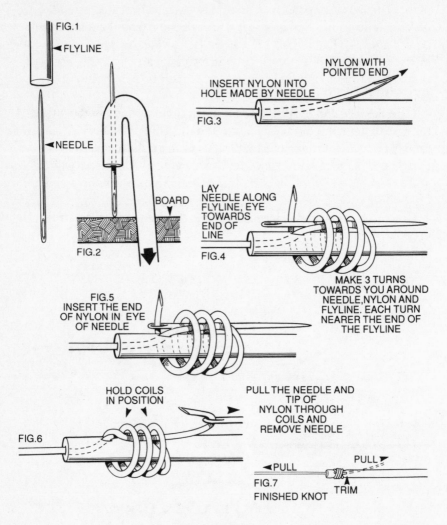

The needle knot

Choose a needle with the eye large enough to accept the diameter of nylon you are using, and make sure it has a good sharp point. Push the needle into the end of the fly-line and out through the side of the line about 4mm from the tip. I find it easier to do this if the eye end of the needle rests on a tile or other hard surface. After the needle is inserted into the line, the line is pulled hard downwards so that the point protrudes through the side.

Some advise heating the needle so as to melt the line coating, but I find that if the needle is left for five minutes or so and rotated a few times before withdrawal, the hole in the line remains open long enough for the nylon to be inserted. It helps if the end of the nylon is cut to a point.

With the tip of the fly-line pointing to the left, insert the nylon into the end of the line and out through the side hole. Pull about 3 inches through.

Lay the needle alongside the line, with the eye pointing towards, and level with, the tip of the line. Holding line, nylon, and needle together in the thumb and first two fingers of the left hand, take the end of the nylon in the right hand. Wind the nylon round itself, the line, and the needle, moving progressively towards the tip of the line. I find it helps to stop each turn unwinding if each is held in place by the second finger of the left hand. Each turn must lie against the previous one, and they must not cross over.

After three turns, push the end of the nylon into the eye of the needle from below. Pull the needle and the end of the nylon through the turns of nylon (to the right), ease the eye of the needle off the end of the nylon, and tighten carefully by pulling both ends of the nylon. Try to keep the coils neat as they tighten. Take care not to over-tighten, or a nasty 'dog-leg' will result.

Cut off the tip of the nylon close to the line, so that it does not constitute an obstruction to easy passage of the knot through the rod-rings. You can give the knot a coat of Vy-Coat liquid PVC if you wish. I don't bother.

The nail knot

If the fly-line is very thin at the tip, as in very fast sinking lines, for example, the needle knot is not a practical proposition for joining leader to line. A large enough needle cannot be inserted into the line. So we use the needle knot without the initial stages of inserting the nylon into the fly-line. Originally, a nail was used alongside the line to give a little space through which the nylon was passed, but it is much better to use a needle.

As with the needle knot, lay the needle along the fly-line with the eye towards, and level with, the end of the line, which should point to the left.

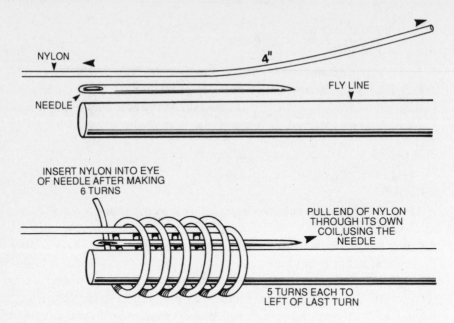

The nail knot

Lay the nylon alongside both line and needle, with about 4 inches pointing towards the right.

Starting about 1cm from the tip of the fly-line, make six turns of the nylon over itself, line, and needle; each turn to the left of the previous turn. Again as with the needle knot, push the end of the nylon into the eye of the needle, and pull it through the turns of nylon. Make sure everything doesn't unwind!

Pull the needle off the nylon, and as you tighten the knot, ease the line through the coils so that the knot finally tightens about 2mm from its tip. The knot must be really tight so that it doesn't slip off the end of the line. A couple of coats of Vy-Coat liquid PVC definitely helps in this instance.

Fly-lines coated with other than PVC, such as the Airflo brand, must utilise braid/sleeve joints.

The loop

I don't know if this knot has a specific name, but I find it the best of all the loop knots. Its main advantage, apart from its strength, is that the end doesn't stick out but lies alongside the nylon.

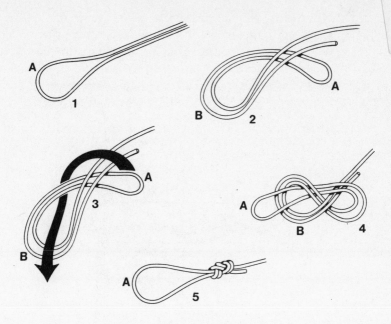

The loop knot

Fold back 4 or 5 inches of the nylon, making a loop pointing left; we'll call this loop **A**. Grip the free end to the main length with thumb and first finger of the right hand. Grip the loop **A** between thumb and first finger of the left hand, and take it to the right and round the back, using the second finger of the left hand as a pivot.

Grip the crossover between thumb and first finger of the left hand and release the grip of the right hand. Then, with thumb and first finger of the right hand, take hold of the loop **A** whilst at the same time gripping the double strands of nylon between second and third fingers of the right hand. Bring the loop **A** up and in front of the double strands, which will then have formed a double-strand loop round the second finger of the left hand. We'll call this double-strand loop **B**.

Temporarily switch the grip on loop **A** to the thumb and first finger of the left hand, and grip the crossover between thumb and first finger of the right hand. Ease the second finger of the left hand out of the loop **B**, and hold the tip of loop **B** between thumb and first finger of the left hand. Push loop **A** up into loop **B** from below, and before you pull the knot tight, check that the actual knot shows a figure 8 configuration – this means you've done it correctly. You can cut off the free end quite close to the knot.

Now for an extra knot, the mooring knot.

This isn't a fishing knot, but a useful boating knot. As well as mooring a boat to a post, chain, or rail, it can be used for attaching a drogue or anchor rope.

Take two turns of the rope around the point of attachment, then two half-hitches round the main rope and pull tight. Safe as houses!

TWICE ROUND
THE POST AND
2 HALF-HITCHES

The mooring knot

Appendix B

Fly Patterns

Although many of my flies are 'specials', original patterns or variations on standard patterns, I do use some standard patterns as well. As these are readily available in fly-tying textbooks, I am not giving the dressings here of, for example, Silver Invicta, Wickham's Fancy, Ginger Quill or Black & Peacock Spider, etc., etc. *Robson's Guide* (Beekay Publishers) is as good a source as any for standard stillwater patterns. The following are my special dressings of flies mentioned in the text:

Bill's Viva

Hook: Mustad 9672, sizes 8 or 10.
Tying thread: black Monocord.
Tail: Glo-Brite floss, shade 12.
Rib: silver oval tinsel.
Body: dubbed black Antron or seal fur.
Beard hackle: Glo-Brite floss, shade 12.

Blae & Black

Hook: Partridge L2A, size 12, 14, or 16.
Tying thread: black Monocord.
Tail: Glo-Brite floss, shade 3 or 4.
Rib: silver wire.
Body: dubbed black Antron or seal fur.
Beard hackle: dyed black hen.
Wing: starling secondaries.

Bloodworm

Hook: Partridge K4A, sizes 10 or 12.
Tying thread: Flymaster, shade 505 (fire orange).
Tail: Glo-Brite floss, shade 4.
Rib: Flymaster tying thread, black.
Body: Glo-Brite Floss, shade 4.

Caddis Grub

Hook: Mustad 9672, sizes 8 or 10.
Tying thread: black Monocord.
Weight: lead wire wound along whole of shank.

Rib: gold wire.
Body: hare body fur, dubbed heavily and well picked out.
Thorax: cream floss.
Hackle: black hen.

Claret Palmer

Hook: Partridge L2A or CS7, sizes 10 or 12.
Tying thread: black Monocord.
Tail: Glo-Brite floss, shade 4 or 7.
Rib: gold wire.
Palmer: light red-brown cock hackle.
Body: claret Antron or seal-fur dubbing.

Claret & Black Mini-Muddler

Hook: Partridge L2A or CS7, size 10, 12 or 14.
Tying thread: black Monocord.
Rib: gold wire.
Body: dubbed claret seal fur or Antron.
Wing: dyed black squirrel-tail hair.
Head: clipped deer hair.

Concrete Bowl

Hook: Mustad 9672, sizes 8 or 10.
Tying thread: Monocord, colour to match body.
Weight: 6–8 turns fine lead wire at the thorax.
Tail: arctic fox body hair, colour to match body.
Rib: oval silver tinsel.
Palmer: hen hackle, colour to match body.
Body: chenille in black, white, or olive.
Thorax: built up thicker than the body with Glo-Brite suede chenille,
    shade 12 (signal green).

Crystal Peach Doll

Hook: Mustad 9672, size 8 or 10.
Tying thread: orange Monocord.
Tail and back: Crystal Hair, orange.
Rib: gold wire.
Body: apricot GlowBug yarn.

Damsel-fly Nymph

Hook: Mustad 9672, size 10.
Tying thread: olive Monocord.
Tails: three olive cock-hackle points, evenly spread.
Butt: Glo-Brite floss, shade 13.

Rib: fine oval gold tinsel.
Body: dubbed a blend of 60 per cent medium-olive/40 per cent golden-olive seal fur or Antron.
Thorax cover: cock pheasant centre-tail fibres.
Thorax: as body.
Beard hackle: grey partridge dyed golden-olive.
This pattern designed by Mike Huffer.

Drone-fly

Hook: Partridge L2A, size 12.
Tying thread: yellow Monocord.
Rib: black Danville flat floss.
Body: yellow wool.
Wings: two natural blue-dun cock-hackle points (preferably Metz), tied flat, pointing back in a slight 'V'.
Hackle: ginger cock.
Head: Glo-Brite floss, shade 4.

Dry flies

Hook: Partridge L3A or L3B, sizes 10, 12, 14, or 16.
Tying thread: suitably-coloured Monocord.
Body: dubbed Antron or seal fur in either black, fiery brown, hot orange, or medium olive. Other colours may also be used.
Hackle: white or badger cock.
As soon as the fly is tied, anoint it heavily with Gink flotant. Store the treated dry flies in a small tin.

Fluebrush

Hook: Kamasan B830, size 8 or 10.
Tying thread: black Monocord.
Rib: fine copper wire.
Rear palmer: light red-brown cock hackle.
Middle palmer: white cock hackle.
Front palmer: olive cock hackle.
The palmering should be close. A Lyn Francis pattern.

Green Peter Mini-Muddler

Hook: Partridge L2A, sizes 10 or 12.
Tying thread: olive Monocord.
Rib: gold wire.
Body: dubbed dark green Antron.
Beard hackle: ginger cock.
Wing: hen pheasant secondaries.
Head: clipped deer hair.

Grenadier Palmer

Hook: Partridge L2A, sizes 10, 12, or 14.
Tying thread: orange Monocord.
Tail: Glo-Brite floss, shade 7.
Rib: gold wire.
Palmer: light red-brown cock hackle.
Body: dubbed with a blend of 80 per cent orange/20 per cent red
    Antron or seal fur.
Add a clipped deer-hair head for the Grenadier Mini-Muddler.

Hairwing Dunkeld

Hook: Partridge L2A, GRS2A, or CS7, sizes 10 or 12.
Tying thread: black Monocord.
Tail: Glo-Brite floss, shade 7.
Rib: gold wire.
Palmer: orange or fluorescent arc chrome cock hackle.
Body: gold Lurex or Mylar.
Wing: Parey squirrel tail, or grey squirrel dyed dark brown.
Cheeks: small jungle cock.

Hairwing Mallard & Claret

Hook: Partridge L2A, size 10 or 12.
Tying thread: black Monocord.
Tail: golden-pheasant tippet fibres.
Rib: fine oval gold tinsel.
Body: dubbed claret Antron or seal fur.
Beard hackle: fluorescent neon magenta cock.
Wing: grey squirrel-tail dyed dark brown, or Parey squirrel.
Addition of a tuft of Glo-Brite floss, shade 15, at the tail, turns this
    into the Purple Mallard & Claret.

Hatching Sedge

Hook: Partridge L2A, sizes 8, 10, or 12.
Tying thread: orange Monocord.
Tail: two ginger hen-hackle points, set flat in a 'V'.
Rib: narrow flat gold tinsel.
Body: dubbed gingery hare fur from hare's mask.
Sidewings: strips of cinnamon goose, about 2mm wide and half the
    length of the body, angled out 30° from the body and cut off
    square at the ends.
Wing: sparse white calf-tail hair.
Hackle: ginger hen.

Herl Buzzer Nymph

Hook: Partridge L2A, size 10, 12, 14 or 16.
Tying thread: black Monocord.
Tail: Glo-Brite floss, shade 16.
Rib: finest silver wire.
Body: turkey herl, dyed required colour.
Thorax and cover: cock pheasant centre-tail fibres.
Breather: Glo-Brite floss, shade 16.
Popular body colours are black, olive, grey, insect green.

Honey Buzzer

Hook: Partridge L2A or GRS2A, sizes 12 or 14.
Tying thread: orange Monocord.
Tail: honey (pale ginger) cock-hackle fibres.
Rib: gold wire.
Palmer: honey (pale ginger) cock hackle, preferably Metz.
Body: pale cock pheasant centre-tail fibres.
Wings: slips of grey feather from wings of mallard or teal.

Juicy Lucy

Hook: Mustad 9672, sizes 8 or 10.
Tying thread: Flymaster-Plus, shade 503.
Tail: Glo-Brite Multi-Yarn, shade 7.
Rib: oval silver tinsel.
Body: silver Lurex.
Hackle: dyed red or orange cock.
Wing: orange marabou.

Lake Olive

Hook: Partridge L2A, sizes 12 or 14.
Tying thread: olive Monocord.
Tail: brownish-olive cock-hackle fibres.
Rib: gold wire.
Body: dubbed with a blend of cinnamon and medium-olive (fine
    fibres, e.g., Veniard Seal-fur Substitute).
Wings: starling or similar.
Beard hackle: brownish-olive cock.

Montana Nymph variation

Hook: Mustad 9672, size 10 or 12.
Tying thread: brown Monocord.
Weight: lead wire wound along the shank.
Tail: chocolate-brown cock-hackle fibres.

Body: dark brown chenille.
Palmer for thorax: chocolate-brown cock hackle.
Thorax: fluorescent cream GlowBug yarn.

Ned's Fancy

Hook: Partridge L2A sizes 10, 12, or 14.
Tying thread: black Monocord.
Tail: Glo-Brite floss, shades 2, 4, 7, or 12.
Rib: silver wire.
Body: silver Lurex or flat Mylar.
Thorax: peacock herl.
Hackle: hen hackle, ginger or blue-dun.

Orange-bodied Muddler

Hook: Partridge L2A, size 10 or 12.
Tying thread: orange Monocord.
Tail: slip of hen pheasant wing-quill.
Rib: gold wire.
Body: dubbed orange Antron or seal fur.
Wing: slips of hen pheasant wing-feather.
Ruff: deer hair.
Head: clipped deer hair.

Orange Hare's Ear Nymph

Hook: Kamasan B830, sizes 10 or 12.
Tying thread: Monocord, black if leaded, orange if unleaded.
Weight: (optional) lead wire wound along whole of shank.
Tail: Glo-Brite floss, shade 7.
Rib: oval gold tinsel.
Body: dubbed with a blend of 80 per cent hare body-fur and 20 per
    cent hot orange Antron fibre or seal fur, well picked-out.
Various colours of Glo-Brite floss may be used for the tail; good
shades are 4, 5, 11, 12, and 16. In these variations, the body is solely
hare body-fur.

Orange Marabou Muddler

Hook: Mustad 9672, size 8 or 10, or Partridge L2A, size 10 for Mini-
    Muddler version.
Tying thread: orange Monocord.
Tail: Glo-Brite floss, shade 7.
Rib: gold oval tinsel.
Body: gold Lurex.
Wing: orange marabou or arctic fox hair dyed orange.
Head: orange deer hair, clipped.

BILL'S VIVA

DRY FLY

DAMSELFLY NYMPH

BLOODWORM

BLAE & BLACK

BLACK CONCRETE
BOWL

GREEN PETER
MINI-MUDDLER

CLARET PALMER

FLUEBRUSH

CADDIS GRUB

DRONE FLY

CRYSTAL PEACH DOLL

BLACK & CLARET
MINI-MUDDLER

A

ORANGE HARE'S-EAR NYMPH

GRENADIER PALMER

HAIR-WING DUNKELD

HAIR-WING MALLARD & CLARET

JUICY LUCY

ORANGE-BODIED MUDDLER

NED'S FANCY (GREEN TAIL)

HERL BUZZER NYMPH

LAKE OLIVE

HONEY BUZZER

MONTANA NYMPH VARIATION

HATCHING SEDGE

B

PEETIE

**SAVILLE
SEDGE PUPA**

**PALMERED
GREY BUZZER**

ORANGE TADPOLE

**ORANGE MARABOU
MUDDLER**

PEACH PALMER

PINK NYMPH

RED PALMER

**PEARL-RIB BLACK
BUZZER NYMPH**

SAVILLE CORIXA

PEPPERMINT DOLL

SEDGE PUPA

C

SWEENEY PALMER

SHRIMP

TOM'S TERROR

**TUBED BUZZER
NYMPH (GINGER)**

SPUDDLER

**TUBED BUZZER
NYMPH (BLACK)**

**SUPER
CINNAMON
SEDGE**

SUSIE

**WHITE
WICKHAM'S**

**SILVER
PALMER**

**TWINKLE
BUZZER NYMPH**

**WING-LESS
WICKHAM
MINI-MUDDLER**

D

Orange Tadpole

Hook: Mustad 9672, size 8 or 10.
Tying thread: orange Monocord.
Weight: lead wire, 6–8 turns at the head.
Tail: orange marabou or arctic fox hair dyed orange.
Rib: gold oval tinsel.
Body: Glo-Brite suede chenille, shade 7.
Head: as body, built up into a spherical shape.
For Black Tadpole or White Tadpole: change rib to silver, and tail
and body colours to suit.

Palmered Grey Buzzer

Hook: Partridge GRS2A, sizes 12 or 14.
Tying thread: grey Monocord.
Tail: natural blue-dun cock-hackle fibres.
Rib: silver wire.
Palmer: natural blue-dun cock hackle, preferably Metz.
Body: grey goose herl.
Wings: slips of grey mallard or teal wing-quills.

Peach Palmer

Hook: Partridge L2A, size 10 or 12.
Tying thread: orange Monocord.
Tail: Glo-Brite floss, shade 5.
Rib: gold wire.
Palmer: light red-brown cock hackle.
Body: Glo-Brite Multi-Yarn, shade 8.
The addition of a clipped deer-hair head turns this pattern into a
Peach Muddler.

Pearl-rib Black Buzzer Nymph

Hook: Kamasan B830, sizes 12 or 14.
Tying thread: black Monocord.
Rib: one strand pearl Lureflash Mobile.
Body: black floss.
Rear cheeks: behind thorax, tufts of Glo-Brite floss, shade 7, pointing
back.
Thorax: black floss.
Cheeks: in front of thorax, tufts of Glo-Brite Multi-Yarn, shade 16,
pointing back.

Peetie

Hook: Mustad 9672, size 8 or 10.
Tying thread: black Monocord.
Body: gold Mylar tubing.

Beard hackle: yellow cock-hackle fibres.

Wing: green plain-dyed squirrel-tail with dyed black squirrel-tail over.

Head: built up quite large with tying thread and varnished with black varnish.

Eyes: thin slices of white electric flex from which the wire has been removed, stuck on each side of the head while the varnish is still wet.

Peppermint Doll

Hook: Mustad 9672, size 8 or 10.
Tying thread: white Monocord.
Tail and back: Glo-Brite Multi-Yarn, shade 12 or 13.
Body: Glo-Brite Multi-Yarn, shade 16.
Beard hackle: white cock fibres.

Pink Nymph

Hook: Partridge L2A, sizes 12 or 14.
Tying thread: black Monocord.
Tail: Glo-Brite floss, shade 2.
Rib: gold wire.
Body: Glo-Brite floss, shade 2.
Thorax: peacock herl.
Hackle: blue-dun hen.

Red Palmer

Hook: Partridge L2A or GRS2A, size 10, 12, or 14.
Tying thread: black Monocord.
Tail: Glo-Brite floss, shade 4.
Rib: gold wire.
Palmer: light red-brown cock hackle.
Body: dubbed red seal fur or Antron.
This is virtually the Soldier Palmer, but the body colour should be a bright red rather than the deeper crimson.

Saville Corixa

Hook: Partridge L2A or GRS2A, sizes 10 or 12.
Tying thread: olive Monocord.
Weight: lead wire wound along hook shank.
Paddles: olive condor or turkey-tail fibres, tied at right-angles to the shank.
Back: olive condor or turkey herl.
Rib: silver Lurex.
Body: Glo-Brite suede chenille, shade 11.
Hackle: ginger hen.

Saville Pheasant Tail Nymph

Hook: Partridge L2A, sizes 10, 12, or 14.
Tying thread: black Monocord.
Tail, body, thorax, and wing-case: cock pheasant centre-tail fibres. The thorax must be slim, only slightly thicker than the body.
Beard hackle: ginger hen-hackle fibres.

Saville Sedge Pupa

Hook: Partridge K4A, sizes 10 or 12.
Tying thread: black Monocord.
Rib: black Monocord.
Body: thickly-dubbed Antron, olive or orange.
Beard hackle: fibres of grouse body plumage.
Antennae: two cock pheasant centre-tail fibres, pointing back.

Sedge Pupa

Hook: Partridge L2A, sizes 10 or 12.
Tying thread: brown Monocord.
Rib: gold wire.
Body: cream or pale yellow wool or dubbing.
Thorax: brown wool or dubbing.
Wing-stubs: slips of cinnamon hen wing-quill.
Beard hackle: ginger hen, long.
Antennae: two fibres of barred teal, pointing backwards.
Head: cock pheasant centre-tail fibres.

Shrimp

Hook: Partridge K4A, sizes 10 or 12.
Tying thread: olive or orange Monocord.
Weight: lead wire wound along the shank.
Tail: two olive or orange cock-hackle points.
Rib: green Maxima or clear T-Line monofil, 6lb-test, over both body and back, to give a noticeable segmented effect.
Body: olive or orange Antron dubbing, well picked-out.
Back: clear polythene sheet.

Silver Palmer

Hook: Partridge GRS2A, size 10, 12, or 14.
Tying thread: black Monocord.
Tail: Glo-Brite floss, shade 4.
Rib: silver wire.
Palmer: light red-brown cock hackle.
Body: silver Lurex or flat Mylar.

Spuddler

Hook: Mustad 9672, size 6 or 8.
Tying thread: black Monocord.
Tail: brown calf tail-hair.
Body: cream wool.
Thorax: Glo-Brite Multi-Yarn or suede chenille, shade 4.
Wings: two pairs of well-marked grizzle cock hackles (Metz or D. J. Hackle Farm type) dyed fiery brown, back-to-back.
Ruff: Canadian fox squirrel-tail hair.
Head: clipped deer hair in an oval 'tadpole-head' shape.

Super Cinnamon Sedge

Hook: Partridge L3B or Mustad 94842, sizes 8, 10, or 12.
Tying thread: brown Monocord.
Rib: Glo-Brite floss, shade 8.
Palmer: ginger cock hackle.
Body: cinnamon ostrich herl.
Wings: two hen pheasant body feathers drawn through Cellire No. 1 varnish between finger and thumb, allowed to dry and tied flat in a slight 'V' when viewed from above.
Hackle: two ginger cock hackles.
Antennae: the stems of the above hackles, stripped, curving upwards, and 45° apart.

Susie

Hook: Mustad 9672, size 6, 8, or 10.
Tying thread: white Monocord.
Tail: orange Crystal Hair.
Underbody: silver thread or silver oval tinsel.
Body: pearl Mylar tubing.
Beard hackle: orange Crystal Hair.
Wing: white hair, e.g., goat or ringcat.

Sweeney Palmer

Hook: Mustad 9672 or Kamasan B830, sizes 8 or 10.
Tying thread: black Monocord.
Rib: silver oval tinsel.
Palmer: black hen hackle.
Body: dubbed black Antron or seal fur.
Thorax: dubbed neon magenta Antron.
Beard hackle: guinea-fowl.
Wing: dyed black squirrel-tail hair.

Tom's Terror

Hook: Mustad 9672, size 8 or 10.
Tying thread: black Monocord.
Body: Mylar tubing in silver or pearl.
Beard hackle: white cock, or white hair.
Wing: dyed black squirrel tail, with plain-dyed orange squirrel tail over.
Head: built up quite large with the tying thread, and finished with black varnish.
Eyes: thin slices of white electric flex from which the wire has been removed, stuck on each side of the head while the varnish is still wet.

Tubed Buzzer Nymph

Hook: Partridge GRS2A, sizes 10, 12 or 14.
Tying thread: colour to match body insert.
Body: clear tubing in nylon or polythene; 1.25mm diameter for size 10, 1mm diameter for size 12, .063mm diameter for size 14.
Body insert: horsehair, nylon monofilament, DRF floss, Glo-Brite floss, or tying thread. Colour of insert as required.
Thorax and thorax-cover: cock pheasant centre-tail, or dyed turkey tail.
Wing-stubs: (optional) goose biots, colour as required (orange is popular).
Breathers: Glo-Brite floss, shade 16.

As this pattern requires special tying techniques, follow these instructions:

Locate the hook in the vice so that the dressing can be taken round the bend. Make eight touching turns of waxed thread at the eye. Take about 4 inches of tubing into which has been inserted the chosen insert material, and carefully flatten one end for about 15mm or ½ inch, using the blunt side of a scissor blade on a firm surface. This 'flat' ensures that the tying thread grips the tubing firmly, and gives a neat taper to the finished body. The length to be flattened will vary according to the size of the hook; it will be wound round the shank and halfway round the bend with enough left to start a return journey before the tubing thickens out again, thus forming a tapered rear end of the body.

Tie in the flattened end of the tubing with six close tight turns towards the bend of the hook; make sure the insert is tied down at the same time. The open end of the tubing faces the eye. Leave enough space at the front of the shank to take the thorax, wing-stubs, and breather.

Wind the flattened tubing tightly in touching turns along the shank towards the bend, halfway round the bend, then back over itself towards the eye. Keep the tension constantly tight, and fasten off with a few tight turns of thread; these turns will not be seen because they will be covered by the thorax material. Cut off the surplus tubing.

The goose biots can now be tied in, one on each side. Next, tie in six fibres of cock pheasant centre-tail or turkey tail, by the tips, with the butts facing towards the bend; these will form the thorax-cover. Then tie in a further six fibres, and in the same place tie in a short length of white Glo-Brite floss which has been folded three times (facing forward over the eye). Cut off the loose ends of floss which point backwards. Now wind the tying thread up to the eye of the hook.

To form the thorax, wind three of the fibres towards the eye and tie off. Repeat with the other three fibres, winding over the first layer. By doing this operation in two stages, you will find it easier to shape a better-looking thorax. There is no need to twist the fibres.

Now bring the thorax-cover fibres forward over the thorax, pulling firmly to keep them on top, and tie off. Trim the white floss to about 2mm and fluff the ends out. Whip-finish, making sure you don't trap the floss, and varnish.

Twinkle Buzzer Nymph

Hook: Partridge L2A, sizes 10, 12, or 14.
Tying thread: black Monocord.
Tail: Glo-Brite floss, shade 16.
Body: Lureflash Twinkle or Crystal Hair in required colour.
Thorax: cock pheasant centre-tail or dyed turkey herl, in required colour.
Breather: Glo-Brite floss, shade 16.
Good body colours include black, bronze, or green.

White Wickham's

Hook: Partridge GRS2A, size 10 or 12.
Tying thread: white Monocord.
Tail: Glo-Brite floss, shade 16.
Rib: silver wire.
Palmer: ginger cock hackle.
Body: white floss.
Wings: slips of grey mallard wing-quill.

Wingless Wickham Mini-Muddler

Hook: Partridge L2A or CS7, sizes 10 or 12.
Tying thread: black Monocord.
Tail: Glo-Brite floss, shade 4.
Rib: gold wire.
Palmer: light red-brown cock hackle.
Body: flat gold Mylar or Lurex.
Head: clipped deer hair.

Index

Page numbers in *italic* refer to illustrations in the text

"White lives". p.158